# The Elusive Self

# The Elusive Self

Psyche and Spirit
in Virginia Woolf's Novels

*Louise A. Poresky*

Newark
University of Delaware Press
London and Toronto: Associated University Presses

© 1981 by Associated University Presses, Inc.

Associated University Presses, Inc.
4 Cornwall Drive
East Brunswick, N. J.  08816

Associated University Presses Ltd.
69 Fleet Street
London EC4Y 1EU, England

Associated University Presses
Toronto, Ontario, Canada M5E 1A7


**Library of Congress Cataloging in Publication Data**

Poresky, Louise A
   The elusive self.

   Bibliography: p.
   Includes index.
   1.  Woolf, Virginia Stephen, 1882-1941--
Criticism and interpretation.  2.  Self in
literature.  I.  Title.
PR6045.O72Z863      823'.912      79-64503
ISBN 0-87413-170-7

Printed in the United States of America

*To Helen and Herb*

# Contents

9

# Acknowledgments

Teachers and colleagues provided essential advice and encouragement as I wrote this book. Those who read the entire manuscript and commented on its content and form—Robert Chapman, Virginia Mollenkott, Merrill Skaggs, and John Warner—deserve thanks for their endurance and wisdom. Each added specialized knowledge that helped me solidify ideas and strengthen the prose.

Friends and family worked hard and graciously supported me throughout the years of study and writing. Phyllis Goodfriend spent many arduous hours typing the manuscript, and James Goodfriend generously contributed to its production. They, along with other very special people, continued to believe in me and this work, even through those times when I doubted.

# List of Abbreviations

The following abbreviations are used throughout this book for in-text page references to Woolf's works:

| | |
|---|---|
| *TVO* | *The Voyage Out* |
| *N&D* | *Night and Day* |
| *JR* | *Jacob's Room* |
| *MD* | *Mrs. Dalloway* |
| *TTL* | *To the Lighthouse* |
| *O* | *Orlando* |
| *TW* | *The Waves* |
| *TY* | *The Years* |
| *BTA* | *Between the Acts* |
| *AWD* | *A Writer's Diary* |
| *AROO* | *A Room of One's Own* |
| *TG* | *Three Guineas* |

# Introduction

Many critics explicate and interpret the individual novels by Virginia Woolf. Some analyze the prevalent imagery, such as that of the sea[1] and the globe[2]; others dissect Woolf's style: her use of rhythm and repetition,[3] multilayered point of view,[4] and impressionism[5]; and still others trace themes of feminism,[6] androgyny,[7] and the reconciliation of opposites.[8] In addition, scholars frequently approach Woolf by way of possible literary and philosophical influences: some detect Henri Bergson's philosophy of time in Woolf's novels,[9] while others disagree[10]; some compare Woolf to James Joyce,[11] while others deny the validity of that comparison.[12]

These illustrations provide typical samples of Woolf scholarship. And viewed as a whole, this scholarship seems to reach out in a hundred directions without leading back to a clear focal point. The heart of Virginia Woolf's work is her search for the Self. Once that fact is acknowledged, her imagery, stylistic techniques, themes, and philosophical theories cohere into a pattern.

The Self, that core or center of the human psyche that Woolf's characters seek, differs from the self, one's superficial identity. We can say that a man or a woman who operates strictly in accordance with society's expectations—for instance, a man should assert himself, whereas a woman should remain passive—adopts a particular self. Yet, as Virginia Woolf suggests in her novels, all individuals possess a Self that defies such categorization. This Self constitutes the psychic core of a person. Outside of this core, the ego reigns, the ego that insists on shallow identities. Within the core, however, to which the ego has no access, one finds the profound psychic wholeness that mystics seek. As June Singer says, within the Self exists the "correspondences between the specks of dust we are as individuals, and the immeasurable mystery of which we are an integral part."[13] Virginia Woolf's characters seek this mystery, for they wish to participate in it.

A major character in each of Woolf's novels furthers the progress of this search for the Self. One, therefore, can view these particular characters as both separate personalities and as a composite personality that operates throughout all the novels. But the progression of this search does not start with the composite personality completely outside of the Self, then end with full immersion into the Self. Rather, the composite personality consistently moves toward Selfhood, until it reaches it and understands it. Then the personality descends into the self again, for, as Woolf demonstrates, sustained Selfhood is impossible. Woolf shows, in other words, that her composite personality yearns for Selfhood, and therefore works through the many barriers that block its access to the Self. The ego puts up these barriers, all of which stem from the ego's fear of what Singer calls "the immeasurable mystery." Fear, for instance, insists that individuals exhibit only those qualities that society deems appropriate for a man or a woman, or those qualities that the parents instill in their children. Woolf's composite personality struggles against these expectations placed on its existence, so as to reach the Self that remains independent of such demands. It does reach the Self, and there it finds God in the place of the ego and androgyny in the place of gender identification. But this discovery does not assure that the composite personality can permanently become an integral part of this mystery. As

Woolf makes clear in *The Waves*, the spiritually fallen nature of humankind prevents sustained Selfhood. Consequently, an individual can only hope to catch momentary glimpses of the Self and to heal himself somewhat from the human separation from God. *Between the Acts* demonstrates that love supplies humanity with the only means to regain the psychic wholeness experienced in androgyny and the spiritual wholeness experienced through God's grace.

In Virginia Woolf's first novel, *The Voyage Out*, the composite personality, embodied in Rachel Vinrace, meets the force of socialization. Though she yearns for peace, and achieves it through her music, Rachel cannot overcome the restrictive demands placed on her by society. She thus lets herself die, for only in death can she protect herself from psychic disintegration. Katharine Hilbery, in *Night and Day*, furthers the personality's battle with socialization. She does not permit society to overwhelm her; rather, she seeks the safety of solitude where she can, if only for one brief moment, intuit the presence of her Self. In *Jacob's Room* and *Mrs. Dalloway*, Woolf depicts those particular forces that determine society's traditional roles based on gender. Every individual, Woolf suggests, must confront those forces, the parental figures, as they manifest themselves within the individual's unconscious, and overcome them. Jacob Flanders and Clarissa Dalloway do exactly this. Therefore, Lily Briscoe, in *To the Lighthouse*, can artistically render the wholeness indigenous to the Self. In the process of acquiring this vision, Lily discovers that the Self contains the internalized powers of God. The God within comprises the first major component of the Self. With *Orlando*, one finds that the Self possesses also an androgynous nature. Yet, despite these revelations, *The Waves* shows that the composite personality must fall back into the fragmented world of superficial identities because, with humankind's fall from God's grace in the garden of Eden, self-consciousness took over. And with self-consciousness the ego ascends into power, asserting the domi-

nion of the "I." *The Years* depicts Eleanor Pargiter's struggle for a vision of wholeness, despite all the emotional separation between individuals and psychic fragmentation within
individuals. And finally, *Between the Acts* proposes love as
humankind's only means to heal itself.

Virginia Woolf's style complements the psychological progression in the nine novels. The composite personality that
searches for its Self throughout the novels operates primarily
on the conscious level in *The Voyage Out* and *Night and Day*,
so Woolf writes these first two novels in a realistic style. Once
this personality descends into its unconscious in order to
dispel the parental forces, as in *Jacob's Room* and *Mrs.
Dalloway*, the literary mode turns more impressionistic. In
*To the Lighthouse* the style, with its complexity of point of
view, parallels the emotional struggle to uncover the Self's
wholeness. With the vision achieved, *Orlando* shows total
disregard for all temporal and sexual limitations. To convey
the isolation and loneliness that result from humankind's fall
from divine grace, Woolf unfolds *The Waves* through the interior monologues of the six characters. And because the ego
reasserts its strengths in *The Years*, Woolf returns to her
realistic style so as to reflect the merely conscious concerns of
society. Then Woolf emphasizes the consequent self-
deception and fragmentation with the apparent stylistic
disunity in *Between the Acts*.

## NOTES

1.  Bernard Blackstone, *Virginia Woolf: A Commentary* (New York: Harcourt Brace
Jovanovich, Inc., 1949). Blackstone says the sea is Virginia Woolf's most enduring image for it implies both permanence and change (p. 232).

   Peter and Margaret Havard-Williams, "*Bateau-Ivre*: The Symbol of the Sea in
Virginia Woolf's *The Waves*," *English Studies* 34 (February 1953): 9-17. The authors
refer to the sea as symbolizing the activity of the unconscious mind.

2.  Dorothy Brewster, *Virginia Woolf* (New York: New York University Press, 1962).
Brewster considers the globe Woolf's central symbol: "Several of Mrs. Woolf's leading

characters take this globe in their hands at some stage in their experience of life" (p. 79). The symbol of the globe, according to Brewster, represents "the interplay between the inner and the outer, the Internal and the External, the individual and 'life in general,' Night and Day" (p. 80).

3. Allen McLaurin, *Virginia Woolf: The Echoes Enslaved* (London: Cambridge University Press, 1973).

4. Mitchell A. Leaska, *Virginia Woolf's Lighthouse: A Study in Critical Method* (New York: Columbia University Press, 1970). Leaska analyzes the shifting point of view in *To the Lighthouse*.

5. James Naremore, *The World without a Self: Virginia Woolf and the Novel* (New Haven, Conn.: Yale University Press, 1973). Naremore says, "her most highly experimental fiction, from *Mrs. Dalloway* to *The Waves*, reflects a steady movement away from the more-or-less direct rendition of thought streams toward methods which allow her considerable latitude to express what lies outside the character's ego" (p. 71).

6. Nancy Topping Bazin, *Virginia Woolf and the Androgynous Vision* (New Brunswick, N.J.: Rutgers University Press, 1973). Bazin writes that "as a female, [Woolf] believed that her vision, though ideally bisexual, should on the whole be distinctly feminine, that is, 'woman-manly' as opposed to 'man-womanly' " (p. 5).

Ruth Gruber, *Virginia Woolf: A Study* (Leipzig: Verlag von Bernhard Tauehnitz, 1935). Woolf sees woman as the genius of life (p. 94), says Gruber.

Mary Electra Kelsey, "Virgina Woolf and the She-Condition," *Sewanee Review* 39 (October-December 1931): 425-44.

Herbert Marder, *Feminism and Art: A Study of Virginia Woolf* (Chicago: University of Chicago Press, 1968).

7. Geoffrey H. Hartman, "Virginia's Web," *Chicago Review* 14 (Spring 1961): 20-32. The only fully developed character in Woolf's novels is the androgynous mind (p. 23), believes Hartman.

Vijay Lakshmi, "The Solid and the Intangible: Virginia Woolf's Theory of the Androgynous Mind," *Literary Criterion* 10 (Winter 1971): 28-34. Lakshmi says that in Woolf's fiction only the androgynous mind can grasp wholeness (p. 34).

8. Alice van Buren Kelley, *The Novels of Virginia Woolf: Fact and Vision* (Chicago: University of Chicago Press, 1971). The author writes that the characters in Woolf's novels are either fact- or vision-oriented. But, she continues, "Fact needs vision to help it transcend the limits of objective, physical truth. Vision needs fact as the solid base from which to leap into unity" (p. 5).

Jean O. Love, *Worlds in Consciousness: Mythopoetic Thought in the Novels of Virginia Woolf* (Berkeley, Calif.: University of California Press, 1970). Love discusses many dialectics in Woolf's novels, one of which is that of life and death. She believes that Woolf's novels "succeed in synthesizing life and death" (p. 79).

9. Floris Delattre, "La Durée Bergsonienne dans le roman de Virginia Woolf." This article originally appeared in *Revue Anglo-Americaine* (December 1931): 97-108. It also is included in *Virginia Woolf: The Critical Heritage*, ed. Robin Majumdar and Allen McLaurin (London: Routledge and Kegan Paul, 1975), pp. 299-300. Delattre discusses how Woolf uses, in her novels, the Bergsonian distinction between quantitative, or actual, time and qualitative, or psychological, time.

Harvena Richter, *Virginia Woolf: The Inward Voyage* (Princeton, N.J.: Princeton University Press, 1970). Richter says that Woolf did not read Bergson, but did read Proust, who was tutored by Bergson and absorbed Bergson's concept of time (p. 38).

10. Jean Guiguet, *Virginia Woolf and Her Works*, trans. Jean Stewart (New York: Harcourt, Brace & World, 1962): "For Virginia Woolf the problem was not the reconciliation of time and duration, any more than of physical space and mental space. . . . We must give up referring to Bergson" (p. 396).

11. M. C. Bradbrook, "Notes on the Style of Mrs. Woolf." Originally this article appeared in *Scrutiny* (May 1932): 33-38. It also is included in *Virginia Woolf: The Critical Heritage*, pp. 308-13. Bradbrook sees the series of cross references in *Mrs. Dalloway* as influenced by Joyce's *Ulysses*, but *Ulysses*, according to Bradbrook, has a far firmer structure (p. 311 in *Critical Heritage*).

12. James Naremore writes, "In Joyce, the meaning of experience is often related to encounters with words . . . . while in Virginia Woolf words seem at times superfluous, sometimes even false to the experience of something that is non-verbal" (*The World without a Self*, p. 37).

13. June Singer, *Androgyny: Toward a New Theory of Sexuality* (Garden City, N.Y.: Doubleday & Co., 1972), p. 113.

# The Elusive Self

1

# The Voyage Out
## To Triumph in the Wind

Virginia Woolf's fiction follows the psychological growth of one individual. Major characters from Woolf's nine novels comprise this single personality, which experiences its first major stage of psychic development in *The Voyage Out* and *Night and Day*. In no way, however, do these two novels duplicate each other. Rather, the first novel begins the stage, whereas the second completes it. Rachel Vinrace, the major character in *The Voyage Out*, turns to death out of despair; she sees no way of achieving psychic integration in her world. To her mind, such Selfhood comes solely through death, which provides the only escape from the social demands that fragment her full identity. Katharine Hilbery, on the other hand, grows successfully through *Night and Day*, so at the end she can, if only briefly, contact her wholeness without leaving society. The fact that Katharine succeeds where Rachel falls short does not indicate Katharine's superiority over Rachel, because they do not start at the same point in their growth process. What Rachel experiences and learns in *The Voyage Out* is a given in Katharine's personality at the opening of *Night and Day*. In other words, Rachel's growth, though aborted, gives Katharine a head start in her own development toward Selfhood.[1]

23

Some critics of *The Voyage Out* concern themselves with structure — either the coherence or the lack of coherence of the elements.[2] But those who see no coherence in the novel miss Woolf's logic, a psychological logic as flawless as a syllogism but that operates on the psychic rather than the rational level. Actually, with *The Voyage Out* one sees the beginning of Woolf's use of a dreamlike concatenation of events that reaches its fullest expression with *The Waves*. One critic who acknowledges the organic unity of the novel is James Hafley. He says, "*The Voyage Out* may be regarded as a finished work of art, and judged as such. There seems to be no special 'struggle' between its form and its content."[3] Nancy Topping Bazin specifically points out a pronounced symmetry in the plot: "There are two major shapes or blocks of material in *The Voyage Out*, that which occurs on the cargo ship, a symbolic island, and that which occurs on the real island of Santa Marina." Then Bazin adds, "On each 'island', there is a major emotional event, on the first a kiss, on the second a death. The kiss is preceded by a storm and followed by a dream. The death is preceded by a hallucination and followed by a storm."[4] Clearly, the novel's elements fall into a distinct pattern.

Lytton Strachey and Virginia Woolf, in their exchange of letters in February 1916, discuss the same point. After complimenting Woolf on the "wit and exquisiteness" of the novel, Strachey writes, "My own criticism is about the conception of it as a whole — which I am doubtful about. As I read I felt that it perhaps lacked the cohesion of a dominating idea — I don't mean in the spirit — but in the action. I wonder if you at all agree about this."[5] Woolf immediately wrote back:

I suspect your criticism about the failure of conception is quite right. I think I had a conception, but I don't think it made itself felt. What I wanted to do was to give the feeling of a vast tumult of life, as various and disorderly as possible, which should be cut short for a moment by the death, and go on again — and the whole was to have a sort of pattern, and be somehow controlled. The difficulty was to keep any sort of coherence.[6]

But the novel does have coherence, a coherence visible only when viewed within the context of an individual's search for the Self. Obviously, this assertion counters Woolf's own evaluation of her book. But perhaps even she would agree, at this point, that she erred in her comments to Strachey. Such a conjecture is based on Woolf's own theory of fiction writing. She asks, in her essay "The Leaning Tower," if "we strain Wordsworth's famous saying about emotion recollected in tranquility when we infer that by tranquility he meant that the writer needs to become unconscious before he can create?"[7] If the writing process emanates from the unconscious, then the conscious statements in Woolf's letter may miss the mark. Actually, just as she says that she intended the whole "to have a sort of pattern," she accomplished just that—despite her conscious acceptance of Strachey's criticism.

The structural and thematic coherence becomes evident once one understands Rachel Vinrace's psychological predicament. In the beginning she knows only of her ego, her conscious personality. And the ego identifies her solely by gender; she must act strictly in accordance with the conventional expectations the world holds for a young woman. Then, as the novel progresses, she meets the masculine element in the world, finds it frightening and repulsive, and finally allows herself to die out of the world that functions according to the socialized roles of male and female. She wants psychic integration, but sees this integration endangered by the dictates of tradition. Consequently, she resorts to death as the only means to retain the integrity of her hidden Selfhood. The title of the novel conveys this theme. Rachel voyages out of the immediate world dominated by societal strictures that assign ego-determined roles to men and women.[8]

In the first chapter, Rachel appears at her most naive stage. She has no concept of the Self; therefore her identity forms

solely out of her conventional role as a young woman. She
derives this role from her position as daughter of Willoughby
Vinrace. For instance, as Rachel waits on board the
Euphrosyne for the arrival of her aunt and uncle, Helen and
Ridley Ambrose, she knows that

> as her father's daughter she must be in some sort prepared to
> entertain them. She looked forward to seeing them as civi-
> lized people generally look forward to the first sight of civi-
> lived people, as though they were of the nature of an ap-
> proaching physical discomfort, — a tight shoe or a draughty
> window. She was already unnaturally braced to receive
> them.[9]

Rachel knows what role society expects her to play—that of
charming hostess—but she finds this role unnatural.

Rachel senses that something more exists in life and that
something else will fulfill her nature. Music satisfies this yearning. But she also knows that her love for music conflicts with
the young woman her aunts expect her to be. The conflict between these two comes out when Helen tells Rachel that Aunt
Bessie "is afraid that you will spoil your arms if you insist upon
so much practicing." Rachel immediately retorts, "The
muscles of the forearm—and then one won't marry?" Of
course, Helen replies, "She didn't put it quite like that," but
both Helen and Rachel know that this is exactly Aunt Bessie's
concern (*TVO*, 20).

In the first chapter then, Rachel is torn between her
natural desires and those others hold for her. Helen wants
Rachel to act like a demure and delicate female, while
Willoughby wants her to take over the role of her dead mother.
Yet both Helen and Willoughby sense that Rachel resists these
roles. As the narrator says, "Much as Willoughby would
doubtless have liked his daughter to praise him she did not; her
eyes were unreflecting as water" (*TVO*, 21). And, at the end of
the chapter, Helen rises to go to bed, expecting Rachel to accompany her, but "Rachel rose, looked vaguely into Helen's face
and remarked with her slight stammer, 'I'm going to t-t-

triumph in the wind' " (*TVO*, 23). Rachel wants to confront nature and to absent herself from the world of civilization that hampers her. Here also appears Rachel's desire for solitude, a desire that increases until it eventually leads to her death. Moreover, her stammer indicates her distrust of idle chatter; she cannot communicate as the others do:

> Each of the ladies, being after the fashion of their sex, highly trained in promoting men's talk without listening to it, could think — about the education of children, about the use of fog sirens in an opera — without betraying herself. Only it struck Helen that Rachel was perhaps too still for a hostess, and that she might have done something with her hands. (*TVO*, 17)

When Rachel goes out to triumph in the wind, leaving her subordinate role that denies her any purpose beyond that of man's emotional support, "Mrs. Ambrose's worst suspicions were confirmed" (*TVO*, 23).

Rachel seeks full development as a person, but she is confused as to how to achieve it. Her predicament likens her to the biblical Rachel, who blames her husband, Jacob, for her own barrenness (Genesis 30:1). Similarly, Rachel Vinrace sees the masculine world as a detriment to her psychological development. The biblical Rachel does eventually become pregnant, but she dies while giving birth to her second son, Benjamin, on her way from her father's house to her new life with Jacob in Ephrath (Genesis 35:18). Not completing the trip symbolizes her inability to complete the transition from the father's world to one of her own. Her reluctance to leave her father also shows up when she departs with Jacob: she secretly carries with her the pagan gods of her father (Genesis 31:34). In other words, she resists the move from her former pagan existence to one of the new God, the God of Israel. Virginia Woolf's Rachel also cannot make her transition; thus she dies before she reaches the psychically integrated Self.

Another name in the novel used symbolically is *Euphrosyne*, the name of the ship that carries the passengers from London to Santa Marina. This ship represents Rachel not only because it, like Rachel, belongs to her father, and not only because it ends its voyage at Santa Marina, as Rachel's death, likewise, ends her voyage at that island. The ship also represents Rachel because of its name. Euphrosyne, whose name means *joy* in Greek, is one of the three Charites or Graces, all of whom have a distinct fondness for music and dance. So Euphrosyne shares two major qualities with Rachel: her femininity and her love of music.

Through music Rachel can reach silence, the silence and stillness that T.S. Eliot speaks of in "Burnt Norton":

> . . . Words, after speech, reach
> Into the silence. Only by the form, the pattern,
> Can words or music reach
> The stillness . . .[10]


Rachel tries to retain her stillness despite the social demands placed on her. The society that Rachel confronts appears in the form of Richard and Clarissa Dalloway: he once occupied a seat in Parliament, and she is the daughter of a peer (*TVO*, 39). The two exercise their social power, for instance, when they gain passage on the *Euphrosyne*. When they hear that the *Euphrosyne* carries primarily cargo and only takes passengers "by special arrangement," these words encourage the Dalloways, "for they came of a class where almost everything was specially arranged, or could be if necessary" (*TVO*, 40). But the social power they wield makes Rachel feel insecure: "She had come to the depressing conclusion, since the arrival of the Dalloways, that her face was not the face she wanted, and in all probability never would be" (*TVO*, 41).

Richard Dalloway runs his life along distinct sexist lines. Although Rachel resists his blatant sexism somewhat, she does so demurely. For instance, he vehemently objects to woman's suffrage: "May I be in my grave before a woman has the right to vote in England! (*TVO*, 43). He sees woman merely as an adjunct to man and significant only as his inspiration; the woman, Richard believes, should exist in delusion and concern herself with only mundane duties, so that she provides a comfortable refuge for the man who returns home from his job:

> I never allow my wife to talk politics . . . It is impossible for human beings, constituted as they are, both to fight and to have ideals. If I have preserved mine, as I am thankful to say that in great measure I have, it is due to the fact that I have been able to come home to my wife in the evening and to find that she has spent her day in calling, music, play with the children, domestic duties — what you will; her illusions have not been destroyed. She gives me courage to go on. The strain of public life is very great. (*TVO*, 65)

Rachel wishes to argue this point with Richard, "although to talk to a man of such worth and authority made her heart beat" (*TVO*, 65). Nevertheless, she takes one stab when she suggests the figure of a lonely widow whose affections politicians ignore. Richard responds by depicting the state as a complicated machine in which he serves as an essential component. This response misses Rachel's point completely: "It was impossible to combine the image of a lean black widow, gazing out of her window, and longing for someone to talk to, with the image of a vast machine, such as one sees at South Kensington, thumping, thumping, thumping. The attempt at communication had been a failure" (*TVO*, 66).

Richard's insistence on categorizing people according to traditional roles gains support from those women who accept such categorization. Helen Ambrose, for one, wishes to guide Rachel through her growth into maturity, but Helen bases her definition of maturity on society's conventional criteria. And Clarissa Dalloway willingly denigrates herself in Richard's presence:

> "Dick, you're better than I am," said Clarissa. "You see round, where I only see *there*." She pressed a point on the

back of his hand.

"That's my business, as I tried to explain at dinner."

"What I like about you, Dick," she continued, "is that you're always the same, and I'm a creature of moods."

"You're a pretty creature, anyhow," he said, gazing at her with deeper eyes. (*TVO*, 51)

A few minutes later Clarissa muses over her dependence on Richard, which she justifies by considering him her moral superior: "I suppose I feel for him what my mother and women of her generation felt for Christ. It just shows that one can't do without *something*" (*TVO*, 52). Clarissa's reliance on Richard for that *something* she needs reveals her limited concept of life.

Clarissa then compares her younger self to Rachel and implies that when Rachel grows up she will see things correctly, the way Clarissa now sees them. So Clarissa assumes a maternal role with Rachel and Rachel innocently accepts her relative position as ingenue. For Rachel erroneously sees in Clarissa a model of a fully matured woman. Clarissa, by taking on a maternal role, fills the void in Rachel's life created by Mrs. Vinrace's death thirteen years before. Finally, Rachel, now twenty-four years old, establishes a relationship with a maternal figure: "At that moment, standing out in the fresh breeze, with the sun upon the waves, and Mrs. Dalloway's hand upon her arm, it seemed indeed as if life which had been unnamed before was infinitely wonderful, and too good to be true" (*TVO*, 61). This belated union of mother and daughter, even though Clarissa proves herself a victim of social convention, triggers Rachel's movement toward Selfhood. The affirmative love Rachel lacked in not having a mother for better than half her life is now hers. And this union fortifies Rachel to confront Richard Dalloway on issues of politics. She does so with her suggestion that politicians ignore the affections of a lonely widow.

Then the wind comes up and the second major storm of the novel occurs. Richard struggles against the wind as he climbs onto the deck. Then suddenly he collides with Rachel. They both turn into her room to escape the heavy winds. The details in this scene closely align this storm to the first. With the first, Rachel says she will go out to triumph in the wind; and with the second, she comes out of the tempest saying, "Fine, isn't it?" The narrator then tells the reader "Certainly the struggle and wind had given her a decision she lacked; red was in her cheeks, and her hair was down" (*TVO*, 75). Therefore, Rachel seems to return now from the storm she entered at the end of the first chapter. She has, to put it another way, spent chapters 2 through 5 in the storm.

Woolf tells directly what the storm signifies: the activities of the unconscious mind. She presents this definition when she describes people's reaction to the storm during an intermittent calm: "After their view of the strange under-world, inhabited by phantoms, people began to live among tea-pots and loaves of bread with greater zest than ever" (*TVO*, 72). So, if Rachel spends chapters 2 through 5 in the storm in her attempt to triumph in the wind, she has symbolically entered her own unconscious. In that unconscious she contacts the mother long denied to her when she relates to Clarissa Dalloway. Moreover, in the unconscious Rachel collides with a paternal figure — Richard Dalloway. Just as Clarissa supplies Rachel with the closeness to a mother she has lacked, Richard offers Rachel an intimacy that her actual father forbids: Willoughby's face is "more fitted to withstand assaults of the weather than to express sentiments and emotions, or to respond to them in others" (*TVO*, 20-21); conversely, "Richard took her in his arms and kissed her. Holding her tight, he kissed her passionately . . . 'You tempt me,' he said. The tone of his voice was terrifying. He seemed choked in fight" (*TVO*, 76).

The kiss breaks the seal of naiveté that has surrounded Rachel and thus frees her to grow into self-awareness. The first step in growth involves Rachel's handling her immediate reactions to Richard's kiss. Initially, "Life seemed to hold infinite

possibilities she had never guessed at" (*TVO*, 76). But guilt
must appear, because Richard psychically fills the role of
father. So, "At dinner . . . she did not feel exalted, but merely
uncomfortable, as if she and Richard had seen something
together which is hidden in ordinary life, so that they did not
like to look at each other" (*TVO*, 77).

The discomfort grows. That night Rachel has a dream that
adds another dimension to Richard's psychic significance.
Besides father figure, Richard becomes also the projection of
Rachel's own masculine component. This component had lain
dormant when Rachel lived under the care of her aunts,
because they objected, for example, to Rachel's piano playing,
which might develop her forearms in an unladylike way. For-
bidden conscious access to her own masculinity, she compensates by dreaming about it. According to the Jungian
psychologist M.-L. von Franz, dreams contain "aspects of one's
own personality that for various reasons one has preferred not
to look at too closely. This is what Jung called 'the realization
of the shadow.' " [11] Never knowing her own masculine potential, therefore, Rachel finds it frightening:

> She dreamt that she was walking down a long tunnel, which
> grew so narrow by degrees that she could touch the damp
> bricks on either side. At length the tunnel opened and
> became a vault; she found herself trapped in it, bricks
> meeting her wherever she turned, alone with a little deform-
> ed man who squatted on the floor gibbering, with long nails.
> His face was pitted and like the face of an animal. The wall
> behind him oozed with damp, which collected into drops
> and slid down. Still and cold as death she lay, not daring to
> move, until she broke the agony by tossing herself across the
> bed, and woke crying 'Oh!' (*TVO*, 77)

In her descent into her unconscious, symbolized by the vault at
the end of the tunnel, she meets her masculine component that
Richard's kiss arouses. But because it lay unrecognized for so
long, when finally sighted it appears grotesque. As a result,
upon waking, Rachel feels as if this demonic force pursues her:

"All night long barbarian men harrassed the ship; they came scuffling down the passages, and stopped to snuffle at her door. She could not sleep again" (*TVO*, 77).

Hence, her dream, an expression of her unconscious thoughts, completes the stage in growth Rachel makes during the span of time between the first and second storms, when she attempts to triumph in the wind. During this time she contacts parental figures and discovers her own masculine component, that specific force tempering Rachel's feminine identity that has prescribed how she should act. This unconscious complementary element, if integrated with Rachel's feminine identity, can lead to psychic wholeness. Carl Jung explains this phenomenon as one of compensation: "The unconscious processes stand in a compensatory relation to the conscious mind. . . . conscious and unconscious . . . complement one another to form a totality, which is the *self*."[12] Rachel tries to integrate this complementary force so as to become whole, and she does this through her relationships with those people she meets in Santa Marina.

Now Rachel's emotional life extends beyond the perimeter of her immediate family, aunts, uncles, and figures in society who act as parental projections. Because she has made the necessary contact with her parental forces, her psychic scope expands into the social world where she must evaluate various life orientations and her relationship to them. Through all of this she wants to know, "What is the truth? What's the truth of it all?" (*TVO*, 123). She eventually finds the truth after her encounters with several significant characters—St. John Hirst, Terence Hewet, Evelyn Murgatroyd, and Miss Allan—and after three major events in her life—the picnic, the dance, and the trip into the jungle.

Rachel first learns a little about "truth" in the company of Hirst and Hewet. Her growth appears, for instance, in her reaction to Hirst's sexist remark: "About Gibbon . . . D'you think you'll be able to appreciate him? He's the test, of course. It's awfully difficult to tell about women . . . how much, I

mean, is due to lack of training, and how much is native in-
capacity" (*TVO*, 154). After Hirst leaves and Rachel remains
alone in the garden, she exclaims, "Damn that man! . . .
Damn his insolence!" (*TVO*, 155). Hirst offends her in-
,telligence, and she reacts accordingly. Her freedom to feel
outright anger now, which she holds back earlier in the novel
when faced with Richard's sexism, signals Rachel's emotional
growth. This growth also comes out when Rachel spends some
time with Terence. At the picnic, Rachel and Terence, alone
on a walk, accidently see Susan and Arthur embrace. Rachel
flatly states, "I don't like that" (*TVO*, 140). Then, " 'Love's an
odd thing, isn't it, making one's heart beat. . . . And it makes
one sorry for them too,' Rachel continued, as though she were
tracing the course of her feelings" (*TVO*, 140). She does, indeed, trace the course of her own feelings. She first relives her
negative reaction to Richard's kiss. Because of this past incident and the more recent sexist insult hurled at her by Hirst,
she presently concludes that men and women should live
separately, because "we cannot understand each other; we only
bring out what's worst" (*TVO*, 156).

Although Rachel rejects physical intimacy between a male
and female, she nevertheless experiences the same unity but on
a mystical level. At the dance in the hotel, once the musicians
stop, the dancers insist that Rachel play the piano. Consent-
ing, she begins with a few pieces of dance music she knows,
but then moves on to a sonata, then a minuet, then "old
English hunting songs, carols, and hymn tunes" (*TVO*, 166).
At first the guests object that they cannot dance to this kind of
music. But Rachel retorts, "Invent the steps" (*TVO*, 166). And
so they do, losing all self-consciousness as they permit their
bodies to freely relate to the rhythm. Not only do the dancers
drop their demands for conventional dance tunes, but they
also ignore social conventions — women dance with
women — and sexual distinctions — Terence dances like a
woman — while all join in a common movement:

Helen caught the idea; seized Miss Allan by the arm, and whirled round the room, now curtseying, now spinning round, now tripping this way and that like a child skipping through a meadow . . . St. John Hirst hopped with incredible swiftness first on his left leg, then on his right; the tune flowed melodiously; Hewet, swaying his arms and holding out the tails of his coat, swam down the room in imitation of the voluptuous dreamy dance of an Indian maiden dancing before her Rajah . . . By degrees every person in the room was tripping and turning in pairs or alone. (*TVO*, 166)

With her music Rachel harmonizes disparate personalities outside of her own being. She also achieves a psychic integration within herself. In general terms, she brings her private love of music out into the social world so as to unite the two. But, more specifically, she unifies her projections on and reactions to all of these people; she thereby integrates her unconscious contents.

Critics agree that Rachel experiences a freedom at the dance. This freedom, according to Jean Alexander, comes from the combination of the "conventional world (dances are proper) and of . . . her subjective being (music)."[13] But one must also consider the novel's suggestion of the unconscious. Woolf states that once the dancers "fell in with the rhythm they showed a complete lack of self-consciousness" (*TVO*, 166). One also notices that they dance throughout the night — the world of dreams and the unconscious. And, as Susan remarks, music "seems to say all the things one can't say oneself" (*TVO*, 167). The unconscious, likewise, contains all those elements that determine behavior, but which the individual often cannot consciously articulate. Therefore, Woolf again recalls the spirit of Eliot's "Burnt Norton," where he says, "At the still point of the turning world. / . . . at the still point, there the dance is."[14] Rachel creates this still point at the dance. Then she also experiences it in solitude, as she walks off alone dreamily. During this walk she comes upon a symbol from nature, a tree, that represents her integrated Self:

It was an ordinary tree, but to her it appeared so strange
that it might have been the only tree in the world. Dark was
the trunk in the middle, and the branches sprang here and
there, leaving jagged intervals of light between them as
distinctly as if it had but that second risen from the ground.
Having seen a sight that would last her for a lifetime, and
for a lifetime would preserve that second, the tree once more
sank into the ordinary ranks of trees. (*TVO*, 174)

From a grove of trees arises a single tree, complete unto itself,
as from the crowd of dancers arises a single integrated psyche,
Rachel's.

If the dancers represent Rachel's unconscious contents, to
understand Rachel one must investigate her relationship with
these people. From knowledge of Hirst, one can conclude that
he represents the intolerant masculine element in Rachel, that
part of her psychic make-up instilled by the sexist orientation
of her father. This element in Rachel's make-up conflicts with
her essential nature. Bernard Blackstone explains the conflict
as between intuition and reason,[15] but one can also see the
antithesis as operating between socialization and individuality.

Helen Ambrose also fits into the traditional pattern, but not
completely. She can grow, and does somewhat. For example,
at first in her search for a man to help her educate Rachel in
the ways of society, she sees Hirst as just the right person
(*TVO*, 163). But later she realizes the error in her assumption;
she finds Rachel has "a will of her own" (*TVO*, 207). So Helen
represents that part of Rachel that must struggle out of its
cultural conditioning, and she shows signs of having the potential to do so.

Miss Allan, a prisoner to a time schedule dictated by her
father's watch and to her work on her *Primer of English
Literature*, seems nevertheless happy. As Mrs. Elliot notes,
"she seems pretty cheerful" (*TVO*, 115). Miss Allan serves as
an antithesis to Evelyn Murgatroyd. When one first sees Evelyn
she cannot choose between two men who want to marry her.

To use Woolf's terms, Evelyn has become involved in a "profusion of love affairs" (*TVO*, 248). In contrast, Miss Allan stays a solitary figure, deeply involved only in her manuscripts—"Age of Chaucer; Age of Elizabeth; Age of Dryden" (*TVO*, 253). And, as Rachel notices, "Miss Allan's room was very unlike Evelyn's room. There were no variously coloured hatpins on her dressing-table; no scent-bottles; no narrow curved pairs of scissors; no great variety of shoes and boots; no silk petticoats lying on the chairs. The room was extremely neat. There seemed to be two pairs of everything" (*TVO*, 253). And whereas Evelyn remains imprisoned in her own identity—"tormented by the little spark of life in her which was always trying to work through to other people, and was always rebuffed" (*TVO*, 251)—Miss Allan extends herself to Rachel—she "looked at Rachel with great kindness and simplicity, as though she would do her utmost to provide anything she wished to have" (*TVO*, 253). By contacting both these women, Rachel confronts opposites within her own nature: Evelyn represents the socialized Rachel, and Miss Allan stands for the Rachel that exists outside the woman's traditional role. But both women suffer in their respective life styles: Evelyn cannot escape her vanity and Miss Allan cannot escape her compulsions.

In Evelyn's room, Rachel faces the woman her father expects of her, the woman Helen wishes to cultivate in her, the woman Richard reacts to in her. Then, in Miss Allan's room, she faces her solitary self, that part of her she hides from the society that cruelly insists on conformity. Woolf symbolizes the predicament of both these women in her picture of the animal slaughter. Rachel, having just left Evelyn's room, stands alone at the end of a passageway where she stares out a window down into the hotel's kitchen premises. There she watches large women, in cotton dresses besmeared with blood, slaughter and pluck chickens. These chickens symbolize both Evelyn and Miss Allan. Evelyn describes her "Profusion of love affairs" as "a muddle, a detestable, horrible, disgusting muddle!" (*TVO*, 246), while in the kitchen premises the bird chased by the old woman "ran this way and that in sharp angles" (*TVO*, 252). Similarly, just as Miss Allan strips her room and dress of all feminine accounterments, so the woman plucks the chicken's body until it hangs limp in its bare yellow skin. The scene outside the kitchen, therefore, symbolizes Rachel's confused and tortured psychic life.

Rachel hopes that by visiting people she "might remove the mystery which burdened her" (*TVO*, 252). But after her visits to Evelyn and Miss Allan, Rachel remarks to Helen, "It's so unpleasant, being cooped up with people one hardly knows" (*TVO*, 262). Then she adds, "Oh, it's only what's the matter with every one! . . . No one feels—no one does anything but hurt. I tell you, Helen, the world's bad. It's an agony, living, wanting" (*TVO*, 263). From these comments it appears that Rachel suffers from great disillusionment because she has seen in Evelyn and Miss Allan the victims of society's unyielding standards for women. She seeks her own psychic relief by visiting these women, but, as she explains, "One goes from one to another, and it's all the same. One never gets what one wants out of any of them" (*TVO*, 263). Her next step, therefore, must take her deeper into the unconscious to see if any identity resides beyond her acculturated feminine self.

The novel shows this step as the journey into the jungle. There Rachel unites with the psychic element that can help actualize her wholeness. Terence Hewet represents that element. The jungle, as Jean O. Love says, suggests "the chaos of sights and sounds of primordial consciousness."[16] This interpretation finds confirmation in the image Woolf uses to describe the jungle—"The heart of the night" (*TVO*, 265), or the very depths of the psyche. Only at these depths can Rachel clearly see her psychic tie with Hewet, and only here can she accept that element in her that Hewet represents. They can emotionally unite now because they have left the conscious world of society and have entered the primordial one of the jungle.

Before they travel into the jungle, they cannot emotionally meet at any one point. For instance, when Hewet asks Rachel how she spends her day, she questions his reasons for asking. He answers that he has asked "partly because you're a woman" (*TVO*, 215). Rachel objects to what she considers a label, so her anger at Terence grows: "No, she would not consent to be pinned down by any second person in the whole world" (*TVO*, 215). She then turns her glance to the sea; consequently, "a feeling of extreme depression came over him" (*TVO*, 215). Then, immediately afterwards, the flip side of this scene occurs. Terence speaks of the novel he wants to write, "Silence, or the Things People Don't Say." Thoughts of his fiction relieve him of his emotional dependence on Rachel: "In his turn he looked out to sea. She was instantly depressed" (*TVO*, 216). In sum, these twin scenes show the couple's failure to make emotional contact, and the distance between them prevails as long as they remain in the conscious world of society.

In the jungle, however, they silently agree to take a walk together, and as they go deeper into the forest, "silence seemed to have fallen upon the world" (*TVO*, 271). Only in the silence, distanced from the useless and superficial chatter of the social world, can Terence and Rachel truly meet each other:

> "We are happy together." He did not seem to be speaking, or she to be hearing.
> "Very happy," she answered.
> They continued to walk for some time in silence. Their steps unconsciously quickened.
> "We love each other," Terence said.
> "We love each other," she repeated.
> The silence was then broken by their voices which joined in tones of strange unfamiliar sound which formed no words. (*TVO*, 271)

Though they speak to each other before this jungle scene, their words never penetrated through their respective solipsistic shells. Now, they speak with those inarticulate words that lie behind speech, and they communicate. So they know each other through "silence or the things people don't say."

But after the walk in the forest, each succeeding day separates Rachel and Hewet more and more. They now take divergent routes. Terence again becomes preoccupied with the distinctions between male and female and begins to question Rachel about the notes he has taken on the peculiar qualities of women:

> "Not really vainer than men. Lack of self-confidence at the base of most serious faults. Dislike of own sex traditional, or founded on fact? Every woman not so much a rake at heart, as an optimist, because they don't think . . . Again, it's the fashion now to say that women are more practical and less idealistic than men, also that they have considerable organising ability but no sense of honour" — query, what is meant by masculine term honour? — what corresponds to it in your sex? Eh? (*TVO*, 291)

Terence assumes an inherent temperamental gap between the sexes.

And Rachel finds herself emotionally self-sufficient and thus independent of man. She makes this discovery at the point that she and Terence wrestle: "He caught her in his arms as she passed him, and they fought for mastery, imagining a rock, and the sea heaving beneath them. At last she was thrown to the floor, where she lay gasping, and crying for mercy" (*TVO*, 298). The two sexes struggle with each other on a rock, a symbol for the conscious portion of the psyche that stands above the primordial waters. There, the masculine overpowers the feminine. But once Rachel is "flung into the sea, to be washed hither and thither, and driven about the roots of the world," an idea that "was incoherently delightful" to her, she triumphantly cries out "I'm a mermaid! I can swim . . . so the game's up" (*TVO*, 298). She finds she can maneuver on her own in the depths of the churning unconscious, for she has the qualities of both a woman and a fish. The mermaid image portrays her Selfhood: her personal womanliness attracts

Terence's intellect and arouses Richard's passion, while her identification with the holy symbol of the fish underscores her highly spiritual nature. Realizing that she has this spiritual nature, Rachel no longer can find satisfaction in the conscious social world that sees her only as woman. The "truth" she seeks lies deep within her own unconscious.

As a mermaid, Rachel contains a union of opposites — personal with archetypal, gender with no gender. Thus, she loses all need for Terence: "She seemed to be able to cut herself adrift from him, and to pass away to unknown places where she had no need of him" (*TVO*, 302). Rachel "wanted many more things than the love of one human being — the sea, the sky. She turned again and looked at the distant blue, which was so smooth and serene where the sky met the sea; she could not possibly want only one human being" (*TVO*, 302). Rachel gets a glimpse of her wholeness, her Self, where the heavenly sky meets the deep sea, where conscious meets unconscious, so she needs nothing beyond herself. Rachel has achieved union with her Self under the exact terms June Singer prescribes: "One must accept oneself as a total and complete being, else each will be looking for another person who will fill out the inner empty places. This must make the individual the victim of his own emotional dependence." [17] Terence still needs Rachel to fill out his psychic voids, whereas Rachel has achieved total self acceptance.

If Rachel acquires at-oneness with her Self, why does Woolf end Rachel's life so early? [18] The key to Rachel's death lies in the passage from *Comus* that Terence recites aloud. In John Milton's masque, Sabrina liberates a young lady from Comus's spell. Rachel, like the young lady, feels helplessly bound to one who wishes to possess her, Terence. So Rachel needs a power that will liberate her, like Sabrina, whom Milton describes as "swift/ To aid a virgin . . ./ In hard besetting need."[19] When Rachel lies in bed, supposedly ill from jungle fever, she preoccupies herself with trying to remember these lines from *Comus*:

Under the glassy, cool, translucent wave,
In twisted braids of lilies knitting
The loose train of thy amber dropping hair;
(*TVO*, 329)

These lines come from a song to invoke Sabrina. Rachel's reactions to the words show that she identifies not only with the virgin in need of help, but also with the liberating power, Sabrina: "The glassy, cool, translucent wave was almost visible before her, curling up at the end of the bed, and as it was refreshingly cool she tried to keep her mind fixed upon it" (*TVO*, 329). Rachel associates herself with Sabrina, and thereby recalls the delight she feels when she identifies with a mermaid. Both figures dwell in water, an image Woolf uses for the unconscious in *The Voyage Out* as well as in other novels. Thus, in her illness Rachel approaches the truth she seeks throughout the book, the true power of her Self that she contains within, which she cannot acquire in her relationships with others. To become fully immersed in this power within, therefore, Rachel must liberate herself from the binding spell of society.

In her illness, however, Rachel fluctuates between her conscious and her unconscious minds. Slipping into her unconscious, she identifies with Sabrina; then rising into the conscious again, she sees "a nurse in spectacles, whose face vaguely recalled something that she had once seen. She had seen her in the chapel" (*TVO*, 330). The incident Rachel recalls occurs when Mr. Bax gives his sermon on evil:

She ceased to listen, and fixed her eyes on the face of a woman near her, a hospital nurse, whose expression of devout attention seemed to prove that she was at any rate receiving satisfaction. But looking at her carefully she came to the conclusion that the hospital nurse was only slavishly acquiescent, and that the look of satisfaction was produced by no splendid conception of God within her. (*TVO*, 228)

The nurse represents the hypocrisy that Rachel struggles with. The appearance of devotion that covers a spiritual void frightens Rachel, for the same hypocrisy exists in the social world where so many words pass but never touch truth. Consequently, while Rachel lies in bed and sees this nurse, whose figure casts a peaked shadow on the ceiling, all of Rachel's energy "was concentrated upon the desire that this shadow should move. But the shadow and the woman seemed to be eternally fixed above her. She shut her eyes" (*TVO*, 331). Rachel, in other words, closes her eyes to her own superficial identity characterized by hypocrisy, so that she can commune with the spiritual Self she possesses in her psychic depths.

But she cannot escape the conflict between the nurse and Sabrina figures by just closing her eyes. Despite her attempts to escape this conflict, she drops further into it. For instance, she hallucinates a scene that peculiarly mirrors her earlier dream of the deformed man. In the hallucination, Rachel "found herself walking through a tunnel under the Thames, where there were little deformed women sitting in archways playing cards, while the bricks of which the wall was made oozed with damp, which collected into drops and slid down the wall" (*TVO*, 331). Just as in the dream of the deformed man she sees her masculine component as frighteningly grotesque, now in this hallucination she sees her feminine component as equally unattractive. She seeks her Self, but finds only deformity. And such ugliness continues to plague Rachel in her frequent recollections of the old women chopping heads off chickens. She sees heads rolling and the old woman with the knife (*TVO*, 333); and later, when Terence kisses her, she opens her eyes, but she sees only "an old woman slicing a man's head off with a knife" (*TVO*, 339). Hypocrisy fills Rachel's world, and the grotesque continually haunts her. Consequently, Rachel has no choice but to let herself sink into a death-like state, the only asylum for her tormented mind:

> . . . she fell into a deep pool of sticky water, which eventually
> closed over her head. She saw nothing and heard nothing
> but a faint booming sound, which was the sound of the sea
> rolling over her head. While all her tormentors thought that
> she was dead, she was not dead, but curled up at the bottom
> of the sea. There she lay, sometimes seeing darkness,
> sometimes light, while every now and then some one turned
> her over at the bottom of the sea. (*TVO*, 341)

Soon thereafter Rachel allows herself to die, because "she wished to be alone. She wished for nothing else in the world"
(*TVO*, 347). She departs from the social world that has no
cognizance of the spirit, so she can enter the solitude that offers
the spiritual integrity she craves. In the opening of the novel
Rachel leaves her company to triumph in the wind. Here again
she departs, also to triumph.

As she dies, Terence sits by her. So strongly tied to her
psychically, Terence experiences on a conscious level the feelings of release and ensuing calm that Rachel achieves through
death:

> An immense feeling of peace came over Terence, so that he
> had no wish to move or to speak. The terrible torture and
> unreality of the last days were over, and he had come out
> now into perfect certainty and peace. His mind began to
> work naturally again and with great ease. The longer he sat
> there the more profoundly was he conscious of the peace in-
> vading every corner of his soul. Once he held his breath and
> listened acutely; she was still breathing; he went on thinking
> for some time; they seemed to be thinking together; he
> seemed to be Rachel as well as himself; and then he listened
> again; no, she had ceased to breathe. So much the bet-
> ter—this was death. It was nothing; it was to cease to
> breathe. It was happiness, it was perfect happiness. (*TVO*,
> 353)

Through Terence one learns of the perfect happiness that
Rachel finds in death's solitude.

With the novel's last chapter comes the final storm. Virginia
Woolf uses the storm to depict the overwhelming forces of

nature, death being the greatest of such forces. In contrast, the pursuits and concerns of society appear miniscule and insignificant. Rachel recognized this contrast when she discovered that the "truth" she sought lay way beyond the feckless behavior of society. So Rachel departs from this world permanently now, as she did momentarily in the novel's first chapter, to triumph in the raging winds. Meanwhile, the social world remains huddled together out of fear of the natural force: "While the storm continued . . . they collected in little groups under the central skylight . . . looking upwards. Now and again their faces became white, as the lightning flashed, and finally a terrific crash came, making the panes of the skylight lift at the joints" (*TVO*, 369). The overwhelming power of the storm's natural force draws everyone together out of fear. But when the storm subsides and the electricity comes on, the people see themselves in artificial light. For the first time they see the artificiality of their existence, the same artificiality that drives Rachel into death; so "they turned at once and began to move away" (*TVO*, 369). Lines from Milton's "On the Morning of Christ's Nativity," the poem Ridley Ambrose recites just before Rachel's death, perfectly capture the atmosphere at the end of *The Voyage Out*:

> So when the Sun in bed,
> Curtain'd with cloudy red,
>     Pillows his chin upon an Orient wave,
> The flocking shadows pale
> Troop to th'infernall jail,
>     Each fetter'd Ghost slips to his severall grave. [20]

# NOTES

1. Many critics see a connection between these two novels, but they often doubt the works' creative success. For instance, D. S. Savage says, in *The Withered Branch: Six Studies in the Modern Novel* (London: Eyre & Spottiswoode, 1950), that *The Voyage Out* and *Night and Day* are dull and inferior novels (p. 71).    Also, David

Daiches, in *Virginia Woolf*, 2nd ed. (New York: New Directions, 1942), calls the story lines in both novels "simple," and claims that they function as "opportunities for the careful presentation of moods and states of mind" (p. 33).

2. For instance, David Daiches writes, in *Virginia Woolf*, that "throughout the book something is continually breaking up the solidarity of events; the characters suddenly cease being real and become more and more fantastic, then lurch back into reality again" (p. 14).

3. James Hafley, *The Glass Roof: Virginia Woolf as Novelist* (New York: Russell & Russell, 1963), p. 26.

4. Nancy Topping Bazin, *Virginia Woolf and the Androgynous Vision* (New Brunswick, N.J.: Rutgers University Press, 1973), p. 64.

5. Leonard Woolf and James Strachey, eds., *Virginia Woolf & Lytton Strachey: Letters* (New York: Harcourt, Brace and Co., 1956), p. 73.

6. Ibid., p. 75.

7. Virginia Woolf, *The Moment and Other Essays* (New York: Harcourt Brace Jovanovich, 1948), p. 134.

8. Avrom Fleishman views the significance of the title in a similar manner. He says that Rachel's voyage helps her to see "less from the conventional perspective . . . and more in accord with the rhythm of life and death." See *Virginia Woolf: A Critical Reading* (Baltimore, Md.: Johns Hopkins Press, 1975), p. 3.

N. C. Thakur takes quite a different position. To him, the voyage takes Rachel "into the world of love and adventure" and "into the world of experience and comprehension of life." See *The Symbolism of Virginia Woolf* (London: Oxford University Press, 1965), p. 13.

9. Virginia Woolf, *The Voyage Out* (New York: Harcourt, Brace & World, 1920), p. 14. All further quotations and references to the novel will be cited within the text as *TVO*.

10. T. S. Eliot, "Burnt Norton," *Chief Modern Poets of England & America*, ed. Gerald Dewett Saunders, John Herbert Nelson, and M. L. Rosenthal, 4th ed. (New York: Macmillan, 1929), 2: 296.

11. C. G. Jung, ed., *Man and His Symbols* (Garden City, N.Y.: Doubleday & Co., 1964), p. 168.

12. C. G. Jung, *Two Essays on Analytical Psychology*, trans. R. F. C. Hull, 2d ed. (Princeton, N.J.: Princeton University Press, 1966), p. 177.

13. Jean Alexander, *The Venture of Form in the Novels of Virginia Woolf* (Port Washington, N.Y.: Kennikat Press, 1974), p. 47.

14. Eliot, "Burnt Norton," *Chief Modern Poets of England & America*, 2: 294.

15. Bernard Blackstone, *Virginia Woolf: A Commentary* London: Longmans, Green, 1952), p. 26.

16. Jean O. Love, *Worlds in Consciousness* (Berkeley, Calif.: University of California Press, 1970), p. 94.

17. June Singer, *Androgyny: Toward a New Theory of Sexuality* (Garden City, N.Y.: Doubleday & Co., 1976), pp. 323-24.

18. Critics interpret Rachel's death in various ways. For instance, Avrom Fleishman believes in *Virginia Woolf: A Critical Reading*, that Rachel's death confirms her initiation and symbolizes the highest stage of her development (p. 5).

Mitchell A. Leaska, in "Virginia Woolf's *The Voyage Out*: Character Deduction and the Function of Ambiguity," *Virginia Woolf Quarterly* 1 (Winter 1073), says Rachel withdraws into death as a means to protect herself from the life of uncertainty that would result from her marriage to Terence (p. 39).

19. Lines 855-57 from John Milton, *A Mask* in *The Complete English Poetry of John Milton*, ed. John T. Shawcross (New York: New York University Press, 1963), p. 110.

20. Lines 229-34 from John Milton, "On the Morning of Christ's Nativity" in *The Complete English Poetry of John Milton*, p. 49.

## 2

# *Night and Day*
## A Halo of Illusion

The development of the Self picks up in *Night and Day* where it leaves off in *The Voyage Out*.[1] Rachel Vinrace in *The Voyage Out* does advance from her position as an innocent girl in her father's world to a young woman in the social world. But Rachel dies at this point because she cannot sustain her Selfhood while also trying to function in society. She therefore withdraws into death, the only safety zone available. With Katharine Hilbery, in *Night and Day*, the composite personality in Virginia Woolf's novels starts at the exact point Rachel reaches just before her death — the individual in society. Katharine, however, does not despair at the prospect of achieving integration in the living world. She has a great many psychological barriers to hurdle, but she does hurdle them, and thus by the end of the novel she brings Woolf's composite personality to a higher stage of development.

In addition to the fact that *Night and Day* continues the psychological progression from Woolf's first novel, it also seems that the author has greater control of her material in her second novel. Thematic patterns appear with greater clarity, and the transitions between parts flow more smoothly. Most readers of Woolf's first two books agree that *Night and Day* shows definite improvement. Even Woolf comes to the same conclusion when she records in her diary that the *Times Literary Supplement* judged *Night and Day* as having greater depth than *The Voyage Out*. After noting the *Times's* reaction, Woolf adds that she agrees.[2] Even in an earlier diary entry, Woolf states, "In my own opinion *N&D* is a much more mature and finished and satisfactory book than *The Voyage Out*" (*AWD*, 10).

In regard to theme, one critic sees a philosophical rather than a social profundity in the novel. Manly Johnson says that "*Night and Day* embodies one of mankind's most ancient insights into the nature of the relationship between man and woman: the concept of the universe as a system of two powerful forces interacting and complementary."[3] The androgynous concept of the universe surely exists throughout antiquity, for most mythical accounts of creation, including that in the Bible, tell of a male-female unity that stands at the origin of the world. Though fascinating, this topic is not pertinent here. But it does meaningfully correlate with an interest in psychology; just as the universe originated, according to various mythologems, from an androgynous unit, so the psyche has an androgynous core, the Self. The wholeness of the psyche depends upon this union of complementary forces. Woolf's composite being seeks this wholeness.

The title of the novel conveys this concept of complementary forces. One must first go beyond a superficial consideration of the title that uncovers opposites, for night and day also involve complements. As indicated in the preceding chapter, Carl Jung defines psychic totality not as the union of opposites, but as the coalescence of complements (see note 12). Woolf apparently maintains the same theory about totality, because she suggests that just as nighttime or daytime individually makes up only half the day, so masculine and feminine outlooks need each other to complete the psychic whole.

Robert Ornstein, in his work *The Psychology of Consciousness*, charts many associations to the complementary energies of night and day.[4]

WHO PROPOSED IT?

| MANY SOURCES | DAY | NIGHT |
|---|---|---|
| Blackburn | Intellectual | Sensuous |
| Oppenheimer | Time, History | Eternity, Timelessness |
| Deikman | Active | Receptive |
| Polanyi | Explicit | Tacit |
| Levy, Sperry | Analytic | Gestalt |
| Domhoff | Right (side of body) | Left (side of body) |
| Many sources | Left hemisphere | Right hemisphere |
| Bogan | Propositional | Appositional |
| Lee | Lineal | Nonlineal |
| Luria | Sequential | Simultaneous |
| Semmes | Focal | Diffuse |
| *I Ching* | The Creative: heaven, masculine, Yang | The Receptive: earth, feminine, Yin |
| *I Ching* | Light | Dark |
| *I Ching* | Time | Space |
| Many sources | Verbal | Spatial |
| Many sources | Intellectual | Intuitive |
| Vedanta | Buddhi | Manas |
| Jung | Causal | Acausal |
| Bacon | Argument | Experience |

Ornstein's chart contains a pool of typical theories. Clearly, there is no basis upon which to firmly attach Virginia Woolf's theory to any one of the above. But one can get a hint of the world of apparent dichotomies that she entered when Woolf chose the title for her second novel. And these complementary units apply not only to *Night and Day* but to all her fiction.

Woolf consistently focuses on the relationship between the male and the female forces, and in the process of doing so she generally characterizes man as, for example, intellectual and analytic, and woman as sensuous and intuitive. Woolf stresses this theme through her title, *Night and Day*, in which critic Manly Johnson sees a suggestion of the yin-yang totality: "The Taoist *yin-yang* is implicit in the title and in the supporting imagery of light and dark throughout the novel." Johnson then goes on convincingly, "*Night and Day* is essentially the account of two human natures striving to overcome the deceptive self-sufficiency of their individual selves to achieve a combination of forces representing true strength."[5] The evolution of Woolf's composite being into "true strength" emerges as Katharine Hilbery and Ralph Denham travel parallel courses for much of the novel and then finally merge. Their courses parallel each other because they complement each other. One may imagine a total Self split at the outset but integrated by the end.

When the novel begins Katharine is pouring tea. Yet her role as hostess at a Sunday evening tea party holds little of her interest: "Perhaps a fifth part of her mind was thus occupied."[6] As Ralph Denham watches Katharine pour tea he senses the truth about her: "Denham noticed that, although silent, she kept sufficient control of the situation to answer immediately her mother appealed to her for help, and yet it was obvious to him that she attended only with the surface skin of her mind" (*N&D*, 13). Ralph's ability to intuit the truth about Katharine's state establishes, from the very beginning, the psychic tie between these two people.

This tie does not, however, always manifest itself in empathy. Many times an antipathy works between them. For example, Woolf refers to "Katharine's rather malicious determination not to help this young man, in whose upright and resolute bearing she detected something hostile to her surroundings, by any of the usual feminine amenities" (*N&D*, 14). Further hostility between Katharine and Ralph arises when she shows him the room in the house reserved for the writing materials of her dead grandfather, the great poet Richard Alardyce. Katharine senses Ralph's antagonism towards her; she feels it continually, except when her own thoughts become lost in recollection of her grandfather and of his possessions.

The next few occurrences of hostility between these two people reveal the causes of this antagonism. First, when Katharine refers to traditions within her family, Ralph says, "you see, we don't have traditions in our family." Katharine retorts, "You sound very dull," to which Ralph answers, "Merely middle class" (*N&D*, 19). Ralph shows here his feelings of inadequacy when faced with the upper-class status of the Hilberys. Katharine embodies the social power that makes Ralph insecure, so he must attack her to protect himself: " 'You'll never know anything at first hand,' he began, almost savagely. 'It's all been done for you. You'll never know the pleasure of buying things after saving up for them, or reading books for the first time, or making discoveries' " (*N&D*, 19). Ralph's real disapproval, however, aims at his own relatively low social class. As the events in *Night and Day* unfold, Ralph gradually conquers his self-hatred.

The next incident of hostility uncovers the impediment to full maturity peculiar to Katharine: "She wished to annoy him, to waft him away from her on some light current of ridicule or satire, as she was wont to do with these intermittent young men of her father's" (*N&D*, 20). She seems to resent these men because they are men, and thereby enjoy a certain relationship with her father denied because of her gender. Consequently, she throws her anger, aroused by social restrictions, at the very person she envies. In order for Katharine to grow she must learn to accept and approve of her own masculine element, regardless of society's edicts concerning the proper behavior for a young woman. She eventually does accept it by letting Ralph into her life and loving him. But she initially tries to ease this conflict through escape.

Katharine's wish to escape stems from the same discomfort in society that Rachel Vinrace feels in *The Voyage Out*. Katharine has no death wish, as does Rachel, yet her escape routes resemble death in that they provide a way out of immediate existence. In her first means of escape, Katharine allows herself to become preoccupied with the past. The assistance Katharine gives her mother on the biography of Richard Alardyce supplies the occasion and the materials for Katharine's preoccupation with the past:

> The glorious past, in which men and women grew to unexampled size, intruded too much upon the present, and

dwarfed it too consistently, to be altogether encouraging to
one forced to make her experiment in living when the great
age was dead.

She was drawn to dwell upon these matters more than was
natural, in the first place owing to her mother's absorption
in them, and in the second because a great part of her time
was spent in imagination with the dead, since she was help-
ing her mother to produce a life of the great poet. (*N&D*,
39)

Katharine's work with the past grows to an unhealthy degree,
and she knows this: "Sometimes she felt that it was necessary
for her very existence that she should free herself from the past;
at others, that the past had completely displaced the present"
(*N&D*, 43).

Though Katharine recognizes that her absorption in the past
fetters her personality, she cannot seem to alter the situation.
The immersion in past grandeur apparently satisfies two needs.
One, it offers a relationship with her grandfather that
resembles the one those "intermittent young men" have with
her father. As a result, her envy of these young men lessens as
long as her masculine nature finds expression. Second, by the
same token, she exercises her much-denied masculinity in the
detail work she does on the biography. Katharine knows that
someone has to apply some order to the writing process to
counter her mother's diffuse and disorganized manner. So, in a
fastidious way, one that Ornstein's chart identifies as
masculine, Katharine sets down rules of composition: she and
her mother should sit down punctually every morning at ten
o'clock and resist any temptation to converse until the hourly
ten-minute break (*N&D*, 41). The two reasons, therefore, for
Katharine's deep involvement with the past actually serve one
common purpose, that of freeing her repressed masculine component. Just as Rachel Vinrace escapes into her music to free
her Self of social demands, so Katharine escapes into the past
where she can comfortably use her innate masculine attributes.

Katharine's second means of escape from reality entails her
work on mathematics. She hides her love for mathematics from

everyone. She could tolerate exposing her fantasies of the "taming of wild ponies upon the American prairies, or the conduct of a vast ship in a hurricane round a black promontory of rock," or any other fantasy that is "marked by her complete emancipation from her present surroundings" (*N&D*, 45) but she could not bear anyone knowing of her math. Woolf explicitly states why Katharine's work with figures demands such secrecy: "Perhaps the unwomanly nature of the science made her instinctively wish to conceal her love of it. But the more profound reason was that in her mind mathematics were directly opposed to literature" (*N&D*, 46). Again there are two reasons for one of Katharine's means of escape, and again they amount to the same thing. Not only does she emotionally nourish herself with activity typically masculine, activity which would arouse much disapprobation from her society-conscious parents, but she, through math, becomes liberated from her mother whose first love is literature. As Woolf writes, "Her mother was the last person she wished to resemble, much though she admired her" (*N&D*, 46). Thus, Katharine's second escape route, like her first, allows for the expression of her masculine qualities.

The third and last way in which Katharine escapes consists of her imagined "magnanimous hero." This fantasy figure originates in her desire to know love but results in her inability to experience love. Woolf clearly presents this paradox when she says of Katharine, "Not having experience of it herself, her mind had unconsciously occupied itself for some years in dressing up an image of love, and the marriage that was the outcome of love, and the man who inspired love, which naturally dwarfed any examples that came her way" (*N&D*, 107). This fantasy protects Katharine from intimacy, for no one could ever compete with such an enormously romantic figure who accompanies Katharine on thrilling horseback rides through the forests and along the shore of the sea. Not only does this fantasy guarantee distance between Katharine and realistic intimacy, but it also forces upon her a picture of "a perfectly loveless marriage, as the thing one did actually in real life"

(*N&D*, 107-8). With all this, Katharine protects herself from the romantic expectations of the men around her. But why? For the same reason she submerges herself in the past and withdraws to her room to work on mathematics. Katharine envisions romantic advances made towards her as necessitating that she respond in a typically female way. Because her sophisticated upbringing overloads her with demands to act as a proper woman, her unconscious compensates with defense mechanisms that keep her masculine element safe from the onslaught.

Ralph runs a parallel course to Katharine's, for he operates as her masculine complement. As a mirror reflection of Katharine, who struggles with a masculinity that yearns to be expressed, Ralph needs the feminine so much in his life that he raises Katharine to the eminence of a goddess. He wishes her mind "to be exalted and infallible, and of such independence that it was only in the case of Ralph Denham that it swerved from its high, swift flight, but where he was concerned, though fastidious at first, she finally swooped from her eminence to crown him with her approval" (*N&D*, 24-25). Consequently, Ralph views Katharine in a purely fantastic atmosphere:

> For ever since he had visited the Hilberys he had been much at the mercy of a phantom Katharine, who came to him when he sat alone, and answered him as he would have her answer, and was always beside him to crown those varying triumphs which were transacted almost every night, in imaginary scenes, as he walked through the lamplit streets home from the office. (*N&D*, 93)

So Ralph, like Katharine, constructs a fantastic image that, because of its grandiose dimensions, inevitably creates conflict whenever confronted with reality. And just as Katharine's "magnanimous hero" defends against any anxiety and guilt pursuant to her attaining the love she craves, so Ralph's dream image of Katharine safely distances him from the real woman. Both Katharine and Ralph need each other because each fills a void in the other. Whereas Ralph supplies the masculinity that Katharine has been denied, Katharine provides Ralph "with something the lack of which had left a bare place in his mind for a considerable time" (*N&D*, 25). Until both stop seeing each other as foreign in nature, they continue to delay their union by disfiguring reality with their respective dreams, halos of illusion.

Katharine's passage into psychic liberation rests on her movement through two major stages. These stages involve her relationship with William Rodney and her friendship with Mary Datchet. When the novel begins, Katharine plans to marry William Rodney. Because she lives so deeply within a conventional existence at the beginning, one can understand why she permits such an entrapment. William strictly adheres to the traditional outlook. This is clear, for instance, when he tells Katharine that he recommends marriage for all women: "Not for you only, but for all women. Why, you're nothing at all without it; you're only half alive; using only half your faculties" (*N&D*, 66). Likewise, William's constant fear of rumors that might malign his image characterize him as steeped in traditional attitudes. This concern appears one night when William and Katharine walk together, having just left a meeting at Mary Datchet's home. William says to Katharine, "I can tell you that if any of your friends saw us together at this time of night they would talk about it, and I should find that very disagreeable" (*N&D*, 68). Katharine labels such concerns as nonsense and calls William an "old maid." The fact that she recognizes the ridiculous aspect of social conventions and feels free enough to say so puts her slightly ahead of William in emotional emancipation. Katharine will continue to grow, shedding her relationship with William, which proves dead and useless, yet William never changes. His unwavering conventionality acts as a yardstick by which one can gauge Katharine's growth.

Mary Datchet, unlike William, changes somewhat in her outlook. She leaves her volunteer job in the suffrage office to work on the development of a utopian state; that is, her objectives in life shift from women's liberation to human liberation. Despite this change, Mary's priority on freedom remains a constant. Katharine's growth, therefore, is reflected in her changing attitude toward Mary. In addition, something else remains constant in Mary's personality—her androgynous nature. Woolf expresses this fact when she says, in describing Mary, "It was quite evident that all the feminine instincts of pleasing, soothing, and charming were crossed by others in no way peculiar to her sex" (*N&D*, 48). An incident shortly afterwards emphasizes Mary's androgyny: the fact that Mary reads Emerson surprises Ralph and when Mary asks, "Why shouldn't I read Emerson?", Ralph answers, "There's no reason that I know of. It's the combination that's odd—books and stockings. The combination is very odd" (*N&D*, 50). Due to her androgynous interests, Mary stands for what Katharine could achieve in an emotionally evolved state, one in which Katharine could freely demonstrate her masculine interests side by side with her feminine attributes.

Katharine senses that Mary has achieved what she fears to attempt. This applies not only to Mary's androgyny but also to her devotion to a cause and her participation in public work. When Katharine contrasts herself with Mary on this point, she recognizes passivity as a major weakness in her own personality. Katharine tells Mary that she feels melancholy at the thought that she has never really done anything. Then she says, "I want to assert myself" (*N&D*, 58). The fact that she can admit this signals a significant step in her growth, but to utter a truth takes far less courage than to act on it. Katharine eventually does assert herself, but in the meantime she must endure the conflict between her values and her willingness to work for those values.

Since Katharine's growth depends upon Ralph's and since their lives run parallel courses, Ralph now suffers a conflict similar to Katharine's. His conflict takes place between his work life and his dream life. He turns to his dreams of glory and adventure as a relief from the public opinions and demands placed on him in the solicitor's office. And after he meets Katharine, Ralph's dream life becomes more and more filled with thoughts of her. But just as Katharine does not yet have the courage to act upon her beliefs, Ralph cannot act out his dreams: "To walk through the streets of London until he came to Katharine's house, to look up at the windows and fancy her within, seemed to him possible for a moment; and then he rejected the plan almost with a blush" (*N&D*, 130).

Now that Woolf has brought Katharine and Ralph up to a vital stage in their development, she marks the stage with duplicate scenes for the two of them. Ralph visits Mary and experiences a dilemma. Mary loves him, but he cannot love her. He cannot relate to her because he feels blocked by her masculine nature, the quality which makes her a devotee to her work and to her causes. So, although wishing to tell Mary about his absorption in thoughts of Katharine, Ralph "could not talk to Mary about such thoughts; and he pitied her for knowing nothing of what he was feeling" (*N&D*, 131). Ralph will continue to see the masculine part of Mary's personality as a barrier until his own personality balances with Katharine's. Once Katharine and Ralph unite in love, Ralph's resistance to Mary subsides.

While Ralph goes to Mary but cannot relate to her, Katharine goes to William. And while Ralph wishes to expose his dream world of romance to Mary but cannot, conversely Katharine wishes her intellect to be acknowledged by William. William, however, refuses to budge from his conventional attitudes and thus ends up insulting Katharine's intelligence, as when he reads a part of his play to her. Katharine offers some scholarly criticism, but William says, "My dear Katharine . . . I don't ask you for criticism, as I should ask a scholar . . . But I trust you where feeling is concerned" (*N&D*, 140). William's denial of Katharine's intelligence gives her encouragement in exactly the opposite way than she needs. Katharine needs, instead, an atmosphere in which her masculine side can play freely, rather than hide in the loneliness of her room.

Katharine fully knows the pain of this situation; she has not repressed her true desires that far into unconsciousness. But these desires do not occupy so high a position in consciousness that Katharine wants to alter her conventional life orientation. She therefore "felt certain that she would marry Rodney" (*N&D*, 141). But the more she resigns herself to that end, the more her dream world and the figure of her "magnanimous hero" intrude on her real world:

> Here she sighed, and, putting the thought of marriage away, fell into a dream state, in which she became another person, and the whole world seemed changed . . . so direct, powerful, and unimpeded were her sensations there, compared with those called forth in actual life. There dwelt the things one might have felt, had there been cause; the perfect happiness of which here we taste the fragment; the beauty seen here in flying glimpses only. (*N&D*, 141)

Therefore, the compensatory action of the human psyche between the conscious and the unconscious minds protects Katharine from having to discharge her subliminal desires, those desires that would complete her innate wholeness. Rather, her unconscious provides a dream world in which her hidden wishes can safely reside until they can surface unharmed.

Not much later, in chapters 15 through 19, another pronounced parallel between Katharine's and Ralph's movements appears. During the Christmas season Ralph visits with Mary at Disham near Lincoln. Another village, Lampsher, lies about three miles outside of Lincoln. Here Katharine visits her relatives the Otways for the holidays, and William accompanies her. These scenes do not duplicate each other, as the preceding ones do, but they connect causally. In other words, the emotional advances Katharine makes in this section of the book create a compensatory reaction in her masculine component, Ralph.

In Lampsher, Katharine shows signs of capitulating to societal conventions and thus to Rodney. She decides she can accept marriage with Rodney, but to do so she must view life mathematically, which robs life of its emotional energy. She explains this decision in an imaginary conversation she holds with her cousin Henry, the only person she feels she can confide in. As she walks up and down a gravel path in the garden of Stogdon House, the Otway residence, Katharine thinks, "I'm not domestic, or very practical or sensible, really. And if I could calculate things, and use a telescope, and have to work out figures, and know to a fraction where I was wrong, I should be perfectly happy, and I believe I should give William all he wants" (*N&D*, 195).

Socialization forces a woman to think only of what she can give the man; the success of a relationship rests on the man's comfort, his pleasure with the woman's conversation, and his approval of her physical appearance. Katharine has been trained to conform to all of the demands:

Would she, indeed, give William all he wanted? In order to decide the question, she ran her mind rapidly over her little collection of significant sayings, looks, compliments, gestures, which had marked their intercourse during the last day or two. He had been annoyed because a box, containing some clothes specially chosen by him for her to wear, had been taken to the wrong station, owing to her neglect in the matter of labels. The box had arrived in the nick of time, and he had remarked, as she came downstairs on the first night, that he had never seen her look more beautiful. She outshone all her cousins. He had discovered that she never made an ugly movement; he also said that the shape of her head made it possible for her, unlike most women, to wear her hair low. He had twice reproved her for being silent at dinner; and once for never attending to what he said. He had been surprised at the excellence of her French accent, but he thought it was selfish of her not to go with her mother to call upon the Middletons, because they were old family friends and very nice people. (*N&D*, 195-96)

These are the criteria by which society judges a woman. At no
point does William consider Katharine, or what makes her a
distinct personality, or what might please her.

In order to subdue her internal tumult, Katharine asks for
further training in socialized behavior. Such training would
help her block out any defiant thoughts that would cause a
chaotic fight for liberation. So when her Aunt Charlotte says,
"It's no good being married unless you submit to your
husband" (*N&D*, 211), as Katharine paraphrases her aunt's
message, and when Mrs. Hilbery says, "If you can give way to
your husband . . . a happy marriage is the happiest thing in the
world" (*N&D*, 212), Katharine "wished to induce her mother
and her aunt to go on talking about marriage, for she was in
the mood to feel that other people could help her if they
would" (*N&D*, 212).

Because of the severe suppression Katharine imposes on
herself here, her masculine component suffers enormously.
Katharine's hampered Selfhood must deny entrance to its
masculine part, for its expression would counter everything
William expects of her. Ralph, the representative of her
masculine component, consequently ends up feeling alone and
in need of love. He wants Mary to mother him, wishing "to lay
his head on her shoulder and sob, while she parted his hair
with her fingers and soothed him . . . He felt that he was very
lonely, and that he was afraid of the other people in the room"
(*N&D*, 229). He is indeed alone, since Katharine deserts her
masculine element.

The consolation that Ralph wants from Mary substitutes for
the love and acceptance he needs from Katharine. Katharine
cannot give this love to him until she admits to herself that
nothing holds her to William except convention. Once she admits to her lack of affection for William, she can view Ralph
with compassion rather than resentment. Katharine begins
taking this step when she tells William that their engagement
will not work. William cries when he hears this. To stop his
weeping, Katharine "put her arms about him, drew his head

for a moment upon her shoulder, and led him on, murmuring words of consolation, until he heaved a great sigh" (*N&D*, 243). This scene replays that between Ralph and Mary: just as Ralph feels very lonely, Katharine sees loneliness in William as he stands up and brushes the leaves off his coat. Such duplication in details betokens the eventual union of Katharine and Ralph.

From this point on in the novel the reader watches Woolf's composite being step-by-step reconcile the conflicts that have barred growth. Woolf marks this turning point with references to a particular phenomenon: a woman's life is saved just in time. These references stop the action momentarily so as to capture the present emotional condition of the composite personality. The first reference comes from Katharine's past. As an infant, she was left alone in a perambulator. The red color of the infant's blanket enraged a bull. A gentleman walking by protected Katharine just in time from the bull's anger. Now, when Ralph and Katharine meet in Lincoln over the Chirstmas holidays, Katharine refers to that story. She implies that Ralph acts as the gentleman who saved her in that Ralph helps Mrs. Hilbery locate Katharine after the two women accidentally separate. As Katharine explains the situation, "I was looking for my mother. It happens every time we come to Lincoln . . . Not that it very much matters, because some one always turns up in the nick of time to help us out of our scrapes. Once I was left in a field with a bull" (*N&D*, 235).[7]

The second time this theme comes up is as soon as the Hilberys leave Ralph behind at Lincoln. Just a couple of miles outside of Lampsher, the carriage comes upon "a lonely spot marked by an obelisk of granite, setting forth the gratitude of some great lady of the eighteenth century who had been set upon by highwaymen at this spot and delivered from death just as hope seemed lost" (*N&D*, 237). The picture of being saved in time now includes the figure of William, who acts as a threatening highwayman. Rodney suggests he and Katharine get out of the carriage at this point and walk the rest of the way; he wants to express privately his anger at her. Katharine continues to read silently the inscription on the obelisk until Rodney blurts out, "No one enjoys being made a fool of before other people . . . Every day since we've been here you've done something to make me appear ridiculous" (*N&D*, 238). William, in other words, suddenly attacks Katharine. But no one miraculously saves her from this attack, and she does not know how to rescue herself. She has not yet discovered that the saving power actually exists within her, and so she lets herself fall back into convention. Once again she agrees to marry William.

Having fallen back into convention, Katharine returns to her compensatory escape routes. But she finds them unsatisfactory, even repulsive. This leaves her with only one direction — Mary Datchett:

> If she went by the Strand she would force herself to think out the problem of the future, or some mathematical problem; if she went by the river she would certainly begin to think about things that didn't exist — the forest, the ocean beach, the leafy solitudes, the magnanimous hero. No, no, no! A thousand times no! — it wouldn't do; there was something repulsive in such thoughts at present; she must take something else; she was out of that mood at present. And then she thought of Mary; the thought gave her confidence, even pleasure of a sad sort. . . . (*N&D*, 270)

Thoughts of Mary please Katharine because Mary exercises both her masculine and her feminine attributes, a quality Katharine desperately needs. Mary can love Ralph; Katharine must acquire this same capacity. If she can love Ralph, her masculine complement, she can contact her Self, that core of psychic wholeness that will rescue her from any threatening forces. In the present scene, therefore, when Katharine goes to Mary, she seeks her own potential integration. Up to now, Katharine has found it too difficult to admit to herself that Ralph loves her. So she turns to the woman who embodies her own repressed Selfhood, and this woman tells Katharine, "he's in love with you" (*N&D*, 276). Mary, psychologically speaking, acts as a voice inside Katharine. As a result, Katharine experiences communication between her conscious and unconscious selves. With this long-awaited union accomplished, the two women can enjoy the comfort of silence: "Mary had no wish to speak. In the silence she seemed to have lost her isolation; she was at once the sufferer and the pitiful spectator of suffering; she was happier than she had ever been; she was more bereft; she was rejected, and she was immensely beloved" (*N&D*, 278).

Katharine learns from her exposure to Mary that it is "some littleness of nature" (*N&D*, 283) that goes into the refinements and reserves of conventional behavior. Because "more and more the condition of Mary's mind" seems to her "wonderful and enviable" (*N&D*, 285), Katharine finds no pleasure in society's littleness of nature. She thus tells William that he would probably find greater happiness with someone like her cousin Cassandra. Katharine sees Cassandra as frivolous: "Now it was socialism, now it was silkworms, now it was music" (*N&D*, 283). And because of Cassandra's capricious nature, Katharine assumes that William would find much in common with her. When she makes this suggestion, Katharine demonstrates to William that she has grown emotionally beyond his level. He, therefore, takes no umbrage when Katharine asks if he loves Cassandra, for Cassandra will not revolt against William's superficial expectations.

Katharine has now shed the greatest impediment to her growth — the force that would impose sexist limitations on her personality. It follows, then, that at this point Ralph should join her, which he does. When Ralph knocks at William's door Katharine tells William he must open it; she, in other words, tells her socialized identity to admit a healthy portion of her psyche. Once Ralph walks in and he and Katharine exchange a few words, she realizes, although she cannot remember what Mary said, "that there was a mass of knowledge in her mind which she had not had time to examine — knowledge now lying on the far side of a gulf" (*N&D*, 293). This knowledge is love.

the
pen
she
nd.
by
o-
n-
ic
,
.

she has kept herself ignorant of this love up until
in her image of a gulf. But for the rest of the novel
raverses that gulf, as she and Ralph draw closer un-
ally unite in love.

egins the movement towards this union; he drops
rriers that separate him from love. As he and
e leave William's house together, Ralph wishes to
is negative feelings. He resents Katharine for casting
phantoms and pitfalls across his path"; and he resolves
stion the real Katharine until they can both justify her
ance over him, or she renounces it. In short, he wants to
ont his dream world with the real world. Katharine, on
other hand, knows only that she feels a certain anger
ard him because of something she vaguely recalls Mary
d. Although she only vaguely recalls Mary's clear declara-
n that Ralph loves Katharine, she remembers enough to
islike Ralph for it; she has not yet learned to accept herself,
and so cannot accept his love. Only when she learns to like
herself can she stop blaming Ralph for loving her. Ralph,
however, continues to advance emotionally as he brings his
private world of dreams and phantoms out into the open and
confronts the real Katharine with them: "I've dreamt about
you; I've thought of nothing but you; you represent to me the
only reality in the world" (*N&D*, 297). This truth overwhelms
Katharine. She sidesteps the impact by filling her mind with
algebraic symbols. Because the truth tenaciously resists
dismissal, however, it penetrates Katharine's mind on some
level. As a result, she finds herself bifurcated into two bodies,
"one walking by the river with Denham, the other concentrated to a silver globe" (*N&D*, 300). The first opposes what
Ralph tells her while the other listens and exults in a perfect
joy. Nevertheless, "that her condition was due to him, or to
anything that he had said, she had no consciousness at all"
(*N&D*, 301).

Katharine's fear of love prevents her from joining these two
bodies. Even additional symptoms of her bifurcation appear

later on. As she goes through some letters intended for Alardyce biography, she cannot continue her work. Her remaining suspended in the air, "almost surreptitiously slipped a clean sheet in front of her, and her hand, desce ing, began drawing square boxes halved and quartered straight lines, and then circles which underwent the same p cess of dissection" (*N&D*, 306). Here she works with the co ponents of the mandala, an archetypal symbol for psych wholeness.[8] But she draws the parts detached from each othe rather than superimposed on each other as in the mandala Moreover, she dissects the circles and squares. In other words Katharine can now conceive of wholeness, knows the parts tha compose that wholeness, but approaches these parts through analysis rather than synthesis.

Although continuing to act out of fear of love, "the more she looked into the confusion of lives" the more she saw that they, "instead of running parallel, had suddenly intersected each other" (*N&D*, 313). Specifically, she begins to see patterns, especially between the people most important to her now: "Her mind, passing from Mary to Denham, from William to Cassandra, and from Denham to herself—if, as she rather doubted, Denham's state of mind was connected with herself—seemed to be tracing out the lines of some symmetrical pattern, some arrangement of life" (*N&D*, 314). This vision marks Katharine's first substantial glimpse into her own totality. Each individual in her vision represents a part of her wholeness. Mary corresponds to her potential integration of male and female capable of love for Ralph; Ralph signifies her masculine portion that she needs to incorporate; and Cassandra and William stand for her socialized identity that she must relinquish so it no longer cripples her Selfhood.

The progress Katharine makes shows up on that Saturday when she and Ralph meet at the lake in Kew Gardens. They finally converse without the intrusion of phantom figures and without the disruption of hostility caused by fear. Here Ralph explains to Katharine about the different types of trees and flowers, and Katharine "wished he would go on for ever" because nature showed an order independent of human rules and expectations. These rules have long victimized her social- ized self, but now she wants the more that lies outside of society:

> Circumstances had long forced her, as they force most women in the flower of youth, to consider, painfully and minutely, all that part of life which is conspicuously without order; she had had to consider moods and wishes, degrees of liking or disliking, and their effect upon the destiny of peo- ple dear to her; she had been forced to deny herself any con- templation of that other part of life where thought con- structs a destiny which is independent of human beings. As Denham spoke, she followed his words and considered their bearing with an easy vigor which spoke of a capacity long hoarded and unspent. (*N&D*, 331)

Having lifted her head to see beyond the barriers of society, Katharine exults in the new world open to her. She gains vision into her Self because of her affection for Ralph, and this first significant vision will impel her to see even more. She has, at last, permitted egress to that capacity "long hoarded and un- spent," and with the energy that builds in captivity, this capaci- ty will force its way out of Katharine's unconscious with greater and greater strength.

Katharine's increasing acceptance of Ralph shows when she agrees to go to his home in Highgate for tea. But once she ar- rives, the sight of Ralph's home awakens her fear of love, which she projects onto his home. She "decided that Ralph Denham's family was commonplace, unshapely, lacking in charm, and fitly expressed by the hideous nature of their furniture and decorations" (*N&D*, 375). In reality, Katharine's disgust does not arise from what she considers the crude and tasteless ap- pearance of a social class lower than hers. Instead, she projects her own feelings of inadequacy onto the Denham household. Proof of this projection comes out in Katharine's reaction when Ralph discloses that thoughts of her consume him. She cannot accept this, because she has not yet learned to accept herself.

So she tells him, "Look at me, Ralph . . . I assure you that I'm far more ordinary than I appear." Then she says, "Now you can't separate me from the person you've imagined me to be. You call that, I suppose, being in love; as a matter of fact it's being in delusion" (*N&D*, 381). She throws up all possible roadblocks because she cannot believe he loves her. This is a struggle with a fully understandable doubt. After all, she has been trained to extend a superficial image of herself to friends and suitors by attracting them with dress and poise and flattering them with pleasing conversation. Katharine knows that such dress and talk contain nothing of a person's true personality. So when Ralph says that he truly loves her, she cannot believe he sees her true Self. Despite her protests, she nevertheless intuits from his words, or in the way he speaks them, something else. She wonders, does he see "something she had never shown to anybody? Was it not something so profound that the notion of his seeing it almost shocked her?" (*N&D*, 383).

Woolf proceeds to show Katharine's evolution by switching to the effect it has on Ralph. In the last scene Katharine is conflicted over her apparent and true identies, concerned that she may be as commonplace as she fears. The next step in her growth, then, demands she accept herself. Ralph, accordingly, wrestles with the possible discrepancy between Katharine's apparent self and his idealized notion of her. He decides to test one against the other. Figuring that her actual beauty could not stand up under deep examination, he compares it to some photographs he has of Greek statues. This exercise, however, confirms not the difference but the similarities between Katharine and the figure in his dreams. No matter how he conjures up her faults, they melt away in the beauty of this splendid union:

> Once more he told over conscientiously her faults, both of face and character; they were clearly known to him; but they merged themselves in the flawless union that was born

of their association. They surveyed life to its uttermost limits. How deep it was when looked at from this height! How sublime! How the commonest things moved him almost to tears! Thus, he forgot the inevitable limitations; he forgot her absence, he thought it of no account whether she married him or another; nothing mattered, save that she should exist, and that he should love her. (*N&D*, 386)

Thrilled with this discovery, Ralph feels driven to tell someone. He first rushes to Mary, and then to Rodney. Unsatisfied and fatigued, he momentarily stops at the Embankment, and there is enlightened by a vision: "An odd image came to his mind of a lighthouse besieged by the flying bodies of lost birds, who were dashed senseless, by the gale, against the glass" (*N&D*, 394). Once when he walks to the Hilbery home and stands outside looking up at the window, the same image occurs, and Ralph identifies the lighthouse with Katharine and the birds with himself: "He seemed curiously to see her as a shape of light, the light itself; he seemed, simplified and exhausted as he was, to be like one of those lost birds fascinated by the lighthouse and held to the glass by the splendor of the blaze" (*N&D*, 395). This vision implies that he must gain admittance into the source of light, Katharine. As Ralph stands under the street lamp outside the Hilbery home, he yearns to enter. Once Katharine finally does permit Ralph to enter her home, "Denham looked half dazed by the strong light, and, buttoned in his overcoat, with his hair ruffled across his forehead by the wind, he seemed like somebody rescued from an open boat out at sea" (*N&D*, 419). This sea imagery certainly follows through on the lighthouse vision, but it also recalls the theme of being saved in the nick of time. Katharine's and Ralph's identities have merged, for he now envisions himself as the saved and she as the savior, whereas earlier the roles were reversed.

Ralph's pursuit of Katharine partially completes their union. The final step depends on Katharine's active pursuit of Ralph. Her passive acceptance does not suffice; she still must satisfy her need to assert herself. Woolf brings back the image of the birds and lighthouse to depict Katharine's present state. Katharine describes the "unreality—the dark—the waiting outside in the wind" (*N&D*, 421-22). Katharine sees herself as waiting, and thus surrounded by darkness. She does not even see a light to turn toward. And she will remain in the darkness of unreality until she unites the conditions of her life to those of her dreams.

To do this, she must first accept her mother. Up to now she has rejected any possible similarities between her mother and herself. Confronted with her mother's feminine social graces, Katharine nurtures her own masculine qualities out of rebellion. But now she realizes that she too possesses a socially feminine character, and if she accepts it voluntarily rather than permit society to foist it on her, this characteristic will not damage her integrity. This realization comes when Cassandra remarks, "How like Aunt Maggie you look!" Katharine immediately replies, "Nonsense"; however, Woolf writes, "In truth, now that her mother was away, Katharine did feel less sensible than usual" (*N&D*, 434). So not only due to all the emotional progress she has made so far, but also due to her mother's absence, and thus the absence of a model against which Katharine fashions herself, Katharine wishes "to change her actual condition for something matching the conditions of her dream" (*N&D*, 434). In other words, she can accept her love for Ralph because the real world can equal her imagined one.

This discovery sets Katharine off on a chase after Ralph. First she rushes to Lincoln's Inn Fields, outside the solicitor's office where Ralph works, and then to his home in Highgate. Not knowing his address, she goes to Mary's, and while there decides to wait a while in the hopes that he might turn up. As she sits at Mary's in silence, Katharine thinks she has "missed him, and knew the bitterness of all failure; she desired him, and knew the torment of all passion. It did not matter what trivial accidents led to this culmination. Nor did she care how extravagant she appeared, nor how openly she showed her feelings" (*N&D*, 448). Directly after admitting her love for Ralph, Katharine rises and announces her decision to go home, to go back into her own Self where Ralph waits for her. When she arrives home and opens the door of the dining room where Ralph sits, she becomes possessed of an "extraordinary clearness of sight." As she looks at him, finally seeing him cleared of all her projections, she is overcome by "a flood of confusion, of relief, of certainty, of humility, of desire no longer to strive and to discriminate, yielding to which, she let herself sink within his arms and confessed her love" (*N&D*, 452).

Unfortunately this union does not last. The ephemerality of the bond stems from Ralph's unevolved attitude toward love: "He wished to dominate her, to possess her" (*N&D*, 489). He needs her more than loves her, and Katharine senses the pressure of this need. She therefore tells Ralph that she has no objection to their staying together, "It's only marriage that's out of the question" (*N&D*, 472). She realizes that Ralph still suffers from the split between the real and the imagined Katharine: "Ralph expressed vehemently . . . that he only loved her shadow and cared nothing for her reality" (*N&D*, 473). Having found her own integrated personality, Katharine needs that personality to be fully acknowledged and unadorned by fantasy.

Not only does Ralph vehemently verbalize his dilemma; he sketches it as well. On a letter to Katharine, in which he says that "if life were no longer circled by an illusion . . . then it would be too dismal an affair to carry to an end" (*N&D*, 487), Ralph doodles a "little dot with the flames round it" (*N&D*, 493). This doodle, for Ralph, "represented by its circumference of smudges surrounding a central blot all that encircling glow which for him surrounded, inexplicably, so many of the objects of life" (*N&D*, 493). Katharine, on the other hand, wishes to rid herself of this halo of illusion, and she wants to contact Ralph's psychic core. But she realizes that when she holds his arm she touches only "the opaque substance surrounding the flame that roared upwards" (*N&D*, 503).

Although Ralph hides his true Self, Katharine wants to reach her own and grasp that core. She, of course, does not want to literally take the core in her hands, but figuratively release it from its hiding place and hold it out in front of her so as to directly expose her conscious identity to inner reality. Katharine has "held in her hands for one brief moment the globe which we spend out lives in trying to shape, round, whole, and entire from the confusion of chaos" (*N&D*, 503). But Ralph has not, and so a portion of Woolf's composite personality still must grow out of illusion.

*Night and Day* ties up with Woolf's next novel, *Jacob's Room*, by way of Ralph's doodle of the dot with flames. Not only does *Jacob's Room* open with a corresponding dot symbolism and later provide even further references to the same image, but in that novel Jacob Flanders continues Ralph Denham's personality. Ralph impedes his development by his dependence on the illusion of Katharine rather than his acceptance of the real Katharine. Jacob confronts a similar conflict and thus brings Woolf's composite personality on to the next major stage in the process of individuation. The imminence of this next step is suggested at the end of *Night and Day*, where Katharine and Ralph "loosed their hands" and bid each other "good night." The fact that each faces the night alone prepares the reader for the next novel's deeply psychological theme and its impressionistic style, which reflects the shadowy activity of the unconscious.

## NOTES

1. Certain critics agree that a thematic connection unites *The Voyage Out* and *Night and Day*. Jean Alexander, in *The Venture of Form*, says that Katharine Hilbery continues Rachel Vinrace's search for self-awareness (p. 55). Jane Novak likewise sees a tie between the two novels—the theme of marriage. See *The Razor Edge of Balance*: *A Study of Virginia Woolf* (Coral Gables, Fla.: University of Miami Press, 1975), p. 84.
2. Virginia Woolf, *A Writer's Diary: Being Extracts from the Diary of Virginia Woolf*, ed. Leonard Woolf (New York: Harcourt Brace Jovanovich, 1953), p. 19. All further quotations and references to this book will be cited within the text as *A WD*.

3. Manly Johnson, *Virginia Woolf* (New York: Frederick Ungar, 1973), p. 33.

4. The following chart is reproduced by June Singer in *Androgyny:Toward a New Theory of Sexuality* (Garden City, N.Y.: Doubleday & Co., 1976), p. 220.

5. Johnson, *Virginia Woolf*, p. 34.

6. Virginia Woolf, *Night and Day* (New York: Harcourt Brace Jovanovich, 1920), p. 9. All further quotations and references to the novel will be cited within the text as *N&D*.

7. June Singer gives an explanation of bull symbolism that supplements Woolf's use of the image. Singer bases her comments on recent archeological findings by James Mellaart, who excavated three prehistoric sites in Anatolia and thereby confirmed that a matriarchal society existed. Mellaart discovered that this society used the symbol of the bull frequently, and from its uses Singer concludes that the bull is a strong sex symbol in a gynocracy and "traditionally represented the male principle in a female-dominated world." See *Androgyny*, p. 66.

8. The mandala is a geometric figure that combines the shapes of the circle and the square. Carl Jung says it "is an archetypal image whose occurrence is attested throughout the ages. It signifies the *wholeness of the self*. This circular image represents the wholeness of the psychic ground or, to put it in mythic terms, the divinity incarnate in man." See Carl Jung,*Memories, Dreams, Reflections,* rec. and ed. Aniela Jaffé, trans, Richard and Clara Winston (New York: Pantheon Books, Div. of Random House, 1961), pp. 334-35.

# 3

# *Jacob's Room*
## Some Buried Discomfort

So far in Virginia Woolf's novels the search for the Self has made significant progress; it has revealed that roles determined by socialization block individuation. Rachel Vinrace, in *The Voyage Out*, recognizes this fact, but unfortunately she cannot conceive of her own identity as strong enough to resist the traditional world. So she permits death to carry her out of society's confines. Katharine Hilbery, in *Night and Day*, on the other hand, continues the search from where Rachel left off, and thus brings Woolf's composite being to the threshold of true Selfhood. At the end of *Night and Day*, Katharine can stand on that threshold and catch a glimpse of the Self free of the whole traditional atmosphere. But her awareness of this Self cannot last, because illusion still intercedes. Therefore, the composite personality must first deal with the forces that create the illusion that hangs about life. The forces are the parental imagoes that an individual incorporates into his own psyche.[1]

Clearly, a young child feels the influence of his parents.

After all, he depends upon them for the source of love, acceptance, discipline, and guidance. As time goes on, the child absorbs the personalities of his parents so thoroughly that eventually he carries them within his own psyche. Carl Jung calls these powers the imagoes. And, as Jung states, they go on working even if the parents die; each imago continues operating "as though it were a spirit existing on its own."[2] It is incorrect, therefore, to say the actual parents put up psychological roadblocks in the way of the individual's growth. Since the individual incorporates the personalities of his parents, he must acknowledge that, in Jung's words, "it is no longer father and mother who are standing in his way, but himself—i.e., an unconscious part of his personality which carries on the role of father and mother."[3] Even this realization alone does not bring total freedom. Jung cautions that a person must also accept these forces, and until he accepts them, they "will leave him no peace and will continue to plague him."[4]

Surely Virginia Woolf knew nothing of Jung's theory since he did not publish it until 1943. But then again, the publication of Jung's theory does not mark the beginning of this psychological phenomenon; it merely marks the presentation of it in theoretical form. The phenomenon has operated as long as parent-child relations have existed; apparently Woolf sensed its existence, because she describes it in her novels. The whole portion of psychological development that involves, first, one's victory over the imagoes, and, second, one's willing acceptance of them, appears in *Jacob's Room* and *Mrs. Dalloway*. In the first novel, Jacob Flanders, the present representative of Woolf's composite personality, overcomes the influence of his mother imago, and, in the second novel, Clarissa Dalloway learns to accept the father imago.

Certain details that come at the conclusion of *Night and Day* dovetail with the theme and style of *Jacob's Room*. First, in *Night and Day*, Ralph Denham blocks his own emotional growth by his wish to dominate Katharine Hilbery and by his need for a halo of illusion; for growth depends on the in-

dividual's independent and free evolution into psychic maturity. It follows, then, that the reader now concentrates on the
masculine, that portion of the composite personality that
manifests fear of growth through its wish to overpower the
feminine. Thus, Woolf uses a man as the protagonist of *Jacob's
Room*. The second link between *Night and Day* and *Jacob's
Room* is the concluding words of the earlier novel: "For a moment they waited, and then loosed their hands. 'Good night,'
he breathed. 'Good night,' she murmured back to him."
Katharine and Ralph, having achieved emotional closeness,
cannot sustain their closeness. So they part and wish each other
a good night. That is, the feminine and the masculine components of the Self separate and individually go into the night,[5]
into the world of darkness where they might meet the seemingly irrational and chaotic elements of the unconscious. Consequently, with *Jacob's Room*, Woolf stylistically abandons the
realistic clarity of her first two novels and adopts an impressionism so as to reflect this step out of the conscious world and
into the dark unconscious, where Jacob can confront his
mother imago.

Woolf records in her diary her intention to change her style
after the realism in *The Voyage Out* and *Night and Day*: "For
I figure that the approach will be entirely different this time;
no scaffolding; scarcely a brick to be seen; all crepuscular, but
the heart, the passion, humour, everything as bright as fire in
the mist" (*A WD*, 22). The very images she uses here to describe
her anticipated technique—twilight, heart, fire—relate her
style to those qualities she attributes elsewhere to the unconscious. For instance, twilight, the threshold between day
and night, captures the precise spot on which Katharine
Hilbery stands as she sees into the unconscious at the end of
Woolf's second novel. The image of fire likewise comes from
*Night and Day*; Katharine gains some insight into Ralph
Denham's fiery psychic core: "She thought of him blazing
splendidly in the night, yet so obscure that to hold his arm, as
she held it, was only to touch the opaque substance surroun-

ding the flame that roared upwards" (*N&D*, 503). Finally, Woolf uses also the heart as an image for the unconscious. For example, in her short story "A Haunted House," a "ghostly couple" roam through their house, now occupied by a new couple, looking for their "buried treasure." Throughout their nighttime search, the "heart of the house" is beating. The heart as the life-giving center of a human body here symbolizes the unconscious center of the human psyche. They find their treasure in the new couple, asleep in bed; these male and female figures represent the total Self buried deep in the sleep-world of the unconscious.[6]

In addition, an even more convincing piece of evidence that explains Woolf's use of the impressionistic texture comes right out of *Jacob's Room* itself:

> . . . life is but a procession of shadows, and God knows why it is that we embrace them so eagerly, and see them depart with such anguish, being shadows. And why, if this and much more than this is true, why are we yet surprised in the window corner by a sudden vision that the young man in the chair is of all things in the world the most real, the most solid, the best known to us—why indeed? For the moment after we know nothing about him.
> Such is the manner of our seeing. Such the conditions of our love.[7]

Here Woolf justifies her use of impressionism: its texture matches that of life and our perception of life.[8] With impressionism as her medium, Woolf follows the course of Jacob's growth as he confronts a variety of female figures upon whom he projects his mother imago.[9] As he gets closer and closer to an acceptance of this maternal force, the projections change and lessen. He goes from resentment toward this force, which manifests itself in his cold and detached attitude toward the women, to a full acceptance of woman. In other words, he eventually becomes liberated from the demands and restrictions of his mother's protectiveness.

But Woolf's impressionism is not pure, for at times she interjects the narrator's voice. On the surface, one may view these interjections as obtrusive and disruptive.[10] But one can confidently assume that Woolf had some purpose when she interjects her narrator, since it appears so distinctly. If she felt uncomfortable with her new medium, she more likely would have reverted to the comfort of realism with which she succeeded in *The Voyage Out* and *Night and Day*. She therefore must have had some purpose. To discover Woolf's intention, the reader must compare passages of the narration to passages where the narrator directly addresses the reader. Such a comparison draws out the difference between the realistic style of the interjections and the impressionism of the actual narration. This difference implies that Woolf intended the narrator's voice to come from the conscious world and thus serve as a standard against which one can judge the depth of Jacob's descent into the unconscious. Though Woolf's intention, if this be it, has value, her means detract from her purpose. In later novels she still wishes to measure the depth of unconsciousness by a consistent standard, but there she does it with imagery, a far more successful and integrative means.

An analysis of the novel's theme best begins with the parallels between Virginia Woolf's Jacob Flanders and the biblical Jacob. Just as in the Bible Jacob's mother, Rebekah, favors him and thus helps him to gain his father's blessing through deception, so Betty Flanders wishes to cushion her son in deceptive illusion. And just as the biblical Jacob toils for fourteen years to free Rachel from her father's household so they can marry, so Woolf's Jacob toils emotionally, throughout the novel, to free his view of women of all psychological projections. Freedom from such projections opens the way for the Self to emerge.

In *Night and Day*, Ralph Denham's doodle of a dot with flames around it represents the Self, and this image carries over into *Jacob's Room* where the account of Woolf's composite personality continues. References to dots begin on the first page where Betty Flanders is sitting on the beach, writing to her friend Captain Barfoot. She starts to cry from thoughts of her dead husband, which brings her pen to a halt; as the pen sticks to the paper an ink blot appears and spreads (*JR*, 7). At the same time, Charles Steele paints her portrait, and strikes "the canvas a hasty violet-black dab" because "the landscape needed it" (*JR*, 8). Steele ends up "pleased by the effect of the black—it was just *that* note which brought the rest together" (*JR*, 9). At the same time that Steele and Betty sit on the beach, at the exact moment that Steele decides that the black dot gives his portrait coherence, Jacob climbs down from a rock and espies a "large black woman . . . sitting on the sand" (*JR*, 10). He runs towards her, sobbing out the words, "Nanny! Nanny!" because he thinks the woman is his nurse, whom Woolf names Rebecca after the mother of the biblical Jacob. However, as he approaches the large spot of blackness, it becomes not his Nanny, but a rock. Woolf explains that "he was lost"; he no longer runs, but stands still, lost, for he finds a rock where he wished to find love. Thus Woolf establishes Jacob as emotionally paralyzed in the absence of a loving maternal figure.

The imagery of dots and rocks, associated with the upcoming images of the skull, the crab, the brooch, and the mountain, suggests Jacob's search for Selfhood. Many of these images appear in the beach scene. First Jacob climbs a black rock, and he comes upon a hollow filled with water in which a crab swims. He plunges his hand deep into the hollow, pulls out the crab, and puts the crab in his bucket. Just as he prepares to jump, he sees "an enormous man and woman" rigidly stretched out on the sand side by side (*JR*, 9). He jumps down and now thinks he sees Rebecca, but actually sees a rock. The rapidity with which these events occur, and the concentrated area in which these symbols—crab, man and woman, rock—appear, create a pattern. At this point, however, one only knows certain isolated aspects of the pattern. For instance, one can point out the theme of depth (the hollow in the rock), a treasure in the depth (the crab), the apparent death of the sexes (the man and woman lying rigidly side by side), and a pair of rocks (the one Jacob climbs and the one he mistakes for Rebecca). The only common threads that run through all this are Jacob's curiosity and his need for love.

The very next event enlarges our understanding a little more. As Jacob rejoins his mother and his brother Archer, he comes upon a skull. Mrs. Flanders says, "What has he got hold of? Put it down, Jacob! Drop it this moment! Something horrid, I know" (*JR*, 10). The first contact between Jacob and his mother, therefore, reveals Mrs. Flanders's intolerance for the things that mean the most to Jacob—exploration and discovery. From this one can understand Jacob's preference for solitude and separation from his mother. And it now is clear why he mistakes a rock for Nanny—he runs to the one maternal figure that can offer the love and acceptance he so desperately needs; yet, because his actual mother frustrates these needs, Jacob can envision "mother" as only cold, hard, and dark. The beach scene, then, gives one essential quality to "mother" within Jacob's psychological constellation: intolerance.

Regardless of Betty Flanders's intolerant attitude toward her son's interests, Jacob does not relinquish them entirely. He retains at least a small portion of them, as symbolized by the sheep's jaw that he holds onto, although he complies with his mother's commands to drop the skull. Jacob's defiance of her orders leaves Betty with a sense of "some buried discomfort" (*JR*, 10). The word "buried" here ties the concept of discomfort to the symbols of the crab, which journeys along the sandy bottom of the water-filled hollow in the rock, and the skull, which lies "among the black sticks and straw under the cliff" (*JR*, 10). The imagery thus becomes circular: Betty experiences discomfort at Jacob's defiance, which arises from his own discomfort caused by her intolerance.

But here the two characters diverge—Jacob wishes to disinter the discomfort he suffers but Betty covers it over with layers of illusion and maternal protectiveness. For instance, in the novel's opening scene, Betty writes to Captain Barfoot about her late husband, Seabrook. Thoughts of her husband draw out tears that distort Betty's view of her surroundings: "The entire bay quivered; the lighthouse wobbled; and she had the illusion that the mast of Mr. Connor's little yacht was bending like a wax candle in the sun" (*JR*, 7). The reality of her husband's death evokes not only sadness, but also a protective film over Betty's eyes that causes everything in her view to take on an illusory appearance.

Betty's confining protectiveness triggers Jacob's rebellion. He keeps the sheep's jaw and even brings it to bed with him. And he takes the crab home, which he leaves outside in the bucket. Not only do these objects represent the treasures Jacob uncovers through his curiosity, but Woolf suggests that, in particular, the crab represents Jacob; just as Jacob struggles to flee the narrowness of his mother's world, as when he insists on leaving her to play by himself on the beach, so the crab fights to climb the walls of the bucket. Another connection between Jacob and the crab comes when "Jacob lay asleep, fast asleep, profoundly unconscious." He has descended into the depths of his psyche. At the same time, the crab in the bucket "slowly circled round the bottom" (*JR*, 14). Thus, both men roam the depths in search of a way out.

While Jacob sleeps, Woolf clearly defines the maternal qualities that psychologically immure Jacob. The first of these involves Betty Flanders's reliance on illusion. On her husband's tombstone she has inscribed the epitaph "Merchant of this city"; yet "he had only sat behind an office window for three months, and before that had broken horses, ridden to hounds, farmed a few fields, and run a little wild." She rationalizes the false glory of this inscription by claiming that "she had to call him something. An example for the boys" (*JR*, 16). Despite the fact that she did what she thought best, the illusory effect of her lie ends up crushed by the very weight of the lie itself. Her sons, once having seen through the lie, must then contend with two discomforts: the truth about their father and the fact that their mother deceived them. Jacob alone seems to have advanced to this point already, at least unconsciously, for he senses the deception.

Betty's second quality entails her severe repression of any passion. She protects herself from any passion that would demand she act upon it. This repression comes out in the scene where her son Johnny chases the geese. The sequence of events reveals Betty's restriction on passion. First she reads a note from Mr. Floyd in which he says that he loves her. This arouses the thoughts of Seabrook, her dead husband. Then suddenly her thoughts are interrupted by three geese frantically scuttling across the lawn with Johnny chasing after them, stick in hand. This infuriates Betty, even though Johnny explains that the geese escaped. As she yells at Johnny for chasing the geese, she crumbles Mr. Floyd's letter in her hand (*JR*, 21). Betty reacts angrily because the escaped geese, the running Johnny, and the flailing stick all scare her; she connects them with Floyd's passion and with the passion she fears he expects of her in return. She therefore crumbles the note as she herds the geese back into the orchard. And then, typically, she finds excuses for not marrying Floyd: she dislikes red hair in men and he is far too young for her. The next reference to her dislike of red hair accompanies another symbol of her repression: that evening, stroking the cat Topaz that Mr. Floyd gave to the Flanders, Betty "smiled, thinking how she had had him gelded, and how she did not like red hair in men. Smiling, she went into the kitchen" (*JR*, 22–23). This association between the gelded cat and Betty's dislike of red hair reinforces the fact that she severely represses her own passion and that in others. Thus there is another quality of Betty Flanders that Jacob must exorcise from his own psychic makeup.

With Betty's reliance on repression and illusion established, Woolf now portrays Jacob's resistance toward his mother in a dreamlike sequence. Jacob is deep in the woods, chasing butterflies. He captures one and examines it with the same interest and delight as when he catches the crab and finds the skull on the beach. He thus chances upon a third treasure, this one buried in the heart of the woods, as the crab was in the hollow and the skull in the brush. And, again, Jacob's curious mind discomforts Betty, for as he walks towards the house she mistakes the noise for that of an approaching burglar. So, as before, Jacob's gestures of independence frighten Betty and thus this scene parallels the one on the beach. And Jacob's discovery and examination of the butterfly, the crab, and the skull symbolize his wish to discover his Self.

Until Jacob uncovers the mother imago and all the stifling qualities that go along with it, his conscious existence falls victim to it and his Self eludes him. As victim, he projects the qualities of the imago on the women he meets. For instance, he projects his hatred for his mother on the women at King's College Chapel:

> . . . why allow women to take part in it? . . . No one would think of bringing a dog into church. For though a dog is all very well on a gravel path . . . a dog destroys the service completely. So do these women . . . Heaven knows why it is. For one thing, thought Jacob, they're as ugly as sin. (*JR*, 32-33)

Jacob disparages women because he fears them; just as he kept a distance from his mother, so he wishes to keep all women out of his life. Woolf pictures this with a variation on an image used in *Night and Day*. A moment before Jacob equates women with dogs, he imagines, "If you stand a lantern under a tree every insect in the forest creeps up to it—a curious assembly, since though they scramble and swing and knock their heads against the glass, they seem to have no purpose—something senseless inspires them" (*JR*, 32). The similar image in *Night and Day*—the birds and the lighthouse—shares the meaning of one element denied entrance into another. Whereas Ralph Denham in the earlier novel uses this image to describe his wish to gain entrance into Katharine Hilbery's home, Jacob uses it here to show his resistance toward any and all women.

Jacob craves independence. He demonstrates this fact by his

frequent flights into solitude. More instances of this come into
view now. For example, Jacob exclaims, "Oh God, oh God, oh
God!" when he leaves the Sunday luncheon held by the Cambridge don, Mr. Plumer (*JR*, 35). This exclamation mixes his
anger at the stuffy and stifling atmosphere of the luncheon and
his relief at his final release. A third message carried by Jacob's
repeated exclamation of "Oh God!" does not become clear until later in the novel. This involves Jacob's yearning for God
and all that God represents — wholeness, knowledge, and freedom from the ego that generates fears, insecurities, and
deceits. At this point, in any case, it is very clear that
Jacob yearns for independence. He therefore follows up his
initial exclamation with another, "Bloody beastly!," and scans
the "street for lilac or bicycle — anything to restore his sense of
freedom" (*JR*, 35).

Jacob's need for God, or at least for a greater spiritual life,
begins to emerge in the counterpoint between his thoughts of
Julian the Apostate and his vision of the veiled lady. This
counterpoint concludes the scene in which Jacob's college
friends participate in a deeply intellectual conversation. Jacob,
although in the same room with these other students, does not
engage in the conversation, but rather catches parts of it in a
desultory fashion as he stands looking out the window. The one
fragment that he does retain from the conversation, after
everyone leaves except Simeon, is "Julian the Apostate." As
Jacob still stands by the window, this phrase alternates with a
vision of a veiled female figure personifying the wind that
"lifted unseen leaves and blurred everything" (*JR*, 45). With
the appearance of the wind, the small vestige of the all-male
intellectual conversation becomes muffled. And when that
vestige reasserts itself, the wind subsides. The two cannot exist
together. In psychological terms, Jacob pictures his masculine
self, his conscious self, as incompatible with any female element. But the "veiled lady" means more than just woman.
This figure has spiritual significance by its association with the
wind, a common symbol for God.[11] Moreover, her veil recalls

that which Christ rends so as to unite the holy with the holiest of holies (Matthew 27:51). In like manner, Jacob must unveil this woman, because she stands for the spirituality that his mother has denied him.

A significant shift in the novel's imagery now takes place. Jacob transfers his energy away from his exploration of the depths, which indicates his wish to uncover some buried discomfort, to a fascination with heights, which exhibits his aspiration toward ascendancy intc the Self's freedom from these discomforts. But there has been no change in Jacob's goals; rather, the descent must precede the ascent. The descent tells Jacob that wholeness exists, as symbolized by the crab, the skull, and the butterfly, while the ascent signifies his active pursuit after that whole Self. Having reached into the depths, he now needs to climb to the heights. The catalyst for this shift comes with the veiled figure, from which Jacob learns that he must yet attain an essential element to complete his individuation — the feminine element. So he will ascend his hills and mountains, and in his last ascent he will reach an accord with a real veiled feminine figure.

Chapter 4 begins the string of ascent imagery. The chapter opens with Jacob and Timmy Durrant sailing. When they first sight the Scilly Isles, which were "lying like mountaintops almost a-wash," Jacob shows little interest because he and Timmy have quarreled (*JR*, 47). But a few pages later comes the second reference to the Scilly Isles, and with it an abrupt allusion to God. This allusion interrupts Timmy's and Jacob's playful repartee:

> "What is there about Masham that makes one laugh?" said Timmy.
> "Hang it all — a man who swallows his tie-pin," said Jacob.
> "Lord Chancellor before he's fifty," said Timmy.
> "The Duke of Wellington was a gentleman," said Timmy.
> "Keats wasn't."
> "Lord Salisbury was."
> "And what about God?" said Jacob. (*JR*, 51)

Immediately following this exchange the narrator comments, "The Scilly Isles now appeared as if directly pointed at by a golden finger issuing from a cloud" (*JR*, 51). Jacob's interjection, "And what about God?", jumps out of his spiritual questions that lie behind all of his actions and words. He wants to know where he can find spiritual wholeness. The immediate reappearance of the Scilly Isles, pointed at by what seems the awesome, portentous finger of God, answers Jacob's questions: wholeness, a God-like quality, waits for Jacob at the top of a mountain. Jacob makes this connection subliminally because instinctively he begins to chant, "Rock of Ages, cleft for me, Let me hide myself in thee" (*JR*, 52). These chanted lines indicate Jacob's wish to know God.

On the same summer vacation with the Durrants, Jacob goes with Timmy's sister, Clara, out into the greenhouse to pick grapes. For the first time Jacob has positive feelings for a woman. He can permit them now because of his vision of the veiled lady whose presence inspires Jacob to see the correlation between his wholeness and a woman. As Jacob stands at the bottom of the ladder, Clara climbs down carrying grapes: "'One bunch of white, and two of purple,' she said, and she placed two great leaves over them where they lay curled warm in the basket" (*JR*, 62). The color purple has a spiritual connotation because of the Bible's allusion to the purple robe Christ wears while on the cross (Mark 15:17), and to Lazarus, "a certain rich man, which was clothed in purple" (Luke 16:19), whom Christ restores to life (John 11:43-44). Each of these biblical allusions to purple, furthermore, implies a resurrection — both Christ and Lazarus arise from their burial caves, reborn into life. Thus the two bunches of purple grapes can symbolize Christ and Lazarus, while the while bunch may refer to Jacob and his potential for a similar resurrection. Or the two purple bunches can refer to Jacob and Clara, and the white to the wholeness they can create by their psychic union. Jacob takes one small step towards this union when he tries to tell Clara that he loves her, but she stops him. Woolf does not now reveal Clara's motive. One knows at this point only that Jacob can feel love for a woman. Woolf signals this growth by repeating the thought, "the leathern curtain of the heart has flapped wide" (*JR*, 66), for Jacob can now feel.

Jacob next becomes involved with Florinda. She represents his burgeoning femininity, which still possesses an unevolved nature, since it has just newly separated from the mother imago. Florinda exhibits her innocence by her repeated references to her virginity—which was just lost the night before (*JR*, 77)—and her intellectual ignorance (*JR*, 78–79). Despite her unevolved personality, Florinda possesses one very important attribute that Jacob needs now. He already has the intellect but he lacks passion; this Florinda can offer. This difference between the two of them is seen when she lays her hand on his knee. As she does, Jacob makes up the excuse that his head aches so he can avoid, if only temporarily, the passion that has remained repressed for so long. This repression constitutes the last vestige of the mother imago. Once he rids himself of this, he can fully and truly love a woman. Florinda brings him through this stage.

The closer Jacob gets to liberation, the harder his ego's old patterns of behavior assert themselves. Thus, in the ego's final attempts to contain Jacob, it conjures up Mrs. Flanders's presence with even greater strength. She writes him letters, and in these letters tries to recall Jacob to her power. The narrator says that though Betty chatters in her letters, she really wants to say, "Don't go with bad women, do be a good boy; wear your thick shirts; and come back, come back, come back to me" (*JR*, 90). One such letter from Betty sits near the biscuit-tin in the antechamber, while Jacob and Florinda make love in the bedroom. The passion Jacob has learned to express can finally sever him from his mother; consequently, the mother agonizes:

if the pale blue envelope lying by the biscuit-box had the feelings of a mother, the heart was torn by the little creak, the sudden stir . . . Better, perhaps, burst in and face it than sit in the antechamber listening to the little creak, the sudden stir, for her heart was swollen, and pain threaded it. My son, my son—such would be her cry, uttered to hide her vision of him stretched with Florinda, inexcusable, irrational. (*JR*, 92)

Before making love with Florinda, Jacob shows no interest in his mother's letter. He can accept what she has to say only after he executes the last blow to her psychic hold on him. Then, as the couple steps out of the bedroom, he comes out first, "amiable, authoritative, beautifully healthy, like a baby after an airing, with an eye clear as running water" (*JR*, 92). Now, refreshed and reborn, Jacob goes to the table to read his mother's letter.

Woolf conveys Jacob's new-found freedom through passion both imagistically and thematically. The image consists of a horse and rider that merge into one seamless whole as the horse takes a jump: "Then as if your own body ran into the horse's body and it was your own forelegs grown with his that sprang, rushing through the air you go, the ground resilient, bodies a mass of muscles, yet you have command too, upright stillness, eyes accurately judging" (*JR*, 101). This unity of human being and animal depicts Jacob's newly acquired reconciliation between his rational faculties and his passionate powers. Neither one takes precedence. Although the jump involves physical strength, it also entails great mental command. In Woolf's thematic representation of Jacob's new-found freedom, a complementary combination of the intellect and the body takes place. Bonamy and Jacob converse in intellectual jargon—"common ground" and "objective something," as Mrs. Papworth overhears the words—but complete their communion by wrestling (*JR*, 102). No longer does Jacob compartmentalize aspects of his life in order to keep the intellectual distinct from the physical. His recently developed psychic balance brings him closer to wholeness. And, as indicated by the wrestling, Jacob comes closer to God; for the biblical Jacob wrestles with the angel of God as an initiation into his divinely assigned role as leader of the Israelites ( Genesis 32:24). At that point the angel gives Jacob the name of "Israel," to impress on him that he contains a nation, a totality.[12] Jacob Flanders will likewise soon realize his own totality.

The wrestling with Bonamy signals the onset of Jacob's initiation. Jacob's actual initiation into Selfhood, however, entails several steps. Each step introduces him to a different potential identity for his feminine complement. When he finds the proper one, he will have encountered the part of his personality that can complete his search for the Self. First, he visits with Miss Perry and Miss Rosseter (*JR*, 102-4), who are friends of his mother. Jacob visits them to discover if the identity for his feminine complement lies within his mother's world. But the conversation with these women turns stilted and formal. Consequently, Jacob feels uncomfortable, and thus realizes the unsuitability of this particular world. Immediately afterwards, Jacob visits a prostitute as the second possible identity for his feminine self. This alternative indicates a severe reaction against his mother's world. Jacob appears more comfortable in Laurette's presence and with her somewhat intelligent conversation. But in the Madame Jacob notices "that leer, that lewdness, that quake of the surface (visible in the eyes chiefly), which threatens to spill the whole bag of ordure, with difficulty held together, over the pavement. In short, something was wrong" (*JR*, 105). Consequently, the baseness of the situation makes this second alternative also inappropriate. In reaction against the failure of these first two potential identities, Jacob turns to his last alternative, the intellectual world. Where Miss Perry stands for the maternal identity for Jacob's femininity and Laurette the passionate identity, Julia Hedge, in the British Museum, represents an intellectual identity. But he finds this third possibility also wrong, for "Julia Hedge disliked him naturally enough" (*JR*, 107).

All three alternatives fail because all three stem from past patterns that evolve from the mother image. Miss Perry, being Betty's friend and sharing the same repressed nature, replicates Jacob's life with his mother, against which he rebels. Laurette, in turn, duplicates Florinda; the passion she offers supplies Jacob with the necessary release from his mother's repression. But to turn away from his mother binds him as much to her as if he turned towards her, for his reaction takes its form solely from the personality against which he rebels. Jacob's pursuit of the intellect comes also as a reaction against his mother by demonstrating his wish for solitude, the only means he has to escape his mother.

So far Jacob has found the need for a feminine force in his life but cannot discover its appropriate identity. As a result, he sits enclosed in his room reading Plato. Meanwhile, a drunken woman under his window cries, "Let me in! Let me in!" (*JR*, 109). This scene recalls Jacob's imagined figure of a lantern in the woods around which the insects gather as they try to get inside the glassed-in container. Because Jacob is very uncomfortable with all of the alternative identities for his feminine part, or at least all those he knows of at this point, he secludes himself from the feminine entirely and ignores its call for admittance. But this time that Jacob seeks solitude, he is not satisfied. He finishes Plato's argument, but then his "mind continues alone, onwards, into the darkness" (*JR*, 110). His mind enters a realm beyond the intellect. The darkness of this realm, paradoxically, gives him clarity of sight: "getting up, he parted the curtains and saw, with astonishing clearness, how the Springetts opposite had gone to bed; how it rained; how the Jews and the foreign woman, at the end of the street, stood by the pillar-box, arguing" (*JR*, 110). Ironically, until now Jacob thought clarity of sight came from the intellect. Now he discovers that the intellect has actually blinded him. Real clarity of sight, Jacob learns, means what lies outside of himself, outside of his room. It follows, then, that the wholeness exists beyond one's self. No longer needing to seclude himself in his insulated room, Jacob can now go to Paris and then go to Greece, where he will climb his mountain.

By leaving London, Jacob takes a large step away from his

mother's influence and from his need for her. Now, in Paris, he begins to find himself and exercise his own judgments. And the more he learns, the less he can relate to his mother. For example, in Paris he meets Cruttendon and Mallinson, two painters, and Jinny Carslake, an English woman who also wishes to escape her parents' psychic hold on her. But Jacob could not tell his mother anything about these people: "Jacob had nothing to hide from his mother. It was only that he could make no sense himself of his extraordinary excitement" (*JR*, 131). Then, Woolf immediately moves to Betty Flanders and Mrs. Jarvis. Mrs. Jarvis says "Jacob's letters are so like him," and Betty agrees (*JR*, 131). Jacob's mother will always see him as the same, despite any growth he may experience, because, for one thing, she refuses to see otherwise, and, for another, Jacob realizes he cannot tell her any differently.

Mrs. Flanders's blindness to her son's growth arises from her refusal to uncover her buried discomfort. The discomfort has its source in Jacob, but Betty leaves it buried and thus unidentified. Woolf expresses this idea through the image of the garnet brooch. While standing on Dods Hill with Mrs. Jarvis, Betty recalls the brooch that Jacob bought for her. Some time before, she brought Mr. Parker up to the hill to see the view; she then accidentally dropped the brooch (*JR*, 132). Betty never mentions that she looked for it; rather, she leaves this material symbol of Jacob's love buried and, as a result, suffers the psychological pain of its repression.

This understanding of the brooch clears up some other ostensibly vague references in the novel. A similarity shows up between Betty's disregard for her son's love and Clara Durrant's refusal to hear Jacob tell her of his love. This similarity between the two women appears in Jacob's recollections of Clara. The first recollection occurs when he sits with Fanny Elmer, who tries to impress him by her fondness for *Tom Jones*. As she talks, he thinks of Clara, deciding that of all women, he honored her the most (*JR*, 123). The idea of honor suggests that he thinks of Clara as one might think of a parent. On the train to Greece, Jacob recalls Clara a second time and again equates her with his mother. Here he thinks, "Clara Durrant had left him at a party to talk to an American called Pilchard. And he had come all the way to Greece and left her" (*JR*, 138). Clara's withdrawal from Jacob at the party reenacts Betty Flanders's emotional withdrawal from her son. Jacob, therefore, travels to Greece as the final escape from any reminder of this love-denying mother.

To break out of such confines is necessary, but not conclusive; Jacob must not only escape his mother, but also find and then accept his own feminine identity. Woolf conveys this concept when she brings back the figure of the old woman who pleads beneath Jacob's window for admittance to his room. She, if not the exact woman, then precisely the same symbolic figure, appears again outside his room in Greece and "refused to budge" (*JR*, 138). Jacob now does accept this figure, or the psychological concept she embodies, in the form of Sandra Wentworth Williams. Sandra combines several qualities, all of which Jacob needs to achieve Selfhood. First, of course, she provides the feminine aspect needed to complete Jacob's personality. Second, Jacob can relate to her without projecting out of his mother imago because he has distanced himself from his mother. And third, Woolf frequently refers to Sandra as veiled, so she actualizes Jacob's imagined figure of the "veiled lady" that personifies the wind, a symbol of God. In sum, Sandra represents all that Jacob seeks. As a result, he feels much freer with Sandra than with the other women he has known: "Mrs. Williams said things straight out. He was surprised by his own knowledge of the rules of behaviour; how much more can be said than one thought; how open one can be with a woman; and how little he had known himself before" (*JR*, 146). Sandra's influence, and Jacob's love for her, will help him discover his own Selfhood.

In Jacob's two trips to the Acropolis, he replays the whole emotional gamut he follows throughout the novel. In the first trip he seeks solitude, but meets with Madame Lucien Gravé, who disrupts his peace. He sees in her all the intolerance and insensitivity of his mother. As she jumps down from a block of marble, Jacob thinks, "Damn these women—damn these women! . . . How they spoil things" (*JR*, 151). He now verbalizes his annoyance and hatred for his mother that have accumulated throughout the years. In Jacob's second climb to the Acropolis, this one with Sandra, he wishes to overcome the effects of his mother. To do this he brings to the place where he has sought solitude the feminine force that, up to now, has either disgusted or failed to interest him. Or, as Woolf writes, "He had in him the seeds of extreme disillusionment, which would come to him from women in middle life. Perhaps if one strove hard enough to reach the top of the hill it need not come to him—this disillusionment from women in middle life" (*JR*, 159). Here is a direct reference to Jacob's buried discomfort and the content of the discomfort. Here is also the poultice for his pain—the joining together of the complements within his personality that contend for his attention: his wish for solitude and his need for the feminine. Furthermore, Sandra also recognizes that to acquire totality she needs Jacob; she asks herself, "what do I want from him? Perhaps it is something that I have missed . . ." (*JR*, 159; Woolf's ellipsis). They each need wholeness, and only together can they attain it.

Woolf's description of the Acropolis renders the psychological stages Jacob plays out in his two visits to the site: "the beauty is sufficiently humane to weaken us, to stir the deep deposit of mud—memories, abandonments, regrets, sentimental devotions" (*JR*, 148). This description suggests what happens to Jacob on his initial trip to the Acropolis—the presence of Madame Lucien stirs up Jacob's memories of his mother. Yet Jacob returns to the Parthenon with Sandra so he can attain all that lies beyond these memories. Woolf's additional description of the Parthenon captures this stage in Jacob's growth: "Far from being decayed, the Parthenon appears, on the contrary, likely to outlast the entire world" (*JR*,

148). The sense of eternity suggesting God and psychic wholeness, that the Parthenon offers, diametrically contrasts with Betty Flanders's personality. Woolf poignantly illustrates this contrast by weaving a picture of Betty right into the scene of Jacob and Sandra at the Acropolis. In this picture of the mother Woolf says, "The salt gale blew in at Betty Flanders's bedroom window, and the widow lady, raising herself slightly on her elbow, sighed like one who realizes, but would fain ward off a little longer—oh, a little longer!—the oppression of eternity" (*JR*, 160). Betty avoids wholeness because she fears it. Conversely, Jacob seeks eternity, and in doing so, he frees himself from his mother.

Toward the end of the novel there are quick views of the women Jacob has known. Clara calls out for him, crying "Jacob! Jacob!" (*JR*, 166). Her words remind the reader of Archer's unanswered cry for his brother on the novel's opening pages. Then Clara sees a horse run by without a rider. This sight recalls the vision Jacob has earlier of a horse and rider that have become one entity. The absence of the rider and the silence that follows Clara's call both underscore Jacob's absence. Julia Eliot also sees the horse (*JR*, 167). And Florinda thinks she sees Jacob, but the figure only reminds her of him. Jacob is gone. Sandra sits alone with her memories of the night at the Acropolis, left with only Jacob's book of Donne's poetry. And finally, Fanny Elmer retains only an idea of Jacob that "was more statuesque, noble, and eyeless than ever" (*JR*, 170). So all of the women Jacob has known continue on, but without him. He, meanwhile, sits alone in Hyde Park drawing a plan of the Parthenon in the dust. Since Jacob has contacted his own feminine identity during that night with Sandra at the Acropolis, he no longer participates in the lives of these women. He has acquired complete freedom from his mother. Woolf, thus, shows Betty Flanders alone, still denying reality to herself. For, although the war has begun and Betty can hear the artillery fire, she deludes herself by thinking "nocturnal women were beating great carpets" (*JR*, 175).

Our scan of the women left alone without Jacob reflects his psychological absence from their lives. But the last chapter, even more poignantly, combines his psychological with his physical absence, for Jacob dies in the war. Bonamy stands by the window and, as he watches the traffic outside, a wind starts: "suddenly all the leaves seemed to raise themselves." With this Bonamy calls out for Jacob, but no one answers, and the "leaves sank down again" (*JR*, 176). The image of the leaves rising and falling recalls two earlier scenes. In one, the narrator says, "The words we seek hang close to the tree. We come at dawn and find them sweet beneath the leaf" (*JR*, 93). Bonamy hopes to communicate with Jacob through these words, but the sinking leaves bring silence. Silence, however, does not preclude communication, as Woolf states repeatedly throughout her novels. Bonamy does experience Jacob's presence, but not in the form Bonamy expects. Rather, Jacob appears to Bonamy as the veiled figure that earlier appears before Jacob. Only this time the wind is disembodied. Jacob's physical nature has been sacrificed to the war, but his spiritual identity lives on in the wind. Bonamy witnesses this phenomenon but does not understand it. Betty, moreover, remains totally ignorant of it, as she has always been blind and deaf to Jacob's spirituality. Betty's only concern centers on Jacob's shoes: "What am I to do with these, Mr. Bonamy?" (*JR*, 176), she asks. Betty's bewilderment over the shoes evidences her empty and helpless regard for her son.

As the end of *Night and Day* implies, Woolf's composite being must free itself from the parental imagoes. Jacob Flanders completes half of this goal: he escapes the mother imago. But the goal's other half remains. Woolf's composite personality accomplishes this task in *Mrs. Dalloway*.

# NOTES

1. "Imago" is a term used by C. G. Jung for behavior-determining psychic content. He most frequently connects this term with that unconscious part of the personality that carries on the roles of father and mother. See *Two Essays on Analytical Psychology*, trans. R. F. C. Hull, 2d ed. (Princeton, N.J.: Princeton University Press, 1956), p. 60

2. Ibid., p. 186.

3. Ibid., p. 60.

4. Ibid.

5. June Singer, in *Androgyny: Toward a New Theory of Sexuality* (Garden City, N.Y.: Doubleday & Co., 1976), says the night world "appears to transcend the three-dimensional as it dreams its dreams and experiences in other ways the lowering of consciousness and the free flow of unconscious contents" (p. 217).

6. Virginia Woolf, *A Haunted House and Other Short Stories* (New York: Harcourt, Brace & World, 1921), pp. 3-5.

7. Virginia Woolf, *Jacob's Room* in *Jacob's Room & The Waves* (New York: Harcourt, Brace & World, 1923), p. 72. All further quotations and references to the novel will be cited within the text as *JR*.

8. Not all critics see value in the impressionistic style that Woolf uses in *Jacob's Room*. For instance, Arnold Bennett, in his essay "Is the Novel Decaying?", which provoked Woolf to write her "Mr. Bennett and Mrs. Brown," labels the style of *Jacob's Room* as mere cleverness. See *Virginia Woolf:The Critical Heritage*, eds. Robin Majumdar and Allen McLaurin (London,: Routledge and Kegan Paul, 1975), p. 113.

On the other hand, R. L. Chambers allows for some pattern behind the novel's not obviously related details. See *The Novels of Virginia Woolf* (New York: Russell & Russell, 1947), p. 29.

Because of Woolf's use of impressionism, some critics fault the novel for its lack of thematic focus. Though the book's title refers to the character Jacob Flanders, E. D. Pendry contends, Woolf focuses more on the many women who affect Jacob's life. See *The New Feminism of English Fiction: A Study in Contemporary Women-Novelists* (Tokyo: Kenkyusha, 1956), p. 37.

J. K. Johnstone, similarly, says that the reader is not given a coordinated and whole picture of Jacob. See *The Bloomsbury Group: A Study of E. M. Forster, Lytton Strachey, Virginia Woolf, and their Circle* (New York: Noonday Press, 1954), p. 334.

Nancy Topping Bazin, on the other hand, appreciates the novel's stylistic technique: "Making his presence incidental helps to suggest that the reality (the soul or essence) of Jacob exists apart from the actuality (or facts) of his life, yet that one must somehow get at his 'reality' through these facts." See *Virginia Woolf and the Androgynous Vision* (New Brunswick, N.J.: Rutgers University Press, 1973), p. 93.

9. C. G. Jung explains that it is natural for young men to "transfer the imagos of their parents to more suitable substitute figures." Jung then continues, "Although this is not a fundamental solution, it is yet a practical road which the normal man treads unconsciously and therefore with no notable inhibitions and resistances." See *Two Essays*, p. 60.

10. David Daiches says, "There is discernible here a certain lack of confidence on the author's part in her own technique. She has to introduce herself at intervals, *in propria persona*, to explain her doubts and difficulties to the reader, and enlist his sympathy." See *Virginia Woolf*, 2d ed. (New York: New Directions, 1942), p. 60.

In contrast, Barry Morgenstern sees the narrator's presence as integral to the story: "The story she tells has two plots: Jacob's growth and death, and the narrator's learning about him." See "The Self-Conscious Narrator in *Jacob's Room*," *Modern Fiction Studies* 18 (Autumn 1972): 353.

11. C. G. Jung translates Greek, Hebrew, and Arabic words for God and thereby shows that in all three a definition of God contains a reference to the wind. He then concludes that, archetypally, "God is the wind, stronger and mightier than man, an invisible breath-spirit." See *Two Essays*, p. 135.

Similarly, Erich Neumann equates wind with breath and breath with inspiration. He also says that the wind takes the form of the dove, the Holy Ghost, that is wafted under the Virgin Mary's robe. These details relate directly to those in *Jacob's Room*: the figure Jacob sees is female and she is veiled, as Mary is robed. See *The Origins and History of Consciousness*, trans. R. F. C. Hull (Princeton, N.J.: Princeton University Press, 1954), p. 22.

12. Thomas Troward presents an interesting linguistic analysis of the name "Israel" that supports Woolf's androgynous concept of the Self. He breaks the word up into its three syllables. He concludes that "Is" carries the "feminine spiritual principle manifesting itself in individuality . . . and it is thus indicative of all that we mean when we speak of the psychic side of nature." And "Ra" is "the complementary of everything that is signified by 'Is.' It is primarily indicative of physical life rather than psychic life, and in general represents the Universal Lifegiving power as distinguished from its manifestation in particular individuality." Lastly, "El" signifies the "Universal Being. It is 'THE,' i.e., The nameless Principle which includes in itself both the masculine and feminine elements, both the physical and the psychic, and is greater than them and gives rise to them." See *Bible Mystery and Bible Meaning* (New York: Dodd, Mead, & Co., 1913), pp. 62-63.

4

# *Mrs. Dalloway*
## The Privacy of the Soul

*Mrs. Dalloway* functions as a companion piece to *Jacob's Room* in that it thematically matches the psychological task accomplished in the earlier novel. Whereas Jacob Flanders overcomes his mother imago, and thus frees himself from all the psychological projections that emanate from that figure, Clarissa Dalloway, in the present novel, battles with and then liberates herself from the father imago. Just because Clarissa's task seems to parallel Jacob's does not mean, however, that the events, characters, and theme of *Mrs. Dalloway* duplicate those things in *Jacob's Room*. Rather, *Mrs. Dalloway* extends the ground won by the composite personality in *Jacob's Room* in a way similar to how Katharine Hilbery's growth in *Night and Day* advances from the point where Rachel Vinrace in *The Voyage Out* leaves off. Actually, one can envision Virginia Woolf's first four novels as all of a piece: the first two works reveal the immediate problem for a psychologically unevolved personality—society's imposition of narrow, social roles—while the third and fourth works portray the personality's struggle with the source of these roles—the parental imagoes. And whereas Katharine benefits from and builds upon what Rachel learns, so Jacob's progress brings Clarissa closer to her goal. Jacob's discovery of his own spiritual wholeness provides Clarissa with a predilection toward such a wholeness. Clarissa's entire story, for that matter, builds towards her party, held at the end of the novel's single day, where she experiences a vision of wholeness that psychologically transforms her.

The theme of *Mrs. Dalloway* has greater complexity than some critics realize. [1] Perhaps the profundity of the novel's theme sometimes goes unacknowledged because the novel's intricats style often deflects critical attention. In *Mrs. Dalloway*, Virginia Woolf refines her stylistic techniques remarkably, and thus smooths out a lot of the roughness that mars *Jacob's Room*. She maintains an impressionistic style, of course, because the composite personality here, as in *Jacob's Room*, roams the unconscious in an attempt to exorcise the imago force. But the ostensible illogic and incoherence of the events and elements in the unconscious are captured with far greater authenticity and with less of a sense of contrivance than in *Jacob's Room*. For instance, Woolf drops the intruding narrator technique for measuring the depth of the unconscious thoughts, and instead introduces the tolling clocks that repeatedly mark the present moment as various characters alternately allow their thoughts to wander through their pasts. Because Clarissa Dalloway carries on the role of Woolf's composite being, the novel focuses on her past and her unconscious associations to that past. Even when other characters reflect, their thoughts fill in the novel's overall picture of Clarissa. Woolf calls this stylistic technique her "tunnelling process" by which, in her words, "I dig out beautiful caves behind my characters: I think that gives exactly what I want; humanity, humour, depth. The idea is that the caves shall connect and each comes to daylight at the present moment" (*A WD*, 59). In a notebook entry, Woolf explains precisely what she wants to accomplish through this technique: "Every scene would build up the idea of C's character. That will give it unity, as well as add to the final effect." [2] The caves that Woolf digs out behind her characters take the reader into their unconscious world where one can meet their essential and ultimate personality. At this point, according to Woolf's notebook, all people connect. This assertion implies that ultimately we participate in a oneness. Woolf hints at this theory in her earlier novels, but she gives her finest expression of it in *The Waves*. With *Mrs. Dalloway*, she begins conscientiously to capture it in her art.

Not only does she convey the interrelationships among the characters and their psyches in *Mrs. Dalloway* itself, but she also shows the psychic connections between personalities in *Jacob's Room* and those in *Mrs. Dalloway*. More particularly, deep in the cave dug behind Septimus Warren Smith, *Mrs. Dalloway's* shell-shocked veteran of World War I, resides the character of Jacob Flanders. The most obvious connection between the two men is their participation in the war. One can argue against this point by saying that Septimus survives the war, though shell-shocked, whereas Jacob dies. But Jacob dies only physically. The last chapter of *Jacob's Room*, where Bonamy senses Jacob's presence in the wind, hints at Jacob's spiritual survival. Complementary evidence comes in *Mrs. Dalloway*, specifically in Septimus's mystical interests and insights. This quality carries over directly from Jacob's personality that, throughout *Jacob's Room*, develops greater spiritual strength. Furthermore, Woolf connects the two men through her use of similar imagery for both: whereas Jacob shows a repeated interest in ascension and heights—the novel opening with him on a rock and concluding with scenes of him on the Acropolis—so Septimus frequently envisions himself as high above humanity, atop the world. By way of these connections between Septimus and Jacob, Virginia Woolf suggests that Jacob's psychic growth predetermines Clarissa Dalloway's, for Septimus inspires her vision of psychic wholeness and thus her psychic transformation.

In addition to the connecting caves behind Jacob and Septimus, even more prominently do the caves connect behind

Clarissa and Septimus. For that matter, even though Clarissa and Septimus never meet, even though he never hears of her and she hears only a quick, indirect reference to him near the novel's conclusion, Woolf unites them ineluctably. Toward the end of the novel Clarissa, having heard that Septimus committed suicide by throwing himself from a window, deeply empathizes and identifies with his act as she emotionally replays it in her own mind. His physical descent to the ground inspires her emotional ascent into a mystical vision.

On the novel's first page Woolf sets the connection between Clarissa and Septimus. As Clarissa shops for flowers for her party she exults in the beauty of the morning. Her exhilaration here portends her mystical one that comes with the news of Septimus's death. Woolf strengthens this connection between the two events by first having Clarissa recall her life at eighteen years old: "What a lark! What a plunge!"[3] Within these phrases Woolf joins Septimus's plunge out the window to Clarissa's resultant exultation. Woolf further stresses the association when she has Clarissa recall the time "she had burst open the French windows and plunged at Bourton into the open air" (*MD*, 3). A third statement on the same point, also on the novel's first page, occurs when Clarissa recollects the sense of solemnity mixed with her youthful joy: she experiences a feeling that "something awful was about to happen." Clarissa predicts Septimus's death.

Septimus represents that part of Clarissa's psychological makeup that has been devastated by the masculine juggernaut of war. Woolf continually portrays war as a masculine force; she does so in *Jacob's Room*, *The Years*, and *Between the Acts*, while her most explicit statement appears in *Three Guineas*: "For though many instincts are held more or less in common by both sexes, to fight has always been the man's habit, not the woman's. Law and practice have developed that difference, whether innate or accidental."[4] And just as Septimus suffers from the tortures of war, so Clarissa faces a battle against a masculine force, that of her father imago. As explained in the previous chapter (see note 2), the destructive effect of this imago does not in the least depend upon the presence of an individual's father; it continues its influence even after the parent's death because it actually operates out of the individual's own psyche. Therefore, Clarissa Dalloway is beleaguered by thoughts of inadequacy brought on by the intimidating power she projects onto the general masculine force operating in the world. She confronts the force and fights her battle against it all through the day, and eventually defuses it through her empathic replay of Septimus's death. To identify with the devastated Septimus amounts, for Clarissa, to an acceptance of that part of herself that has been emotionally shell-shocked by the world's masculine attitude.

In the novel's opening scene, Clarissa demonstrates her first instance of projection: she attributes to Hugh Whitbread far greater power over her than in reality he possesses, because she views him through her own projections. She accidentally meets Hugh in the park and cannot see beyond "his very well-covered, manly, extremely handsome, perfectly upholstered body" (*MD*, 7). He impeccably exhibits his manhood, which instantly robs Clarissa of all her self-confidence. She feels oddly self-conscious:

> Not the right hat for the early morning, was that it? For Hugh always made her feel, as he bustled on, raising his hat rather extravagantly and assuring her that she might be a girl of eighteen . . . she always felt a little skimpy beside Hugh; schoolgirlish; but attached to him, partly from having known him always. (*MD*, 8)

Hugh's mere presence stirs up Clarissa's insecurities. He says nothing and does nothing directly that insults Clarissa's maturity and integrity; her rapid slide into an adolescent state results from her own sense of inadequacy in the presence of a man.

Clarissa's fear of man's power makes her dependent upon a certain distance between herself and a man. Only through this distance can she at all feel comfortable. This fact even determines her choice in husbands. Peter Walsh wanted to marry her, but Clarissa found it intolerable that "with Peter everything had to be shared; everything gone into" (*MD*, 10). Clarissa views the very close intimacy Peter wantcd as an infringement on her freedom. But, in fact, no one can rob another of freedom; freedom is a gift one gives one's self, regardless of outside demands. Clarissa places the blame on Peter's personality, because she projects upon Peter the qualities of a stifling masculine force. She, consequently, accepts Richard Dalloway as a husband, "for in marriage a little licence, a little independence there must be between people living together day in day out in the same house; which Richard gave her, and she him. (Where was he this morning for instance? Some committee, she never asked what.)" (*MD*, 10). In reality, the little licence Clarissa gets in her marriage with Richard provides her with only the outward trappings of the independence that she cannot fully actualize until she stops the masculine force from victimizing her.

The next important scene in the novel combines the two major phenomena in Clarissa's personality: her psychic tie with Septimus and her self-doubts. Clarissa has a presentiment of her own death: "Did it matter that she must inevitably cease completely; all this must go on without her; did she resent it; or did it not become consoling to believe that death ended absolutely?" (*MD*, 12). Her thoughts of her own death unite her with Septimus who will soon die. She next wonders, as she looks into a bookstore's window, "What was she trying to recover?" (*MD*, 12). Thus a connection appears between death and the wish to regain something. Clarissa lacks self-acceptance and the ability to assert her own integrity. Apparently, then, Clarissa senses that she once possessed these vital qualities, and that perhaps death will help her get them back. As the end of the novel indicates, Clarissa does recover these qualities through her identification with Septimus's death.

In a book opened for display in Hatchard's window, Clarissa

reads, "Fear no more the heat o' the sun/ Nor the furious winter's rages" (*MD*, 13). These two lines of poetry come from the funeral dirge in Shakespeare's *Cymbeline* (4, 2, 258-59). The incidents in the play suggest the psychological occurrences in *Mrs. Dalloway*. Briefly, Posthumus, acting out of jealousy, orders his servant, Pisanio, to kill Imogen, Posthumus's wife. Pisanio, instead, disguises Imogen in man's apparel and supplies her with a drug that will give her masculine strength. This drug, however, throws her into a death-like state, which thus occasions the funeral dirge. As the play's plot unfolds, Posthumus discovers that he had been duped into thoughts of jealousy, Imogen awakes from her death-like state, and the lovers reunite. The scantiness of this plot summary does little justice to Shakespeare's play, but it nevertheless highlights Woolf's reason for using the words, "Fear no more . . ." The paradox that Imogen escapes death through a masculine disguise, yet also enters an apparent death, portrays exactly Clarissa's dilemma. To escape the psychic death threatened by the external masculine attitude, Clarissa identifies with the damaged masculine portion within her own personality, represented by Septimus. And to raise herself above that ever-present threat, Clarissa mystically plays out a death from which she emerges transformed.

The heat of the sun and the fury of the winter's rages symbolize extremes in passion, that sort of passion that arises out of an intimate relationship. As Woolf shows shortly before these Shakespearean lines come up, Clarissa fears intimacy. This fear leads her to choose Richard for a husband, to whom she can relate from an emotional distance and thus protect herself against any extremes in passion. Furthermore, the concept that Clarissa's fear of intimacy originates from her unwilling submission to masculine expectations also appears in these lines, for the sun represents the masculine force. Religious symbolism and mythologems uniformly attribute masculine powers to the sun.[5] Hence, the words from *Cymbeline* suggest Clarissa's fear of intimacy and her submission to the masculine. These two personality traits block Clarissa from a true realization of the Self.[6]

Clarissa's discomfort in her present psychological state manifests itself in her thoughts that immediately follow the scene by the bookstore. She wishes "that people should look pleased as she came in" (*MD*, 13), and that she could do things just for themselves rather than "to make people think this or that" (*MD*, 14). In other words, Clarissa wants to act according to her own full personhood, and to assert that personhood. Without this assertion, she feels insignificant:

> She had the oddest sense of being herself invisible; unseen; unknown; there being no more marrying, no more having of children now, but only this astonishing and rather solemn progress with the rest of them, up Bond Street, this being Mrs. Dalloway; not even Clarissa any more; this being Mrs. Richard Dalloway. (*MD*, 14)

Quite simply, Clarissa wants people to recognize her distinct identity, and thus to relate to her as a totality unto herself. At the end of the novel, once she returns to her party guests after her transformative vision, Clarissa appears purely and fully as herself.

Clarissa's present feeling of being invisible erupts in her rage against Miss Kilman. Miss Kilman teaches religion to Elizabeth, Clarissa's daughter, and Clarissa can barely tolerate witnessing it: "Better distemper and tar and all the rest of it than sitting mewed in a stuffy bedroom with a prayer book!" (*MD*, 15). She objects by contending "that the religious ecstasy made people callous (so did causes); dulled their feelings" (*MD*, 16). Clarissa admits that she does not hate the person Doris Kilman, but the attitude she represents:

> For it was not her one hated but the idea of her, which undoubtedly had gathered in to itself a great deal that was not Miss Kilman; had become one of those spectres with which one battles in the night; one of those spectres who stand

astride us and suck up half our life-blood, dominators and
tyrants. . . . (*MD*, 16-17)

Here, in artistic terms, is a remarkably clear description of the
psychological phenomenon of projection. Just as Hugh Whitbread himself does not intimidate Clarissa, but rather the force
she attributes to him, so Miss Kilman herself does not enrage
Clarissa, but the spectre Clarissa unconsciously creates around
the figure of this religious devotee.

The phenomenon of projection, quite simply, arises out of
an individual's repressed thoughts. And, in Jungian ter-
minology, a repressed content comprises the shadow part of the
psyche, "that dark half of the psyche which we invariably get
rid of by means of projection."[7] An individual, in other words,
who cannot tolerate some aspect of his own personality,
represses it out of conscious awareness. But no psychic element
can be repressed out of existence; it demands recognition and
achieves it through projection. Often, then, the hatred one experiences for another person actually amounts to one's self-
hatred; the battle, in reality, rages inside. One, therefore, contains the potential for wholeness within himself, in that psychic
wholeness results from the integration of the conscious and the
repressed contents.

Woolf captures the phenomenon of projection in her plot sequences of the motor car and the aeroplane. In these two
events the reader witnesses the existence of Clarissa's psychic
shadow. Her shadow first appears as the hidden figure in the
motor car. As the car passes through the street, Clarissa and
Septimus draw closer to each other and to the car. Clarissa and
Septimus do not see each other; rather, they both watch the
car in which someone of very great importance sits. Though
the spectators cannot clearly distinguish the figure, they do
clearly feel its presence: "Mystery had brushed them with her
wing; they had heard the voice of authority" (*MD*, 20).
Clarissa and Septimus both react with terror; Clarissa jumps
with fear, and for Septimus "this gradual drawing together of

everything to one centre before his eyes, as if some horror had come almost to the surface and was about to burst into flames, terrified him" (*MD*, 21). Terror strikes them both because, although the integrated shadow often appears as a Godlike image, the dissociated shadow wields an evil power.[8] Thus, the mysterious figure in the motor car, symbol of the shadow, unites Clarissa, the ego or conscious portion of the psyche, with Septimus, Clarissa's unconscious counterpart. Clarissa fears the shadow because she has no awareness of it, while Septimus fears it because he realizes that he, as the unconscious, contains it.

The motor car incident reveals Clarissa's unconscious world to the reader, but not to Clarissa, who will remain ignorant of its existence until the novel's end. The unconscious appears in the form of Septimus, with whom the reader stays now, as Clarissa, the ego, avoids any more confrontation with the shadow. Clarissa goes home after the motor car startles her, and thus she misses the aeroplane. But Septimus stays, for he realizes that he contains the shadow: "It is I who am blocking the way, he thought. Was he not being looked at and pointed at?" (*MD*, 21). He imagines himself as the force that attracts the attention of all the bystanders; he therefore identifies with the motor car that hides the shadow. This realization, as much as it terrifies Septimus, holds him in place to witness the aeroplane, an image that draws him into the collective unconscious and the religious phenomena that reside there.

As Septimus looks up at the sky-writing plane, he imagines that

they are signalling to me. Not indeed in actual words; that is, he could not read the language yet; but it was plain enough, this beauty, this exquisite beauty, and tears filled his eyes as he looked at the smoke words languishing and melting in the sky and bestowing upon him in their inexhaustible charity and laughing goodness one shape after another of unimaginable beauty and signalling their inten-

tion to provide him, for nothing, for ever, for looking merely, with beauty, more beauty! Tears ran down his cheeks.
(*MD*, 31)

All the other spectators try to figure out exactly what the sky-
written letters spell out, while Septimus becomes enrapt in a
mystical vision of "a new religion" (*MD*, 33), out of which an
unseen voice tells him that "there is a God" (*MD*, 35). Septimus
glimpses a wholeness that he equates with God, a psychic
wholeness that he cannot see in the immediate world. The
realities of life intrude on such a vision. In Septimus's case, the
realities of life appear in the form of Evans, Septimus's superior
officer and close friend, who died in the war. Septimus imagines that Evans stands behind him. This imagined presence,
along with Rezia, Septimus's wife, who tries to get his attention, interrupts his vision.

Evans's presence reminds Septimus of the love-denying hor-
rors of war; similarly, Rezia tries to distract Septimus from his
vision because Dr. Holmes, insensitive and intolerant of
anything beyond the calculable and the tangible, advised
Rezia to keep the vision-prone Septimus focused on "real
things" (*MD*, 37). Such insensitivity, evidenced in both the war
and in Dr. Holmes, eventually leads Septimus to his suicide.
Through his suicide Clarissa acquires Septimus's visionary
strength, which empowers her to see beyond the insensitivity
and callousness that she has projected out of her shadow.

The car and plane sequences establish the close psychic
alliance between Clarissa and Septimus. Woolf intended these
two characters as doubles, as she explains in her introduction
to *Mrs. Dalloway*. But Woolf does not explain precisely how
they compare. Leon Edel infers that a repression of feeling
unites Clarissa and Septimus; Clarissa hides her intuitions and
feelings behind her mask of the perfect society hostess, while
Septimus held back emotion at the death of his friend Evans.[9]
Also, both characters struggle to recapture feelings: Septimus
struggles against the insensitive world, represented by the war

and by his doctors, while Clarissa fights against the callousness she projects onto others and with which she defensively surrounds herself. The visions that both have, furthermore, provide that they break through to true feeling. These visions constitute the tie between Clarissa and Septimus.

Woolf even names Septimus, meaning seventh, to connote the power of vision he possesses and transfers to Clarissa. As Mircea Eliade discusses, several mythical rituals use the number seven to indicate wholeness. First, the Buddha takes seven ritual steps that bring him to the cosmic summit.[10] Second, the Siberian shaman ascends to Heaven by climbing the seven steps cut out in the ceremonial birch-tree.[11] And third, the initiates in the mysteries of Mithra mount a ladder with seven rungs.[12] In all these mythical rites, seven provides a means to enter a world of timeless vision. In Woolf's novel, Septimus has this power and Clarissa shares in it.

But first Clarissa must continue to struggle against those forces within herself that attempt to block out the timeless and visionary world. The fact that more of this struggle remains for her becomes evident when she, having returned home from her shopping in London, learns that Millicent Bruton has invited Richard, and not Clarissa, to a luncheon. With Millicent, Clarissa faces another object of her own projections, which possesses the same powers over her as Hugh Whitbread and Doris Kilman: Millicent appears to Clarissa as hard and insensitive, and also makes her feel inadequate. As soon as Lucy, the maid, tells Clarissa of the luncheon, Clarissa instantly recalls the passage, "Fear no more the heat o' the sun." With this line of poetry, Clarissa tries to protect herself against Lady Bruton's social slight; she wishes to restrain any passionate response. By holding this response back, she forces the projection to surface, and thus she reads "on Lady Bruton's face, as if it had been a dial cut in impassive stone, the dwindling of life" (*MD*, 44). But the result of any projection entails a displacement of one's own insecurities, or those things one dislikes about himself, onto another. Therefore, no sooner does Clarissa have this picture of Lady Bruton than she goes upstairs, pauses at the window, and feels "herself suddenly shrivelled, aged, breastless" (*MD*, 45).

Although Clarissa's anxiety over her own inadequacy in the presence of Hugh Whitbread makes her regress to the age of eighteen, her fear that she is unloved when not invited to the Bruton luncheon makes her feel aged and unattractive. In reality, Hugh and Millicent do not directly cause these reactions; rather, they perform as vehicles for Clarissa's own lack of self-acceptance, for she suffers from "an emptiness about the heart of life" (*MD*, 45). She feels as if she possesses no emotional center to sustain her and provide a solid sense of Selfhood. This self-denial arises from the avoidance of self-exploration evidenced by her projections, and it causes her need, earlier in the novel, to be Clarissa, rather than Mrs. Richard Dalloway. This same self-denial appears now, as Clarissa retreats to her attic room and to her solitary bed that becomes "narrower and narrower" (*MD*, 45). Lying there, "she could see what she lacked. It was not beauty; it was not mind. It was something central which permeated; something warm which broke up surfaces and rippled the cold contact of man and woman, or of women together" (*MD*, 46). In psychological terms, Clarissa fears that she has no Selfhood that could generate love in her for others, and lacking this Selfhood, Clarissa fears she also has nothing that could attract the love from others.

She does know, however, of one situation in which she could feel love: that "of a woman, not a girl, of a woman confessing, as to her they often did, some scrape, some folly" (*MD*, 46). It seems from this that only a feminine force can penetrate through all of Clarissa's defenses against intimacy, and thus enter her psychic depths. Clarissa can relinquish all of her defenses in such a situation because a woman appealing to her lets her "feel what men felt" (*MD*, 47). Here rests the key to Clarissa's Selfhood. The dominance of the male principle in her life has forced her into a strictly defined role as woman and as the "perfect hostess" (*MD*, 93). Such an unbalanced emphasis dwarfs psychic growth and causes a compensatory need: the need to "feel what men felt." When Clarissa experiences this sensation, she gets a glimpse that emptiness does not, after all, surround the heart of life:

> It was a sudden revelation, a tinge like a blush which one tried to check and then, as it spread, one yielded to its expansion, and rushed to the farthest verge and there quivered and felt the world come closer, swollen with some astonishing significance, some pressure or rapture, which split its thin skin and gushed and poured with an extraordinary alleviation over the cracks and sores! Then, for that moment, she had seen an illumination; a match burning in a crocus; an inner meaning almost expressed. (*MD*, 47)

The final image in this passage captures the totality of Selfhood that Clarissa seeks. The vessel-shaped crocus suggests the feminine,[13] while the erect and burning match implies the masculine. Clarissa sees, therefore, if only for a moment, that she, a woman, contains a masculine principle within her own femininity.

Still thinking about the sense of completeness she derives from the love of a woman, Clarissa now recalls the freedom she experienced in the past when she and Sally Seton loved each other. The relationship was not sexual; in fact Clarissa felt protective of Sally. With her chivalry appealed to, Clarissa could permit herself a freedom from conventional behavior: "For in those days she was completely reckless; did the most idiotic things out of bravado: bicycled round the parapet on the terrace; smoked cigars" (*MD*, 50). Although now "she could not even get an echo of her old emotion" (*MD*, 51), she can remember feeling in the midst of all this past excitement that "if it were now to die 'twere now to be most happy" (*MD*, 51). These lines from Shakespeare's *Othello* (2, 1. 187-88) describe the peak of Othello's love for Desdemona, before Iago's evil plot takes hold. Innocence pervades his feelings at this point,

an innocence that Clarissa identifies with: "That was her feeling—Othello's feeling, and she felt it, she was convinced, as
strongly as Shakespeare meant Othello to feel it, all because
she was coming down to dinner in a white frock to meet Sally
Seton!" (*MD*, 51). Having her masculine principle tapped, in
other words, gives Clarissa a freedom from any compulsion to
hang onto life, for no longer does emptiness surround the heart
of life.

As Clarissa continues to recall her past with Sally, a memory
of her father surfaces. As mentioned earlier, Clarissa, unlike
Jacob Flanders, does not grapple so much with the imago
figure of her actual father, but with the general masculine
force in the world that inhibits her. Nevertheless, the few
references in the novel to Clarissa's actual father particularize
her psychological dilemma and thereby emphasize it. In the
present memory, Clarissa recalls that her father was attracted
to Sally. Woolf does not explicitly state that Clarissa, upon
realizing her father's attraction, felt usurped by him. But the
concatenation of her memories does imply it, for next she
recalls kissing Sally:

> Then came the most exquisite moment of her whole life
> passing a stone urn with flowers in it. Sally stopped; picked a
> flower; kissed her on the lips. The whole world might have
> turned upside down! The others disappeared; there she was
> alone with Sally. And she felt that she had been given a pre-
> sent, wrapped up, and told just to keep it, not to look at
> it—a diamond, something infinitely precious, wrapped up,
> which, as they walked (up and down, up and down), she un-
> covered, or the radiance burnt through, the revelation, the
> religious feeling! (*MD*, 52-53)

No sooner does Clarissa suspect a threat to her innocent playful
relationship with Sally than she allows it to become sexual. Not
only does she allow it, but she also thrills in it. The precious
treasure that Clarissa receives with the kiss consists of her
masculinity, or more specifically, her identification with her
father. To drop the facile label of lesbian on Clarissa's per-

sonality sidesteps the issue.[14]   Rather, the details in the novel make clear that, as Sydney Janet Kaplan says, "the attraction for Sally allows Clarissa to utilize the masculine side of her consciousness."[15] June Singer, a firm believer that androgyny is inherent to all people, explains that one cause of homosexuality stems from an individual's yearning to escape the demands of a sexist society that assigns roles.[16] With Sally, Clarissa does escape sexism. This escape becomes possible because Clarissa contacts her buried masculine identity. She uncovers that element that can contribute to her psychic wholeness, the potential of which manifests itself, as Jung says, in a spiritual or religious feeling. But Peter and Joseph interrupt and "embitter her moment of happiness" (*MD*, 53).

Peter's sudden appearance at the stone urn in the past threatens to rob Clarissa of her own masculinity, as does his constant handling of his knife in the visit to her home in the present. One may see this knife as a phallic symbol, but to stop one's interpretation there oversimplifies this scene.[17] Pointing out phallic symbols can obscure and violate the meaning of art. Once one discovers a phallic symbol, then a whole host of associations crowds into the fiction and, perhaps, crowds out the author's intention. Woolf tells the reader precisely what the knife signifies. It has little to do with Peter's wishes and more to do with Clarissa's reactions. Clarissa interprets Peter's knife as a criticism of her womanhood: " 'And what's all this?' he said, tilting his penknife towards her green dress. He's very well dressed, thought Clarissa; yet he always criticises *me*" (*MD*, 60). Peter shows no obvious criticism of Clarissa, but the presence of his knife, in which Clarissa sees Peter's masculinity and her own lack of it, arouses her self-criticism. Her Selfhood depends on an affirmation of her masculinity, not a denial of it.

This same theme recurs shortly afterwards. The ubiquitous knife forces Clarissa, or so she thinks, into a strictly feminine role: "What an extraordinary habit that was, Clarissa thought; always playing with a knife. Always making one feel, too, frivolous; empty-minded; a mere silly chatterbox, as he used" (*MD*, 65). Clarissa knows only annoyance as long as Peter handles his knife. But her annoyance and Peter's discomfort finally let go: "He burst into tears; wept; wept without the least shame" (*MD*, 69). Only now, once Peter drops his threat against Clarissa, can she lean forward, take his hand, draw him to her, and kiss him. Free of annoyance, she can extend love, for her masculinity no longer hides in fear.

Clarissa suffers from a severe bifurcation of her feminine and masculine psychic elements. As soon as Peter leaves, the clocks sound, symbolizing Clarissa's bifurcation. First Big Ben strikes the half hour; its "leaden circles dissolved in the air" (*MD*, 72). Two minutes lates St. Margaret's tolls the half hour, but her sound "glides into the recesses of the heart and buries itself in ring after ring of sound" (*MD*, 74). The lack of synchronization between these two clocks suggests the lack of harmony between Clarissa's feminine and masculine principles. But, even more important, Big Ben's leaden circles that dissolve in the air and St. Margaret's sound that glides into the recesses of the heart symbolize Clarissa's need to avoid masculine priorities and welcome feminine ones. Those priorities that Clarissa rejects appear in Woolf's description of Big Ben's sound: it strikes out "with extraordinary vigour, as if a young man, strong, indifferent, inconsiderate, were swinging dumb-bells this way and that" (*MD*, 71). This describes all that Clarissa rejects and all that Peter represents when he first visits her. Conversely, St. Margaret's clock sounds "like something alive which wants to confide itself, to disperse itself, to be, with a tremor of delight, at rest" (*MD*, 74). The chime conveys all that Clarissa craves and what Peter gives her, once he puts aside his knife and weeps. In sum, the clocks not only remind one of the irrevocable passage of time[18] and mark the interstices between appearances of characters,[19] but they also symbolize Clarissa Dalloway's central psychological dilemma.

Now that Peter has entered the story, Woolf follows him out of Clarissa's home. His visit has aroused his memories. So, as he sits in Regent's Park, napping, he dreams of a solitary traveler who sees three different women. As Julia Carlson says, the dream portrays Peter's conflict between his visionary and his realistic view of women.[20]

The first woman the solitary traveler sees appears as a spectral presence who offers Peter "compassion, comprehension, absolution" (*MD*, 86). The dream's fulfillment of his wish for these divine gifts makes him want to give up the real world: "May I never go back to the lamplight; to the sitting-room; never finish my book; never knock out my pipe; never ring for Mrs. Turner to clear away; rather let me walk straight on to this great figure" (*MD*, 86-87). Peter searches, in waking life, for such a magnificent relationship with a woman, as, in the past, he has sought one with Clarissa. Clarissa, however, found such demands intolerable. Back in the dream, the spectral presence remains only as long as the traveler stays in the woods. Once he enters the village he meets a more realistic woman. This village woman, unlike the visionary one, has needs and pains of her own. Whereas the spectral presence gives and soothes, the village woman needs something, for she seems "to seek, over a desert, a lost son; to search for a rider destroyed" (*MD*, 87). This second figure in Peter's dream represents the realistic Clarissa, rather than the ideal one. The realistic Clarissa yearns for the return of her masculine principle. In waking life, Peter could not fulfill Clarissa's need for this principle; only Sally Seton could. So the solitary traveler moves on and enters "indoors among ordinary things," where the landlady takes the marmalade, shuts it in the cupboard, and asks, "There is nothing more to-night, sir?" (*MD*, 87). The landlady serves the traveler in menial ways, as the spectral presence does in divine ways. The dream says, then, that because Peter looks for the spectral presence in women, he is left with only the landlady; and because Peter wants compassion from the spectral presence but feels none for the village woman, he is left with only the landlady. Consequently, Peter Walsh, in his five years away from London, marries a young girl on the boat to India and then falls in love with the wife of a major in the Indian army. He loved the girl on the boat, loves the major's wife, and when that love dissolves will love someone else, for Peter will always remain just on the threshold of love until he gets out of the woods and enters the real life in the village.

Unlike Peter, Septimus is totally preoccupied with mystical and spiritual thoughts; he utters aloud such revelations as "I have been dead, and yet am now alive" and the prophecy of "something tremendous about to happen" (*MD*, 104). He has these thoughts as he sits in Regent's Park, on a seat near where Peter, at the very same time, dreams. Though Peter stands up and walks towards Septimus, he remains totally unaware of any spirituality, as he stays totally unaware of Septimus's presence. Interestingly, though, the closer Peter gets to Septimus, the more sure Septimus becomes that this approaching man in the grey suit is Evans, "the dead man" (*MD*, 105). And Peter, having finally seen Septimus and Rezia, decides, as he passes them, that a lovers' squabble has caused the man's excited utterances (*MD*, 106). Peter sees himself in the superficial appearance of others.

In not recognizing the gravity of Septimus's state, Peter not only exhibits the death of his own soul, but also indirectly suggests the nonexistence of that part of Clarissa's personality that Septimus represents. For indeed, a certain part of Clarissa has died. Clarissa herself says this when she admits that she no longer can feel the excitement over life she once experienced with Sally. The incident of Sylvia's death reinforces this same idea. Sylvia, Clarissa's sister, was tragically killed by a falling tree and Clarissa blames her father for the death. The validity of this blame, however, does not rest on the actual fact that Justin Parry did or did not accidentally kill his daughter. Rather, Clarissa's blame holds psychological, instead of factual, validity. Psychologically, Justin Parry killed a part of Clarissa, Sylvia, a girl "on the verge of life" (*MD*, 118). Consequently, Clarissa died emotionally and spiritually. Peter describes the ramifications of her emotional death: "That was the devilish part of her—this coldness, this woodenness . . . an impenetrability" (*MD*, 91). And her sister's tragic death causes her spiritual death as well; Clarissa's initial bitterness, though directed at her father at first, becomes diffused into a general atheism—"there were no Gods . . . so she evolved this atheist's religion" (*MD*, 118). Although this spiritual part of Clarissa's personality died, it continues to thrive in Septimus, who asserts, "There is a God" (*MD*, 35).

Despite Septimus's spiritual revelations, no one takes him seriously. He may retain that part of Clarissa that had died, but he cannot manifest it openly and acceptably in society, for society holds such utterances suspect. As a result, Septimus appears mad. And of even greater consequence is Septimus's acclimation to society's standards of normality. This crucial damage to his sensibilities occurs in the war: "when Evans was killed . . . Septimus, far from showing any emotion or recognising that here was the end of a friendship, congratulated himself upon feeling very little and very reasonably" (*MD*, 130). The war taught Septimus that to survive he must remain indifferent. When peace came, however, Septimus began to panic over his inability to feel; he thus married Lucrezia merely to prove that he could feel. But the war killed his emotions, so despite his marriage, Septimus retains only his intellect: "He could reason; he could read . . . he could add up his bill; his brain was perfect; it must be the fault of the world then—that he could not feel" (*MD*, 133).

Septimus, thus, turns to his mystical revelations as a source of feeling, and thereby complements Clarissa, who also needs to regain her emotional and spiritual faculties. She will regain them when, at the end of the novel, she identifies with Septimus's suicide. This identification revives Clarissa's capacity for love, an event foreshadowed in the song of a street singer. A battered woman, who stands opposite Regent's Park Tube station, sings of love. The critic J. Hillis Miller tracks the words of the woman's song back to Richard Strauss's *Aller Seelen*.

Strauss's song refers to one day in the year in which the dead are free.[21] Woolf recounts this one day in her novel and shows the freedom of the dead in that moment when Clarissa's dead emotions come to life through her identification with Septimus.

Woolf reveals the cause of emotional death when she says, "it must be the fault of the world then — that he could not feel" (*MD*, 133). Woolf states here, and dramatizes in the rest of the novel, the world's life-denying forces. Not only does the war deprive Septimus of feelings, and not only does the generalized father imago stifle Clarissa's feelings, but all forces in the world that deny individuality also kill emotion. Woolf calls these forces the Goddesses of Proportion and Conversion.

The doctors who supposedly treat Septimus for his apparent madness worship the Goddess of Proportion. Dr. Holmes, the general practitioner, finds nothing wrong with Septimus that some outside interest or hobby could not cure (*MD*, 138). Dr. Bradshaw, the psychiatrist, shows even greater devotion to Proportion. Bradshaw has his creed:

> Health we must have; and health is proportion; so that when a man comes into your room and says he is Christ (a common delusion), and has a message, as they mostly have, and threatens, as they often do, to kill himself, you invoke proportion; order rest in bed; rest in solitude; silence and rest; rest without friends, without books, without messages; six months' rest; until a man who went in weighing seven stone six comes out weighing twelve. (*MD*, 149-150)

Bradshaw's prescription for madness deprives the individual of the very things that make his life meaningful; if a person has a messianic complex and offers a message to the world, then his message supplies him with his primary sense of personal significance. To take away that message is to kill a self. But of course, Bradshaw would not account such a death as a loss; rather, he arrogates the privilege of secluding lunatics, penalizing their despair, and muzzling their views "until they, too, shared his sense of proportion" (*MD*, 150).

Doris Kilman exhibits a similar intolerance in her worship of the Goddess of Conversion. In Woolf's words, this Goddess "feasts on the wills of the weakly, loving to impress, to impose" (*MD*, 151). Such a drive determines Miss Kilman's reaction to Clarissa: "And there rose in her an overmastering desire to overcome her; to unmask her. If she could have felled her it would have eased her. . . . If only she could make her weep; could ruin her; humiliate her; bring her to her knees crying, You are right!" (*MD*, 189).

Holmes, Bradshaw, and Kilman display their devotion to the Goddesses of Proportion and Conversion most blatantly. However, the worship of these Goddesses can manifest itself also in more subtle ways. For instance, Hugh Whitbread worships Proportion in his emphasis on order and exactness. Such an emphasis has grave results when Hugh applies it to sentiments, as he does at Lady Bruton's luncheon. Millicent Bruton has adopted the project of emigrating young people to Canada. She invites Hugh and Richard Dalloway to lunch so they can help her draft a letter to the *Times* that would explain this project. As Lady Bruton rambles about her objectives, Hugh carefully writes capital letters with rings around them down the paper's margin, and organizes her "sentiments in alphabetical order" (*MD*, 167). The lives of the planned emigrants have completely vanished from consciousness while the cause, neatly outlined, takes over. Richard Dalloway, likewise, illustrates the effect of the Goddesses. In the scene of Lady Bruton's luncheon, he appears as their victim. Specifically, when he hears that Peter Walsh has returned to London, he determines to go straight to Clarissa after lunch, wishing to tell her "in so many words, that he loved her" (*MD*, 162). But when Richard arrives home, he cannot "bring himself to say he loved her; not in so many words" (*MD*, 179). Thus, both Clarissa and Septimus see all about them the worshipers and the victims of the Conversion and Proportion Goddesses. The concentration of these forces paradoxically kills Septimus and, in Clarissa, frees the dead.

The forces of these Goddesses converge on Septimus. Dr. Bradshaw intends to send Septimus to a rest home. Just a few hours before Bradshaw plans to call Rezia about the arrangement he has made for Septimus's move, and just as Dr. Holmes climbs the stairs to Septimus's room, Septimus flings himself "vigorously, violently down on to Mrs. Filmer's area railings" (*MD*, 226). Septimus feels he has no other choice; he stands by the window aware of the imminence of Bradshaw's phone call, aware of Holmes's physical proximity. So, just as he prepares to hurl himself out the window, he cries out to Holmes, "I'll give it you!" (*MD*, 226). Septimus, out of despair, offers his life to a representative of the world's destructive force. He sacrifices himself.

Identical to Septimus's situation of standing alone by the window as the destructive forces converge on him and drive him to take his own life is Clarissa's situation at her party. Here the forces converge on Clarissa in the form of Hugh Whitbread, of Dr. and Mrs. William Bradshaw, of Richard Dalloway, of Peter Walsh, and even of Sally Seton, who no longer participates in the free, rebellious life, but has settled into the conventional roles of wife and mother, roles that have deprived her of her old luster (*MD*, 260). And while these forces congregate, Clarissa greets them from her post at the top of the stairs. As one might expect, the more these forces gather, the less Clarissa can feel and the more she is robbed of life: "It was too much of an effort. She was not enjoying it. It was too much like being—just anybody, standing there . . . for oddly enough she had quite forgotten what she looked like, but felt herself a stake driven in at the top of her stairs" (*MD*, 259). As the world's destructive forces take away Septimus's physical life, they, likewise, deprive Clarissa of her emotional life.

The novel's suggestions up to this point—that a psychic tie exists between Clarissa and Septimus—become strengthened by the many parallels between his jump and her party. Whereas Septimus's last cry before his death identifies his suicide as a sacrifice or offering, so Clarissa describes her party as an "offering" (*MD*, 185). Clarissa does not know to whom she makes the offering; she merely knows its purpose: "to combine, to create" (*MD*, 185). This purpose further ties together the lives of Septimus and Clarissa, for, when she hears of his suicide, in a moment apart from her guests, she mystically combines her life with his, and from this combination, creates feeling in herself, long dead until now:

> A thing there was that mattered; a thing, wreathed about with chatter, defaced, obscured in her own life, let drop every day in corruption, lies, chatter. This he had preserved. Death was defiance. Death was an attempt to communicate; people feeling the impossibility of reaching the centre which, mystically, evaded them; closeness drew apart; rapture faded, one was alone. There was an embrace in death. (*MD*, 280-81)

Although when she first hears talk of Septimus's suicide Clarissa reacts as a hostess — "What business had the Bradshaws to talk of death at her party?" (*MD*, 280) — her outrage at this disturbance quickly subsides as she permits feeling to permeate her. But permitting the resurgence of emotion, Clarissa's priorities shift from the propriety of her party to the "thing . . . that mattered" that Septimus preserved. Clarissa can now, once again, experience the ecstasy she once knew in the company of Sally Seton; she can now firmly restate Othello's words, "If it were now to die, 'twere now to be most happy" (*MD*, 281).

An additional parallel that exists between Septimus's plunge and Clarissa's vision of it explains the concept that death supplies the means to reach the "centre." As Septimus stands by the window about to jump, "coming down the staircase opposite an old man stopped and stared at him" (*MD*, 226). Woolf says no more of this man. But she does recall him in the figure of the old woman whom Clarissa sees during her ecstatic reenactment of Septimus's death: "She parted the curtains; she looked. Oh, but how surprising!—in the room opposite the old lady stared straight at her!" (*MD*, 283). When Clarissa earlier sees the old woman, she evisions her as an embodiment of the soul's privacy (*MD*, 192). Through this association one gains greater insight into the probable significance of the old man who stares at Septimus. The old man represents the privacy of the soul that Holmes threatens and that Septimus preserves through his suicide. Likewise, the old woman stands for that which Clarissa has "let drop every day in corruption, lies, chatter." Whereas Septimus preserves it through death, Clarissa recaptures it through her identification with his death. Reaching this "centre," Clarissa need not fear any longer the heat of the sun (*MD*, 283).

Clarissa actually goes through a typically mythical experience of initiation. Mircea Eliade describes an initiation as predicated on a ritual death that involves the initiate's descent into hell.[22] Septimus descends onto Mrs. Filmer's area railings. Also, as Eliade explains, the basic idea of this ritual death is that one life must be sacrificed for the birth of another.[23] Thus Clarissa emerges from her spiritual vision and rejoins her guests as if newly born into life. Peter Walsh witnesses Clarissa's birth:

> What is this terror? what is this ecstasy? he thought to himself. What is it that fills me with extraordinary excitement?
> It is Clarissa, he said.
> For there she was. (*MD*, 296)

The novel's last line—"For there she was"—despite its simplicity, conveys the profundity of the rebirth theme.[24]

With *Mrs. Dalloway*, Virginia Woolf brings her composite being's development up to a most crucial point. In conjunction with *Jacob's Room*, the being has evolved to the point of freedom from the personal and the general parental imagoes. Similiar to Jacob Flanders, Clarissa Dalloway struggles through all of the discomfort and insecurities implanted by the imago force and eventually drops her defenses to embrace that privacy of her soul so long supressed. Lily Briscoe, in *To the Lighthouse*, therefore, can complete the composite personality's search for the Self. Free of the imago restrictions, Lily can reconcile the mother and father in her life and accept them as integral to her own personality.

# NOTES

1. D. S. Savage, for instance, says that the novel rejects spiritual affirmation (*The Withered Branch: Six Studies in the Modern Novel* (London: Eyre & Spottiswoode, 1950), p. 87. David Daiches, on the other hand, says that the novel treats the "unresolvable paradox involved in the individual's need to retain his individuality while at the same time needing some real communion with others" (*Virginia Woolf*, 2d ed. (New York: New Directions, 1942), p. xiii).

2. This entry comes from Woolf's holograph notebook of November 9, 1922 to August 2, 1923, which is held in the Berg Collection of the New York Public Library. The passage is quoted by Charles G. Hoffman in his essay "From Short Story to Novel: The Manuscript Revisions of Virginia Woolf's *Mrs. Dalloway*," *Modern Fiction Studies* 14 (Summer 1968); 183.

3. Virginia Woolf, *Mrs. Dalloway* (New York: Harcourt, Brace & World, 1925), p. 3. All further quotations and references to the novel will be cited within the text as *MD*.

4. Virginia Woolf, *Three Guineas* (New York: Harcourt, Brace & World, 1938), p. 6. All further quotations and references to this work will be cited within the text as *TG*.

5. J. J. Bachofen, through his studies of ancient religions, concludes that the sun represents "the greater glory of the male power." And when the sun is at its zenith, "it is triumphant paternity." See *Myth, Religion, and Mother Right: Selected Writings of J. J. Bachofen*, trans. Ralph Manheim (Princeton, N.J.: Princeton University Press, 1973), p. 114. June Singer also speaks of the sun as masculine, but in terms not as sexist as Bachofen's. Where Bachofen sees the sun as representing the dominating, greater force of the masculine, Singer more objectively says the sun "is Masculine in the sense that a fountain is Masculine. It has qualities of pushing out, thrusting, disseminating and dissipating itself." See *Androgyny:Toward a New Theory of Sexuality* (Garden City, N.Y.: Doubleday & Co., 1976), p. 243.

6. There have been some varying critical reactions to Woolf's use of the dirge from *Cymbeline*. Maud Bodkin contrasts the dirge with Clarissa's exhilaration with the ebullient life in the London streets. Such a juxtaposition, says Bodkin, captures the Jungian theory of "those alternations of vital rhythm—a backward, inward turning of libido following the outward flow." See *Archetypal Patterns in Poetry: Psychological Studies of Imagination* (Oxford: Oxford University Press, 1934), p. 87.

Avrom Fleishman believes that Woolf's use of Shakespeare's lines indicates Clarissa's propensity toward death. See *Virginia Woolf: A Critical Reading* (Baltimore, Md.: Johns Hopkins Press, 1975), p. 86.

J. Hillis Miller takes a similar stand when he says that Clarissa is obsessed with these lines because she sees death as her only means to escape suffering. See "Virginia Woolf's All Soul's Day: The Omniscient Narrator in *Mrs. Dalloway*," *The Shaken Realist: Essays in Modern Literature in Honor of Frederick J. Hoffman*, ed. Melvin J. Friedman and John B. Vickery (Baton Rouge, La.: Louisiana State University Press, 1970), p. 123.

7. .C. G. Jung, *Psychology and Alchemy*, 2d ed., trans. R. F. C. Hull (Princeton, N.J.: Princeton University Press, 1968), p. 29. Here Jung refers to "shadow" in its most general sense, though elsewhere, when speaking of it more specifically, he insists that the shadow figure always appears as the same sex as the individual; a woman's shadow is always female and a man's is always male. Such a restriction evidences the weakness of any system that attempts to place a grid of definitions over the vastly complex human psyche.

8. Jung explains that "the contents of the personal unconscious (i.e., the shadow) are indistinguishably merged with the archetypal contents of the collective unconscious and drag the latter with them when the shadow is brought into consciousness." He follows this up by saying that "the archetypal contents of the collective unconscious can often assume grotesque and horrible forms," while the "psychological elucidation of these images . . . leads logically into the depths of religious phenomenology." See ibid., pp. 32-33.

9. Leon Edel, *The Modern Psychological Novel* (New York: Grosset & Dunlap, 1955), p. 132.

10. Mircea Eliade, *Myths, Dreams and Mysteries: The Encounter between Contemporary Faiths and Archaic Realities*, trans. Philip Mairet (New York: Harper & Row, 1967), p. 111.

11. Ibid., pp. 112-13.

12. Ibid., p. 113.

13. Erich Neumann says, "For obvious reasons woman is experienced as the vessel par excellence. Woman as body-vessel is the natural expression of the human experience of woman bearing the child 'within' her and of man entering 'into' her in the sexual act." See *The Great Mother: An Analysis of the Archetype*, trans. Ralph Manheim (Princeton, N.J.: Princeton University Press, 1955), p. 42.

14. Shalom Rachman, "Clarissa's Attic: Virginia Woolf's *Mrs. Dalloway* Reconsidered," *Twentieth Century Literature* 18 (January 1972): 10.

15. Sydney Janet Kaplan, *Feminine Consciousness in the Modern British Novel* (Urbana, Ill.: University of Illinois Press, 1975), p. 95.

16. Singer explains: "Androgyny is innate in each individual, but it is often the environmental circumstances that trigger homosexual or bisexual behavior. Sometimes, but not always, these types of behavior represent the resolution of a conflict between the psyche's urgings toward androgynous functioning and the demands of a sexist society in which people's sexual differences remain more significant than their human commonalities." See *Andorgyny*, p. 280.

17. Erwin R. Steinberg gives such an interpretation. See "Freudian Symbolism and Communication," *Literature and Psychology* 3 (April 1953): 4.

18. Nancy Topping Bazin, *Virginia Woolf and the Androgynous Vision* (New Brunswick, N.J.: Rutgers University Press, 1973), p. 115.

19. David Daiches, *Virginia Woolf*, p. 65.

20. Julia Carlson, "The Solitary Traveller in *Mrs. Dalloway*," *Virginia Woolf: A Collection of Criticism*, ed. Thomas S. W. Lewis (New York: McGraw-Hill Book Co., 1975), p. 59.

21. J. Hillis Miller provides the English translation of Strauss's song:

Place on the table the perfuming heather, bring
here the last red asters, and let us again speak
of love, as once in May.
　Give me your hand, that I may secretly press it,
and if someone sees, it's all the same to me.
Give me but one of your sweet glances, as once in May.
　It is blooming and breathing perfume today on every
grave. One day in the year is free to the dead.
Come to my heart, that I may have you again, as once
in May, as once in May.

See "Virginia Woolf's All Soul's Day," p. 115, footnote.

22. Eliade, *Myths, Dreams and Mysteries*, pp. 79-80.

23. Ibid., p. 184.

24. Isabel Gamble takes a similar view of the novel's last line. See "The Secret Sharer in *Mrs. Dalloway*," *Accent* 16 (Autumn 1956): 251.

## 5

# *To the Lighthouse*
## The Third Stroke

Virginia Woolf arrives at the most crucial point of her nine novels with *To the Lighthouse*. Here the development of the novels' composite personality reaches a pinnacle from which one can observe all that has transpired up to now and from which one can speculate what lies ahead. In *To the Lighthouse* the composite personality discovers Selfhood, that goal sought but only glimpsed in the preceding novels. With this discovery, the nature of Selfhood reveals itself, and finally one gains some insight into its composition. The reader can expect, then, in the novels that follow *To the Lighthouse*, either a further exploration of the Self or a destruction of that Selfhood by intolerant and fragmenting forces. As it turns out, *Orlando* reveals the Self's androgynous nature, *The Waves* shows why the composite personality cannot sustain a hold on the Self's wholeness and finally, in *The Years* and *Between the Acts* the destructive forces fragment this wholeness.

*To the Lighthouse* occupies more than just a pivotal point in the personality's search for the Self. Actually, this novel gathers all the psychological advances made in the first four novels, concentrates them, and elevates them to a high spiritual significance. The spiritual, or religious, quality of the Self has only been a hint up to this point. The image of the wind, a divine force, makes its first appearance in *The Voyage Out*, where Rachel Vinrace announces that she wishes to "triumph in the wind" (*TVO*, 23) to confront the divine powers in the world. References to the wind also occur two times in *Jacob's Room*: the first implies that divine power rests in a veiled female figure (*JR*, 45), and the second shows Jacob Flander's spiritual self, after he physically dies in the war, appearing to Bonamy as wind that lifts the leaves (*JR*, 176). In these two novels Woolf suggests that some connection exists between an individual's Selfhood and his relationship to God. *Mrs. Dalloway* continues this suggestion by showing Clarissa Dalloway embracing the "centre" (*MD*, 281) or the "privacy of the soul," where she experiences her transforming vision of Septimus Warren Smith's death. But in none of these works does Woolf firmly state that when one reaches the Self one contacts God. In *To the Lighthouse* she does make this statement, however, firmly and unequivocally.

Furthermore, one can assume from Woolf's diary entries that she did not intentionally hold back her theory that God exists in the Self until she wrote *To the Lighthouse*. Rather, Woolf discovers the relationship between God and the Self at the same pace that her composite personality does:

> . . . at last, at last, after that battle *Jacob's Room*, that agony—all agony but the end—*Mrs. Dalloway*, I am now writing as fast and freely as I have written in the whole of my life; more so—20 times more so—than any novel yet. I think this is the proof that I was on the right path; and that what fruit hangs in my soul is to be reached there. (*AWD*, 84)

The freedom Woolf feels in her art testifies, from this diary entry, to the fact that in writing *To the Lighthouse* she makes enormous advances toward the "fruit" in her "soul." In the same entry she writes another comment that further uncovers the nature of her search: "I feel that I can float everything off now; and 'everything' is rather a crowd and weight and confusion in the mind" (*AWD*, 84). In other words, Woolf experiences artistically what her composite personality undergoes psychologically: she relieves the mind of all dross so that she can extract what is valuable. Although the terms she uses in her diary tend toward vagueness, she, in *To the Lighthouse*, clearly presents her philosophical theory that in the Self one finds God. Woolf introduces this theory on many artistic levels: in the novel's stylistic texture, in its structure, in its biblical and literary allusions, in its imagery, and in its plot.

The novel's texture follows the impressionism begun in *Jacob's Room*, but improves on it immensely. Whereas in *Jacob's Room* Woolf surrounds the main character with a vagueness that creates the ambience of the unconscious world, and whereas in *Mrs. Dalloway* she follows the unconscious thoughts of her characters, in *To the Lighthouse* Woolf, even more successfully, captures the texture of the psychic realm. No prominent boundaries circumscribe the thoughts and reactions of the characters, and no obvious device signals the movement from unconscious recollections to present action. In addition, an even greater improvement shows up in Woolf's means for measuring the depths of a character's unconscious thoughts—the lighthouse. In *Jacob's Room*, she uses the obtrusive narrator, while in *Mrs. Dalloway* she uses the clocks. But in *To the Lighthouse* she distances the measuring device even further from the characters. Yet, as far away as the lighthouse physically stands from most of the novel's action, its effect on the action and the characters remains strong and consistent. Thus, with *To the Lighthouse* Woolf tightens her grasp on experience so firmly that a greater concurrence exists between her style and her theme.

The beauty of the lighthouse symbol is not only that it gauges unconscious depths. The lighthouse represents God, and does so in many ways. It provides a light in a world of darkness, since the Lord repeatedly appears as light in the Bible: "The Lord shall be unto thee an everlasting light" (Isaiah

60:19); or "Then spake Jesus again unto them, saying, I am the light of the world: he that followeth me shall not walk in darkness, but shall have the light of life" (John 8:12). Besides the divine significance of light, the lighthouse also symbolizes the Trinity in that it has three distinct lights that stroke the darkness. In addition, and here Woolf suggests the connection between the Self and God, the lighthouse stands firm and steadfast upon its rock base in the midst of the ever-flowing dark sea. The sea archetypally symbolizes the unconscious,[1] while the biblical symbol of the rock usually refers to God or spiritual power — for example, "The Lord is my rock, and my fortress, and my deliverer" (Psalms 18:2), and Christ says, "Therefore whosoever heareth these sayings of mine, and doeth them, I will liken him unto a wise man, which built his house upon a rock" (Matthew 7:24). In this novel God, the rock, stands in the midst of the sea, the unconscious. So, thus far, if only imagistically, one has Woolf's primary thesis: God inhabits the Self. And as the title of *To the Lighthouse* implies, the characters and action move toward that God within.[2]

If the lighthouse represents God within the Self, then the question remains as to what symbol Woolf uses for the self without God, the self comprised of only a superficial identity and void of spiritual essence, the self in need of God. Woolf symbolizes this self by the other house in the novel — that of the Ramsays. By juxtaposing these two houses, Woolf indirectly alludes to Christ's parable of the two houses: Christ likens an individual who follows his teachings to a house built on a rock, while one who does not follow Christ is similar to a house built on earth. The first house, Christ says, can withstand the flood, while the second, with its weaker foundation, will immediately fall into ruin (Luke 6:47-49). The two houses in Woolf's novel, therefore, stand for the two possibilities open to an individual; depending upon one's choice and psychological makeup, he may choose the house without God, bound for ruin, or the one with God, steadily withstanding any onslaught. The lighthouse stands unharmed throughout the novel, while in the book's middle section one witnesses the destruction of the Ramsay's home as "the flood, the profusion of darkness"[3] besets it.

The structure of the novel reinforces this theme of the two selves, the one with and the one without God. The first section, entitled "The Window," centers around the Ramsay home, while the third section, "The Lighthouse," focuses attention on the second house, the one built on rock. These two sections are joined by the middle one, "Times Passes," in which chronological time vanishes and psychological time prevails. The central section, rather than tying the two houses together, and rather than pivoting from one to the other, actually shows that if an individual goes deep enough into the darkness that fills the self without God, behind all the darkness he finds light, the light of God. In other words, no single individual contains all darkness or all light; instead, all people possess the light of God. One's recognition of the God within, however, does depend on a willingness to push away all the heavy darkness and thus see the core of light. As one reads through "Time Passes" he does exactly that—plunges into the darkness. This central section of the novel, then, captures more than just the erosive and devastating effects of time and nature.[4]  For beyond the apparent devastation that reigns in "Time Passes" lies "The Lighthouse," the Self built upon the rock foundation.

The options open to an individual, to live in darkness or to seek out the light behind the darkness, comprise the novel's theme. But Woolf uses more than artistic style, structure, and imagery to convey the theme. She also develops her characters for the same purpose. One character may grow into an awareness of the God within, while another may vacillate between the ego, the conscious realm where God does not exist, and the unconscious where the Self resides. Mr. and Mrs. Ramsay are two such characters. In "The Window" Mr. Ramsay operates strictly on the ego level; yet in "The Lighthouse" he eventually sees beyond his own pride and recognizes a power more vast and of greater strength than his own. Mrs. Ramsay, on the other hand, at times appears divine in her immense generosity and integrative capabilities, while at other times she seems somewhat self-centered. A reader, therefore, errs if he classifies Mr. and Mrs. Ramsay as simply character types; narrow categories deny Mr. Ramsay his growth and Mrs. Ramsay her complexity.

Mr. Ramsay's eventual awareness of a power beyond his own has less effect on him than on Lily Briscoe, the painter. Lily, alone, experiences the transformation in that, concomitant with Mr. Ramsay's landing at the lighthouse, she completes the painting begun ten years before. In that painting she integrates the dark and the light masses by drawing a stroke through them. The stroke in her painting, like "Time Passes" in Woolf's novel, unites the darkness of the God-less with the light of the God-filled. Lily thus achieves the "razor edge of balance between two opposite forces" (*TTL*, 287). In psychological terms, she finds the balance between those opposing psychic forces within herself, and thereby captures the Self's wholeness. *To the Lighthouse* tells Lily Briscoe's story, of how she, the current embodiment of Woolf's composite being, achieves a sustained vision of the divine totality that constitutes Selfhood.

In the very beginning of the novel one sees only a little of Lily Briscoe. Rather, in "The Window" Woolf describes Mr. and Mrs. Ramsay and immediately shows how they differ. Mrs. Ramsay's words open the novel: "Yes, of course, if it's fine tomorrow." To James, her son, these words seem "fringed with joy" and filled with "heavenly bliss" (*TTL*, 9), for his mother has given him hope that they will visit the lighthouse. Then Mr. Ramsay intrudes into their blissful solitude with "But . . . it won't be fine" (*TTL*, 10), for he insists that his children should know the difficulties of life and the uncompromising nature of facts. Conversely, for Mrs. Ramsay, "to pursue truth with such astonishing lack of consideration for other people's feelings, to rend the thin veils of civilization so wantonly, so brutally, was to her so horrible an outrage of human decency that, without replying, dazed and blinded, she bent her head" (*TTL*, 51). Mr. Ramsay's calloused outburst, that dashes

James's hopes and destroys his bliss with his mother, also renders Mrs. Ramsay silent and blind.

Both these qualities—silence and blindness—only partially characterize Mrs. Ramsay. That is, viewed from the outside, from Mr. Ramsay's perspective, and perhaps from the position of other insensitive individuals, Mrs. Ramsay seems silent and blind when compared to her verbal, truth-seeking husband. But actually, Mrs. Ramsay fluctuates between two levels. Often when confronted with vision-denying forces, such as her husband, she manifests a submissive attitude; but deep within her lies a power disinterested in fact, a power out of which her assertiveness and clarity of vision arise. Her fluctuation between the two levels shows up repeatedly throughout "The Window."

An example of this fluctuation occurs when Mr. Ramsay insists that rain will cancel their trip to the lighthouse. As Mrs. Ramsay bends her head, "dazed and blinded," she thinks of how deeply she reveres her husband: "She was not good enough to tie his shoe strings, she felt" (*TTL*, 51). She, here, takes a position to Mr. Ramsay that resembles the one John the Baptist takes to Christ: "I indeed baptize you with water unto repentance: but he that cometh after me is mightier than I, whose shoes I am not worthy to bear: he shall baptize you with the Holy Ghost, and with fire" (Matthew 3:11). Just as John predicts that Christ will come, so spiritual powers within Mrs. Ramsay lift up her reverentially bowed head:

> Mrs. Ramsay, who had been sitting loosely, folding her son in her arm, braced herself, and, half turning, seemed to raise herself with an effort, and at once to pour erect into the air a rain of energy, a column of spray, looking at the same time animated and alive as if all her energies were being fused into force, burning and illuminating. (*TTL*, 58)

As Saint John the Divine proclaims in Revelation, Christ shall lead those who come out of the great tribulation "unto living fountains of waters: and God shall wipe away all tears from their eyes" (7:17). Mrs. Ramsay, therefore, gathers her son James close to her and into her divine powers of salvation. But Mr. Ramsay's assertion of fact intrudes: "Into this delicious fecundity, this fountain and spray of life, the fatal sterility of the male plunged itself, like a beak of brass, barren and bare. He wanted sympathy." Then, Woolf compares this beak of brass to "the arid scimitar of the male, which smote mercilessly, again and again, demanding sympathy" (*TTL*, 59). Thus, Mrs. Ramsay shows two levels to her personality: one, the submissive and reverential, and the other, powerful and fertile. These, of course, do not necessarily contradict each other, for, after all, Christ washes his disciples' feet and then wipes them with his own towel (John 13:5).

The reference to "the arid scimitar of the male" does not suggest the phallic power before which Mrs. Ramsay subordinates herself.[5] Rather, Woolf contrasts the sterile and arid male power to Mrs. Ramsay's ability to create the generating essence of life. In other words, it seems as though Woolf breaks down all sexual distinction in Mrs. Ramsay, though she clearly defines Mr. Ramsay as male. One thus can view Mrs. Ramsay's act as does Annis Pratt: "We might consider Mrs. Ramsay's erection, then, as an act of androgynous creativity in which the hero calls upon the fullest reach of her internal nature."[6] The "rain of energy" that Mrs. Ramsay pours forth pertains not at all to male sexuality. Rather, Mrs. Ramsay displays her creative energy that transcends male and female roles or biological functions. This "rain of energy" and "spray of life" originate from her psychic core, which has no sex, but in which lies the power of God. The differences between Mr. and Mrs. Ramsay, then, appear not only in their life orientation, his factual and hers visionary, and in their creative powers, his sterile and hers fecund, but also in their overall personalities: Mr. Ramsay strikes out with his strictly male identity, whereas Mrs. Ramsay creates and comforts with her androgynous one.

Mr. Ramsay's thoughtless assertion of fact and his irascible insistence that rain will keep the family from the lighthouse blind Mrs. Ramsay as well as silence her. The passage in which she bends her head, "dazed and blinded," supplies only one of many references to the theme of blindness. Woolf often refers to Mrs. Ramsay as short-sighted. For instance, Mrs. Ramsay must crane forward to read an advertisement for a circus soon to visit the town, "for she was short-sighted" (*TTL*, 21). And, Mrs. Ramsay "focused her short-sighted eyes" upon Lily Briscoe and William Bankes who stroll together (*TTL*, 109). But a similar paradox exists in Mrs. Ramsay's short-sightedness as in her submissive silence. Her weak sight classifies her along with such blind visionaries as Homer and Tiresias, who possess an acute in-sight that compensates for their weak out-sight. Mrs. Ramsay, indeed, has exceptionally fine insight, evidenced throughout "The Window."

Mrs. Ramsay's insight comes when she can remove herself from any role demands placed on her as mother or wife. For instance, when James goes to bed, she feels relieved because "children never forget. For this reason, it was so important what one said, and what one did" (*TTL*, 95). Mrs. Ramsay knows that James will remember for all his life how his hopes to go to the lighthouse were dashed. So, when he leaves her, she feels relief that now "she could be herself, by herself" (*TTL*, 95). Free of any demands upon her actions, Mrs. Ramsay can finally fall into silence and solitude, where "one shrunk, with a sense of solemnity, to being oneself, a wedge-shaped core of darkness, something invisible to others" (*TTL*, 95). She can permit her superficial identity to drop away so that she can see her Self—herself as an entity.

Mr. Ramsay, conversely, whom Woolf repeatedly refers to as "long-sighted," may enjoy physical sight but he never, at least not until the novel's end, relinquishes his hold on an objective and factual view of the world. Until then, his sole concern lies with himself not as an entity, but himself as an identity: a scholar and a philosopher. He thus bases his whole self-estimate on his mind's ability to traverse thought as if, figuratively, it traversed the alphabet. But he cannot get beyond Q; R eludes him: "A shutter, like the leathern eyelid of a lizard, flickered over the intensity of his gaze and obscured the letter R" (*TTL*, 54). Unlike Mrs. Ramsay, who sees her Self in darkness, Mr. Ramsay, in the darkness behind the "leathern eyelid," sees nothing, and only hears people saying "he was a failure — that R was beyond him. He would never reach R" (*TTL*, 54). Mr. Ramsay's only emotional security comes when he can stay in the light of reason. If he becomes submerged into emotional darkness, severe self-doubt besieges him; and this forces him to demand sympathy from his wife, before whom he bends his head and "does homage to the beauty of the world" (*TTL*, 57). In other words, Mr. Ramsay, "a man afraid to own his own feelings" (*TTL*, 70), ultimately needs the solace and comfort from the true seer, Mrs. Ramsay. And, not only does he fear his own feelings, but, if one understands his desire to reach R as his desire to reach his own initial, as Avrom Fleishman does, then Mr. Ramsay fears his Self. As Fleishman puts it, "He cannot reach R because his thought is so tied up with his self-images as heroic leader, lonely castaway, and victim of man's transient fame."[7]

Mr. and Mrs. Ramsay's contrary reactions to darkness also appear in their perceptions of the sea. Both perceive themselves in the sea. As Mr. Ramsay stands on a spit of land looking out at the water, he sees "the dark of human ignorance, how we know nothing and the sea eats away the ground we stand on — that was his fate, his gift" (*TTL*, 68-69). He projects all his fears about his own intellectual incompetence and failure onto the sea.

Mrs. Ramsay, also seeing herself in the water, envisions a paradox. For her, the repeated sound of the waves falling on the beach

for the most part beat a measured and soothing tattoo to her thoughts and seemed consolingly to repeat over and over again as she sat with the children the words of some old cradle song, murmured by nature, "I am guarding you — I

am your support, but at other times suddenly and unex-
pectedly, especially when her mind raised itself slightly from
the task actually in hand, had no such kindly meaning, but
like a ghostly roll of drums remorselessly beat the measure of
life, made one think of the destruction of the island and its
engulfment in the sea, and warned her whose day had slipped past in one quick doing after another that it was all
ephemeral as a rainbow. (*TTL*, 27-28)

The sea comforts Mrs. Ramsay, yet also terrifies her. This ambiguity reflects her two identities: the conscious one of her
social role and the unconscious one of her Self. She fears that
the first identity will overpower the second. Knowing that her
Self exists, but afraid that her role as mother will engulf it,
Mrs. Ramsay tenaciously holds onto her privacy. She therefore
objects to Charles Tansley's carrying her bag on their trip into
town (*TTL*, 20), and insists that the windows remain open,
through which she can see, but the doors stay shut (*TTL*, 44),
so that no one can intrude on the privacy of her soul. Only in
that privacy can Mrs. Ramsay attain the freedom and peace to
see her Self, so she must protect it fiercely. As Mrs. Ramsay
relinquishes the ego, that personality others know her by, she
frees her identity from all role expectations; thus she meets her
Self: "She looked out to meet that stroke of the Lighthouse, the
long steady stroke, the last of the three, which was her stroke"
(*TTL*, 96). Here Mrs. Ramsay contacts that reality undistorted
by the world of fact.

When Mrs. Ramsay meets the third stroke of the lighthouse
and identifies with it, she accomplishes that which clearly
distinguishes her from her husband. Mrs. Ramsay, unlike her
husband, can see the light that lies behind the darkness. She
sees her Self, that core of one's identity that escapes all role
playing. In doing so, incidentally, Mrs. Ramsay enacts a
mystical initiation into total Being as experienced in Bud-
dhism. As Mircea Eliade describes it, the initiate undergoes a
ceremonial death in which darkness surrounds him. In this
darkness the initiate sees two lights resembling the moon and

the sun respectively. Then a dazzling third light suddenly awakes him, and, as Eliade explains, in this third light, the initiate meets his own Self and that of the ultimate Being.[8] Moreover, in Mrs. Ramsay's identification with the lighthouse's third stroke she sees not only the illumined core of darkness and the Self within the core, but also the God within that Self. She senses the divine presence, for having reached total absorption in the light, Mrs. Ramsay proclaims, "We are in the hands of the Lord" (*TTL*, 97).

This realization jolts Mrs. Ramsay out of her unconscious musings, and with this jolt comes annoyance at herself for saying such a thing. Here her superficial identity reasserts itself, yet does not blind her as much as it did in the past. For now she re-enters her life oriented around the ego with a new understanding about herself. All of her concern over people marrying — her wish that Paul Rayley and Minta Doyle become engaged and her hopes that Lily Briscoe and William Bankes will also wed — is actually the ego's disguise for her Self's deep-seated concern: the marriage of Mrs. Ramsay to God. She realizes this when she, having awakened into consciousness, returns her gaze to the light: "There rose, and she looked and looked with her needles suspended, there curled up off the floor of the mind, rose from the lake of one's being, a mist, a bride to meet her lover" (*TTL*, 98). The biblical image of the bride reinforces the connection between the Self and God; off of "the floor of the mind," the unconscious that contains the potential for Selfhood, arises the Bible's "new Jerusalem," delivered by God and "prepared as a bride adorned for her husband" (Revelation 21:2). Thus, Mrs. Ramsay's insistence that people must marry, when fully understood, really reflects her own need to integrate her human identity with God, the ultimate reality.

Mr. Ramsay, on the other hand, acts not out of his need for God but out of his delusion that he is God, the angry God of the Old Testament. Mr. Ramsay walks through the garden where he meets Lily and William; he booms at them, "Some

one had blundered!" (*TTL*, 41). This scene strongly resembles that of Adam and Eve, after their fall, when they
hear God's voice as he walks through the garden (Genesis 3:8).
God tells Adam and Eve that they sinned by eating the fruit
of the tree of knowledge, and thus he expels them from Eden
(3:23); similarly, Lily and William meet Mr. Ramsay just as
they step "through the gap in the high hedge" (*TTL*, 41). The
irony, however, of Mr. Ramsay's declaration that someone
has blundered rests on the fact that, actually, he judges
himself. Mr. Ramsay has blundered; he blunders in his
awkward appeals for sympathy and in his thoughtless pro-
nouncements that the family will not visit the lighthouse.

In the first section of *To the Lighthouse*, Lily Briscoe appears caught between the ego-centered priorities of Mr. Ramsay and the spiritual ones of Mrs. Ramsay. The first vic-
timizes her, while she aspires after the second. She imagines
sitting on the floor, with her arms wrapped around Mrs.
Ramsay's knees, while she thinks "how in the chambers of
the mind and heart of the woman who was, physically,
touching her, were stood, like the treasures in the tombs of
kings, tablets bearing sacred inscriptions, which if one could
spell them out, would teach one everything" (*TTL*, 79). Lily,
here, wants to tap Mrs. Ramsay's primeval knowledge of
life's ultimates. Yet Lily's socialized nature makes her a victim of the masculine world's disparagement of women;
therefore, frequently, when Lily tries to capture on canvas
the wholeness she senses in Mrs. Ramsay, she becomes
plagued by Charles Tansley's statement that "women can't
write, women can't paint" (*TTL*, 130).

Another example of Lily's conflict between what she wants
for herself as a human being and what the world expects of her
as a woman, occurs at the dinner. She resents the code of
behavior by which "it behoves the woman, whatever her own
occupation may be, to go to the help of the young man opposite so that he may expose and relieve the thigh bones, the
ribs, of his vanity, of his urgent desire to assert himself" (*TTL*,

137). Yet, she abides by this code in response to Mrs. Ramsay's plea, expressed solely through a glance, that Lily help her to soothe and bolster the male ego. Lily, unlike Minta Doyle, who appeals to Mr. Ramsay by making herself "more ignorant than she was, because he liked telling her she was a fool" (*TTL*, 148), resents the insincerity through which man and woman relate. This insincerity, which Lily views as unavoidable, makes her thankful that "she need not marry . . . she need not undergo that degradation. She was saved from that dilution" (*TTL*, 154). Lily imagines that she must sacrifice her identity in order to relate to a man. But what she senses in the novel's first section, and fully understands in the last section, resolves her conflict. The means to Selfhood do not entail her renunciation of the masculine outlook, but the integration of that outlook, and the recognition that it, at its very depths, participates in the same primal world that Lily imagines Mrs. Ramsay contains.

In "The Window" Lily senses this truth when she envisions her painting as "colour burning on a framework of steel; the light of a butterfly's wing lying upon the arches of a cathedral" (*TTL*, 75). She knows that Paunceforte's etherealizing of shapes and colors can accomplish only half her purpose. The thinness and apparent vagueness of such an artistic style demands the complement of a sturdy framework, just as the ethereal visions of the feminine temperament must share a canvas with the cold, unwavering masculine intellect. Intuiting that her painting will remain incomplete until she successfully integrates these complementary forces, Lily still has no idea of how to make the connection: "It was a question, she remembered, how to connect this mass on the right hand with that on the left" (*TTL*, 82-83). The right, connoting the conscious mind, rationality, light, and the left, connoting the unconscious mind, spirituality, darkness, comprise the essential complements of psychic wholeness: male and female. Lily realizes now that she must unite these forces, but not until "The Lighthouse" will she accomplish it. For the time being, however, as she sits at dinner with the Ramsays and their guests, she experiences a prescient flash of how to connect the two masses in her painting: "I shall put the tree further in the middle; then I shall avoid that awkward space" (*TTL*, 128).

Woolf presents this concept, that an integration of the masculine and feminine comprises psychic totality, in different forms during the Ramsay dinner and during that period right after the dinner that concludes the novel's first section. During dinner, Mr. and Mrs. Ramsay sit at opposite ends of the table. As he speaks of the square root of 1253, she, by luxuriating in "the still space that lies about the heart of things, where one could move or rest" (*TTL*, 158), counterbalances his intellectual talk. For that matter, Mrs. Ramsay alone alternates between her spiritual meditations and her social role as hostess. Woolf seems to dig mystical passageways through Mrs. Ramsay's activities as a hostess, in which Mrs. Ramsay travels as she serves the meal:

> There it was, all around them. It partook, she felt, carefully helping Mr. Bankes to a specially tender piece, of eternity . . . there is a coherence in things, a stability; something, she meant, is immune from change, and shines out . . . in the face of the flowing, the fleeting, the spectral, like a ruby; so that again tonight she had the feeling she had had once today, already, of peace, of rest. Of such moments, she thought, the thing is made that endures.
> "Yes," she assured William Bankes, "there is plenty for everybody."
> "Andrew," she said, "hold your plate lower, or I shall spill it." (The Boeuf en Daube was a perfect triumph.) Here, she felt, putting the spoon down, was the still space that lies about the heart of things, where one could move or rest. (*TTL*, 158)

As Mrs. Ramsay travels through these mystical passageways, her experiences recall those "spots of time" that William Wordsworth speaks of in *The Prelude*:

There are in our existence spots of time,
That with distinct pre-eminence retain
A renovating virtue, whence—depressed
By false opinion and contentious thought,
Or aught of heavier or more deadly weight,
In trivial occupations, and the round
Of ordinary intercourse—our minds
Are nourished and invisibly repaired;[9]

Mrs. Ramsay can now weave in and out of her apparent and her spiritual identities; in the midst of the dinner she can partake in eternity. This accomplishment of integrating the two is not possible earlier in the day when she cannot sink into herself, the "wedge-shaped core of darkness," until James leaves her alone. But since her identification with the lighthouse's third stroke, when she feels that "we are in the hands of the Lord," she can break through the boundary that once separated her conscious from her unconscious worlds.

Another scene, this one after the dinner, also evidences Mrs. Ramsay's ability to integrate the masculine and feminine. When she leaves the dinner table to look in on Cam and James, whom she hopes to find asleep, she sees both her children wide awake as they argue over the boar's skull nailed to the wall: "Cam couldn't go to sleep with it in the room, and James screamed if she touched it" (*TTL*, 171). Cam fears the horn-like shadows the skull projects all over the room, while James cannot tolerate its removal. To appease both her children, Mrs. Ramsay wraps the skull with her green shawl. She, therefore, can tell Cam "how lovely it looked now; how the fairies would love it; it was like a bird's nest; it was like a beautiful mountain" (*TTL*, 172), and then move over to James's bed and whisper, "the boar's skull was still there; they had not touched it; they had done just what he wanted; it was there quite unhurt" (*TTL*, 173). As Mrs. Ramsay learns in her experience with the third stroke of the lighthouse, reality does not have to create terror, for rest and peace ultimately infuse all of life if one perceives correctly. Mrs. Ramsay's love, symbolized by her shawl, and her belief in hope and regeneration, symbolized by the color green, help James and Cam to achieve peace where they once saw conflict.[10]

But during "Time Passes" the war rages. The significance of the war extends far beyond its actual occurrence. It represents the world's anger and the spiritual cost the world must pay in the ego's battle for primacy. Thus, in "Time Passes" one watches the Ramsay home, Woolf's symbol for the self, ravaged egregiously by the ego's fight for victory and fame. This central section of the novel conveys its message symbolically; nevertheless, the battle here duplicates that which takes place in "The Window." In that section, Mr. Ramsay's preoccupation with fame and fantasies of battlefield victories threatens Mrs. Ramsay's "wedge-shaped core of darkness." By expressing the ego's devastation of the self in symbolic terms in "Time Passes," Woolf lifts her theme out of the personal context and displays its universality.

"Time Passes" has no plot line; that is, one does not follow the stages of the war. Rather, Woolf draws the reader deep into the human unconscious. As the characters sleep one sees the activities of their common unconscious mind figured in the house, the objects in the house, and the air that moves through the house. Therefore, chronological time evaporates, or, as Woolf says, "time passes," passes away. Literally, one assumes that ten years elapse, yet on the symbolic level the actual time may only extend one night—the section opens with the characters' going to sleep and ends with their awakening. By eliminating the certainty of chronological time, Woolf insists that the reader drop any superficial ordering devices and allow himself to roam the unconscious as the air roams the house. He, thus, enters "the flood, the profusion of darkness" (*TTL*, 189), and will not rise into consciousness again until Woolf writes that "the sun lifted the curtains, broke the veil on their eyes" (*TTL*, 214).

In travels through the unconscious, where the Self resides, androgyny prevails, for all sexual distinctions fade away.

"There was scarcely anything left of body or mind by which
one could say, 'This is he' or 'This is she' " (*TTL*, 190). In
"Times Passes" one learns the source of this wholeness and
the means to achieve it—"divine goodness" (*TTL*, 192). But
though divine goodness "parted the curtain" and displayed
behind it the components of psychic totality, divine goodness
also, "twitching the cord, draws the curtain," so that it seems
impossible that "we should ever compose from their
fragments a perfect whole or read in the littered pieces the
clear words of truth. For our penitence deserves a glimpse only; our toil respite only" (*TTL*, 193). The ego and pride of the
war deny a sustained gaze into the Self because the war buries
truth beneath heavy layers of human blundering.

And, with a blundering stroke, "one fold of the shawl
loosened and swung to and fro" (*TTL*, 196). The frightening
reality of the boar's skull gradually re-emerges as the fearful
shadows it creates begin to cross the room. Mrs. Ramsay's
shawl of love and hope for regeneration cannot sustain its
hold on reality, because humankind's "nobler powers sleep"
while "the surface glassiness . . . forms in quiescence" (*TTL*,
202). The curtain draws over human sensibilities as
humankind slides across "the surface glassiness" of sleep, ignorant of psychic devastation. Woolf occasionally breaks
through this glassiness with interjections of reality; for instance, "Prue Ramsay died that summer in some illness connected with childbirth" (*TTL*, 199). But Woolf encloses these
announcements with brackets to imply the ego's incidental
cognizance of human life. The Selfhood that Mrs. Ramsay
pursues also disappears behind the curtain of human ignorance, as Woolf's announcement of Mrs. Ramsay's death
falls deep within not only the printed brackets but also the
suggested ones of a subordinate phrase: "Mr. Ramsay,
stumbling along a passage one dark morning, stretched his
arms out, but Mrs. Ramsay having died rather suddenly the
night before, his arms, though stretched out, remained empty" (*TTL*, 194).

The curtain that encloses the Self opens and closes only by

the power of "divine goodness." Though human beings work devastation upon themselves, only "divine goodness" can repair the damage and restore Selfhood. Because of this, Mrs. McNab, notified to prepare the house for the family's return, repeatedly sighs, "there was too much work for one woman" (*TTL*, 206). She cannot single-handedly restore the house. Therefore, weary from her work, Mrs. McNab exclaims, "How long . . . how long shall it endure?" (*TTL*, 197). She, here, repeats the thought of David in Psalm 13:1: "How long wilt thou forget me, O Lord? for ever? how long wilt thou hide thy face from me?" Mrs. McNab calls out for God's assistance. But God's strength will not aid her until, to use David's words again, people's eyes are lightened and they no longer "sleep the sleep of death" (13:3). Therefore, "Time Passes" ends with the sleepers awakening as "the sun lifted the curtains, broke the veil on their eyes" (*TTL*, 214). Because they awake, the lighthouse, symbol of the New Testament God, the trinitarian God, awaits.

The novel's third section, "The Lighthouse," depicts the trip to the lighthouse. Though Lily Briscoe does not physically accompany Mr. Ramsay, Cam, and James on the trip, she psychically does. As a result, she experiences a major transformation: the section opens with Lily's wondering, "What did she feel, come back after all these years and Mrs. Ramsay dead? Nothing, nothing—nothing that she could express at all" (*TTL*, 217); yet it closes with her intense vision of wholeness. The emptiness she initially feels reflects the absence of the Self, caused by Mrs. Ramsay's death. The vision at the end, however, comes from Lily's insight into the divine power that infuses life with feeling and unites apparently opposite forces. Until she gains that insight, Lily suffers with a sense of psychic separation, which robs her of emotion. The concept of separation means one's distance from the inner divine forces; such a distance creates a feeling of loneliness and fear of contact with others.

Besides Lily, others in "The Lighthouse" also suffer from

separation, because the lighthouse has yet to be reached. For instance, Mr. Ramsay suffers enormously with loneliness. He keeps repeating "Perished" and "Alone" (*TTL*, 219), words from William Cowper's "The Castaway." Seeing this line within its whole stanza reveals the source of Mr. Ramsay's loneliness:

> No voice divine the storm allayed,
>    No light propitious shone,
> When, snatched from all effectual aid,
>    We perished, each alone;
> But I beneath a rougher sea,
> And whelmed in a deeper gulfs than he.[11]

When Mr. Ramsay recites Cowper's line, he certainly expresses his own aloneness since his wife perished. But with this line he reveals also the human condition resulting from the war: godlessness. Mr. Ramsay, along with everyone else, will perish alone until he accepts the aid of the divine voice and the propitious light. And until that time, the Self will remain "a house full of unrelated passions" (*TTL*, 221).

In the lonely state of separation, the ego takes over. Solipsism reigns. Mr. Ramsay, therefore, displays an insatiable need for sympathy; he roams about "like a lion seeking whom he could devour" (*TTL*, 233). Woolf uses the words of I Peter 5:8 in which Peter says the devil, "a roaring lion, walketh about, seeking whom he may devour," so as to emphasize the world's temptation to forget God. As Mr. Ramsay stops by Lily, sitting on the lawn in front of her easel, "he seemed to be saying, look at me; and indeed, all the time he was feeling, Think of me, think of me" (*TTL*, 227). And Lily cannot respond to his need, for her dominant ego interprets a gesture of sympathy as a surrender of her entire self (*TTL*, 226). So the more Mr. Ramsay pours out his self-pity, the more Lily draws "her skirts a little closer round her ankles, lest she should get wet" (*TTL*,228). Finally, unable to tolerate Mr. Ramsay's effusive self-pity any longer, Lily exclaims,

"What beautiful boots!" (*TTL*, 229). She breaks through the solipsistic boundaries. Though she feels shame that she could only "praise his boots when he asked her to solace his soul," she nevertheless begins to bridge the separation. Mr. Ramsay smiles, and Lily's heart warms toward him. His pride appealed to, Mr. Ramsay drops to his knees and three times knots Lily's shoes to demonstrate his own flawless knotting technique. Mr. Ramsay's tying Lily's shoes recalls the reverence Mrs. Ramsay feels for her husband in "The Window," when she considers herself "not good enough to tie his shoe strings" (*TTL*, 51). As stated earlier, this act alludes to John the Baptist's prediction of Christ's coming: "He that cometh after me is mightier than I, whose shoes I am not worthy to bear." Mr. Ramsay now implies this prediction, for shortly he and his two children will sail to the lighthouse.

For the rest of the novel, the actions, thoughts, and accomplishments of Lily parallel those of Mr. Ramsay, Cam, and James. She sits on the lawn attempting to finish her painting while the Ramsays sail to the lighthouse. Virginia Woolf records in her diary that she intended "a combination of interest" between Lily and Mr. Ramsay (*AWD*, 98). This "combination of interest" runs primarily one way: Mr. Ramsay functions as part of Lily. He represents that masculine voice inside Lily that constantly plagues her with the declaration that women cannot paint or write. In the last section of the novel the words keep coming back to Lily as an expression of her own self-doubts. In other words, she has accepted the masculine attitude toward women held by such men as Mr. Ramsay who "liked men to work . . . and women to keep house, and sit beside sleeping children indoors, while men were drowned, out there in a storm" (*TTL*, 245). Lily consciously rejects such a sexist attitude, but it still creates doubts in her unconscious. When she tries to paint, the force "emerged stark at the back of appearances and commanded her attention." This force "roused one to perpetual combat, challenged one to a fight in which one was bound to be worsted" (*TTL*, 236). And, whenever these doubts surface, Lily concludes that her painting surely "would be rolled up and stuffed under a sofa. What was the good of doing it then, and she heard some voice saying she couldn't paint, saying she couldn't create" (*TTL*, 237). Lily must conquer this destructive voice or her painting will remain unfinished. But she knows that she cannot fight the force with aggression, for "one was bound to be worsted." She, then, must conquer it by accepting it. She must turn to it and sympathize with it. Thus, "impelled by some curiosity, driven by the discomfort of the sympathy which she held undischarged, she walked a pace or so to the end of the lawn to see whether, down there on the beach, she could see that little company setting sail" (*TTL*, 241). Lily repeatedly turns her glance toward the sea, watching the sailboat draw closer to the lighthouse. The more she can accept Mr. Ramsay's existence, and even identify with it, the clearer her artistic vision of wholeness becomes.

Lily's conflict over her acceptance of or her resistance to the masculine force appears in the drama of James and Cam's relationship with Mr. Ramsay. Before setting sail, the two children agree on a compact "to resist tyranny to the death" (*TTL*, 243). At no cost, they agree, will they permit any sympathy to flow from them to their father. They view him as a devil whose alluring temptations they must resist. Similarly, Lily feels that in order to create, she must reject the voice that says she cannot create. But just as a part of Lily gives in to Mr. Ramsay's insatiable need for sympathy and compliments his boots, so Cam begins to admire her father: "He was so brave, he was so adventurous, Cam thought. But she remembered. There was the compact; to resist tyranny to the death" (*TTL*, 246). By yielding somewhat to her father's need, Cam feels the compact give way. So when Mr. Ramsay tries assiduously to make Cam smile by asking her about the family puppy, James watches and concludes pitilessly, "I shall be left to fight the tyrant alone" (*TTL*, 250). As long as James views the coercive force of Mr. Ramsay as selfish tyranny, he will continue to see his father as godless. With his father as godless, James thus sees himself as Moses, "the lawgiver, with the tablets of eternal wisdom laid open on his knee" (*TTL*, 251), who commands his followers to resist and fight the world's pagan forces. Likewise, a portion of Lily feels roused "to perpetual combat" when faced with the voice that denies her creativity.

Until Lily can give Mr. Ramsay all that undischarged sympathy that weighs her down, her painting will remain incomplete. Lily knows what she must paint in order to complete her work; she knows she must combine opposites, the feminine, or herself, with the masculine, Mr. Ramsay: "Beautiful and bright it should be on the surface, feathery and evanescent, one colour melting into another like the colours on a butterfly's wing; but beneath the fabric must be clamped together with bolts of iron" (*TTL*, 255). When Lily can accept the masculine and thereby disarm it of brutal sexism, she will find the means to fill the space that separates the opposites within her. Woolf clearly depicts Lily's painting as a psychological task, for, while Lily focuses on her painting, Woolf declares that "she went on tunnelling her way into her picture, into the past" (*TTL*, 258).

No matter how deep into the past Lily tunnels, the power with which she can achieve totality through the reconciliation of opposites rests one step beyond the limits of human strength. Lily must see now what Mrs. Ramsay saw in the lighthouse's third stroke, that "we are in the hands of the Lord." No intellect and no humanly contrived means can bring one to this truth; only faith can. So when Lily wants to arouse the sleeping Augustus Carmichael, who represents Lily's dormant masculine component, and ask him "what does it mean? How do you explain it all?" (*TTL*, 266), Carmichael does not stir. But if he did, that is, if the thus far unaccepted masculine strengths within Lily awoke, a sign of faith would mark the occurrence: "Something would emerge. A hand would be shoved up, a blade would be flashed" (*TTL*, 266-67). These details allude to Sir Thomas Malory's *Morte Darthur* in which Arthur receives his sword, Excalibur, as a gift from the Lady of the Lake. When Arthur lies dying from battle, he commands Sir Bedivere to return the sword to the lake. At first Sir Bedivere hesitates because he can see only "harm and loss" resulting if he throws away Arthur's rich sword filled with precious stones. Sir Bedivere sees the sword as materially precious, whereas Arthur no longer has such material priorities. Arthur, rather, wishes to unite with the feminine power that once gave him the sword. When Sir Bedivere finally does throw Excalibur into the lake, he does so as an act of faith. Only faith can replace a material possession with a spiritual gift. And when he does fling the sword out into the lake, a sign of fulfilled faith appears: as Malory writes, "there came an arm and an hand above the water and took it and clutched it."[12] Malory's rendition of Arthur's death strongly resembles Lily Briscoe's situation. She must willingly relinquish her ego, that part of her psyche that so far has convinced her that to yield to Mr. Ramsay's need for sympathy would entail a sacrifice of her integrity. Lily now realizes, from her vision of the sword and hand, that the deceptive safety of her own emotionally separated state stops her far short of psychic integration: "Could things thrust their hands up and grip one; could the blade cut; the fist grasp? Was there no safety? No learning by heart of the ways of the world? No guide, no shelter, but all was miracle, and leaping from the pinnacle of a tower into the air?" (*TTL*, 268). Lily learns that faith alone provides her with the strength needed to relieve her of painful psychic dissociation. But not just undifferentiated faith will do it. As Woolf suggests by her allusion to Satan, who brings Christ to the pinnacle of the temple and tests him by saying, "If thou be the Son of God, cast thyself down" (Matthew 4:5-6), Lily's faith must be in God. She must learn the faith Mrs. Ramsay learned, and by doing so, "the space would fill; those empty flourishes would form into shape" (*TTL*, 268), and thus, she could finish her painting.

Once having acquired this faith, Lily will recognize her own

Christlike qualities. Woolf first introduces a symbol of Christ in the fish that Macalister's boy handles. He cuts a square out of its side so he can bait his hook, then throws the mutilated body back into the sea. But, Woolf says, "it was alive still" (*TTL*, 268), as Christ, though crucified, lived on and returned. Woolf immediately follows up this very brief scene with a view of Lily: "No one had heard her cry that ignominious cry, stop pain, stop!. . . No one had seen her step off her strip of board into the waters of annihilation" (*TTL*, 269). From this pain Lily can retrieve the feelings she could not allow herself to experience in the opening of "The Lighthouse." Her identification with Christ brings back all her sorrow over Mrs. Ramsay. And, as Lily's denial of sorrow dissipates, she experiences not only relief but a vision of Mrs. Ramsay's presence, "a sense of some one there, of Mrs. Ramsay, relieved for a moment of the weight that the world had put on her, staying lightly by her side" (*TTL*, 269). This vision of Mrs. Ramsay, which Lily realizes "must be perpetually remade," helps Lily to look away from her own fear and out to Mr. Ramsay's boat, "a brown spot in the middle of the bay" (*TTL*, 270). On land, Lily contacts the divine power within herself. Now, reconciliation with that tyrannical masculine component awaits.

There, out at sea, Mr. Ramsay reveals himself not as a tyrant, but as one who has gained insight into the divine basis of all life, when he sprinkles the crumbs from his sandwich over the water. This gesture appears in Ecclesiastes 11:1, where the preacher admonishes, "Cast thy bread upon the waters: for thou shalt find it after many days." This passage advises that an individual's attempt to determine his own fate amounts only to vanity. Ultimately, a person must rely on God's protection and acknowledge the limitations of human powers, for one "knowest not the works of God who maketh all" (11:5). Mr. Ramsay's gesture demonstrates his awareness that when he predicts rainy weather, as in the beginning of the novel, he actually reveals his vanity and self-defeating selfishness; as the preacher in Ecclesiastes says, "He that observeth the wind shall not sow; and he that regardeth the clouds shall not reap" (11:4). His prediction of rainy weather reaps for Mr. Ramsay only his children's hatred. Now that he realizes this fact, he no longer has to approach James with words of denial, but can offer words of affirmation: "Well done!" (*TTL*, 306). He compliments his son's steering of the boat, and thus gives him the praise James has always yearned for from his father.

Despite the compliment, James remains imprisoned in his own vanity: "He was so pleased that he was not going to let anybody share a grain of his pleasure" (*TTL*, 306). Because of his vanity, James denies God in himself, in his father, and everywhere. He projects this denial onto his father: when Mr. Ramsay stands in the bow of the boat about to step onto the lighthouse rock, James thinks his father says, "There is no God" (*TTL*, 308). By his inability to see beyond his own atheism, James's interpretations of the world remain solely on the level of ordinary experience. Cam, however, counters James's outlook. She looks at her father standing in the bow and imagines him "leaping into space" (*TTL*, 308), as if he were Christ on the temple's pinnacle prepared to cast himself down, confident of God's power to protect him from harm.

The ordinary and miraculous views of life, held by James and Cam respectively, unify harmoniously in Lily Briscoe's vision and complete her painting. Before she returns to her canvas, Lily strains to see the lighthouse and declares, "He must have reached it" (*TTL*, 308). She senses that Mr. Ramsay has landed at the rock. That is, Lily senses that her own masculine principle has contacted God. With this realization, Lily feels recalled to her canvas where now the prospect of the painting's being hung in the attic and destroyed proves not at all repugnant. Such a fate does not threaten her because psychic wholeness has usurped her ego's reign. Deciding that the popularity of her painting does not matter as much as its composition, "with a sudden intensity, as if she saw it clear for a second, she drew a line there, in the centre. It was done; it was finished" (*TTL*, 310).

The center, which Clarissa Dalloway finds mystically evasive in Woolf's preceding novel, is now captured permanently by Lily. With the line through the center, Lily combines all the opposites that have fought within her until now — Mr. and Mrs. Ramsay, male and female, fact and vision, the ordinary and miraculous. The line creates the "razor edge of balance between two opposite forces," and it does so through the strength of God within the Self. Lily Briscoe, thus, can repeat the words of Christ on the cross — "It is finished" (John 19:30) — confident that "all things were now accomplished, that the scripture might be fulfilled" (John 19:28).

# NOTES

1. See C. G. Jung's *Symbols of Transformation*: *An Analysis of the Prelude to a Case of Schizophrenia*, trans. R. F. C. Hull, 2d ed. (Princeton, N.J.: Princeton University Press, 1956), p. 219.

2. Critics interpret the symbol of the lighthouse in various ways. For instance, Ruth Z. Temple says that it represents the achievement of civilization. See "Never Say 'I': *To the Lighthouse* as Vision and Confession," *Virginia Woolf: A Collection of Critical Essays*, ed. Claire Sprague (Englewood Cliffs, N.J.: Prentice-Hall, Inc., 1971), p. 96.

C. B. Cox takes a different view when he says the lighthouse represents the individual's isolation and independence. See *The Free Spirit*: *A Study of Liberal Humanism in the Novels of George Eliot, Henry James, E. M. Forster, Virginia Woolf, Angus Wilson* (London: Oxford University Press, 1963), p. 112.

Margaret Church becomes more spiritual in her interpretation. She sees the lighthouse as a rare moment of eternity. See *Time and Reality*: *Studies in Contemporary Fiction* (Chapel Hill, N.C.: University of North Carolina Press, 1949), p. 85.

3. Virginia Woolf, *To the Lighthouse* (New York: Harcourt, Brace & World, 1927), p. 189. All further quotations and references to the novel will be cited within the text as *TTL*.

4. Among the critics who hold this view are Jean Alexander, Sharon Kaehele and Howard German, and Jane Novak. Alexander says that "a cosmic orgy" reigns in "Time Passes" to compensate for the "tyranny of reason" that dominates the novel's other two sections. During this orgy, "fertility, sensuality, curiosity, amorality attend the process by which the house is undone by wind, wet, rats, and swallows." See Jean Alexander, *The Venture of Form in the Novels of Virginia Woolf* (Port Washington, N.Y.: Kennikat Press, 1974), p. 125.

Kaehele and German view the Ramsay home as devastated by time. See "*To the Lighthouse*: Symbol and Vision," *Bucknell Review* 10, 1 (1962): 336.

Similarly, Novak says "Time Passes" depicts nature's inexorable destructive process. See *The Razor Edge of Balance* (Coral Gables, Fla.: University of Miami Press, 1975), p. 137.

5. Suzette Henke, "Virginia Woolf's *To the Lighthouse*: In Defense of the Woman Artist," *Virginia Woolf Quarterly* 2 (Winter-Spring 1975): 40-41.

6. Annis Pratt, "Sexual Imagery in *To the Lighthouse*: A New Feminist Approach," *Modern Fiction Studies* 18 (Autumn 1972): 425.

7. Avrom Fleishman, *Virginia Woolf: A Critical Reading* (Baltimore, Md.: Johns Hopkins Press, 1975), p. 109.

8. Mircea Eliade, *The Two and the One*, trans. J. M. Cohen (New York: Harper & Row, 1962), p. 38.

9. William Wordsworth, *The Prelude* (Book 12, lines 208-15), *The Norton Anthology of English Literature*, rev. ed., vol. 2, ed. M. H. Abrams (New York: W. W. Norton & Co., 1962), p. 201.

10. Critics propose some very interesting interpretations of this scene. F. L. Overcarsh, for example, sees Mrs. Ramsay as a Christ figure who, when she ascends to the children's room where the skull hangs, climbs to Golgatha, the place of the skull. See "The Lighthouse, Face to Face," *Accent* 10 (Winter 1950): 115.

Glen Pederson prefers a Freudian interpretaton to a theological one. He claims that Cam's fear of the skull reflects her unconscious fear of marriage, while Jame's protection of the skull shows his Oedipal relationship to his mother. See "Vision in *To the Lighthouse*," *PMLA* 73 (December 1958): 593.

11. William Cowper, "The Castaway" (lines 61-66), *The Norton Anthology of English Literature*, ed. M. H. Abrams rev. ed., vol. 1 (New York: W. W. Norton & Co., 1962), p. 1784.

12. All the details and quotations from *Morte Darthur* come from *The Norton Anthology of English Literature*, vol. 1, pp. 358-59.

# 6

# *Orlando*
## One and Entire

Virginia Woolf's sixth novel stylistically and thematically performs Lily Briscoe's vision that concludes *To the Lighthouse*.
Lily completes her vision when through the center of her painting she draws a line. This line achieves the razor edge of
balance she seeks between the ego-oriented masculine force
embodied in Mr. Ramsay and the God-oriented feminine force
embodied in Mrs. Ramsay. Virginia Woolf stylistically performs Lily's vision by making *Orlando* a biography. To
understand this connection more fully, one must first turn to
an essay Woolf wrote at the same time she worked on *Orlando*.
In this essay, "The New Biography," Woolf explains that the
ultimate goal of biography should entail the writer's blend of
both the truth and the personality of his subject. A chronicler
renders merely truth, while an artist captures personality; a
biographer, according to Woolf, must operate as both. She
conceives of truth as "something of granite-like solidity" and of
personality as "something of rainbow-like intangibility." She
then follows up this distinction with the conclusion that "the
aim of biography is to weld these two into one seamless whole."[1]
This distinction between granite and rainbow easily applies to

a similar distinction Woolf makes in *To the Lighthouse* between the obduracy of Mr. Ramsay's insistence on fact and Mrs. Ramsay's intuitive concern for a person's emotional comfort. Lily Briscoe knows her painting must unite these two forces: "Beautiful and bright it should be on the surface, feathery and evanescent, one colour melting into another like the colours on a butterfly's wing; but beneath the fabric must be clamped together with bolts of iron" (*TTL*, 255). And Virginia Woolf does unite these two in *Orlando: A Biography*. She truthfully chronicles the life of Orlando, while she also artistically conveys Orlando's personality.

Yet, in the process of doing so, Woolf comments on these two life orientations; her handling of the book's material clearly demonstrates that though one must unite granite and rainbow, the insistence on fact proves inadequate in comparison to the pursuit of vision. Fact takes one just so far, at which point one must leap into the world of vision. To convey this idea, Woolf adds fantasy to biography. As biographer Woolf recounts the events in Orlando's life, but, as fantasist, she creates a character whom she introduces as aged sixteen and male in the late sixteenth century and whom she leaves aged thirty-six and female in the early twentieth century. Moreover, Woolf repeatedly admits the inadequacy of biographical fact when faced with visionary fantasy. For instance, when Orlando enters his seven-day trance from which he awakes a woman, the biographer wishes to avoid the whole event, because fact falters when confronted with fantasy: "Would that we might here take the pen and write Finis to our work! Would that we might spare the reader what is to come and say to him in so many words, Orlando died and was buried."[2] The biographer experiences a similar discomfort when the time comes to recount that Orlando gives birth: "Is nothing, then, going to happen this pale March morning to mitigate, to veil, to cover, to conceal, to shroud this undeniable event whatever it may be?" (*0*, 292). Even in her essay "The New Biography," where Woolf advises that a biographer weld granite and rainbow into "one seamless whole," she concludes that "truth of fact and truth of fiction are incompatible."[3]  At the risk of losing both worlds, then, Woolf, in *Orlando*, frequently lets the biographical hold on truth slip, so that the stronger visionary truth of fantasy comes through more clearly. As James Naremore says of *Orlando*, "It is meant to show us the futility of biographical fact and the necessity for art in the depiction of personality."[4]  As one proceeds through Woolf's sixth novel, he will see how her interplay between factual truth and fantastic truth stylistically parallels her overall message: the futility of a masculine outlook on life and the necessity for the feminine.

Not only does *Orlando's* style relate to Lily Briscoe's vision, but so does its theme. Lily has her vision only after she permits the image of Mrs. Ramsay to rise into her consciousness. As long as Lily keeps that image submerged, she can feel no emotion (*TTL*, 217). But toward the end of the novel Lily senses Mrs. Ramsay's spiritual presence, which revivifies her emotions. She has the vision that "must be perpetually remade" (*TTL*, 270), and she remakes it at the novel's end. Woolf's plot in *Orlando* follows the same order: her protagonist appears first as a man, defined by all the egocentricity that Woolf attributes to the masculine outlook. But once Orlando becomes transformed into a woman, she learns of the ego's vanity and chooses instead to pursue the Self. One, however, does not supplant the other. In Lily Briscoe's terms, bolts of iron must clamp together the feathery and evanescent. Likewise, Orlando must first experience masculinity before she develops into full femininity. As Woolf explains in her diary, while planning what to write after *To the Lighthouse*, "future shall somehow blossom out of the past" (*AWD*, 101).

This point is elaborated with greater specificity in *A Room of One's Own*, written shortly after *Orlando*, where Woolf presents her theory on androgyny. The author sketches "a plan of the soul" in which "two powers preside, one male, one female."[5] Although in *A Room of One's Own* she never expresses any concern over emotional one-sidedness in women,

Woolf does show great concern for this problem in the self-assertiveness that appears in the writings of male authors as the overpowering "I" (*AROO*, 103). In one such writer, Woolf sees "some obstacle, some impediment . . . which blocked the fountain of creative energy and shored it within narrow limits" (*AROO*, 104). Virginia Woolf, then, in *Orlando* describes the course of an individual who develops out of the "I" confines and thereby enters the far more expansive province of the "soul," or the Self. *Orlando* dramatizes what *A Room of One's Own* describes: the self-consciousness of the masculine will destroy the soul if unaccompanied by the "renewal of creative power which is in the gift only of the opposite sex to bestow" (*AROO*, 90).

Though in *A Room of One's Own* Woolf makes a clear distinction based on gender between masculine and feminine, in her novels she crosses the biological boundaries. For instance, Mrs. Hilbery in *Night and Day* demonstrates masculine rigidity in her insistence on socialized modes of behavior. On the other hand, Jacob Flanders adopts a feminine priority in his pursuit of spiritual vision and psychic wholeness. Whereas Woolf crosses the boundaries between the sexes in her earlier novels, with *Orlando* she completely destroys all such distinction. Therefore, one must at this point distinguish between *feminine* and *Feminine, masculine* and *Masculine*. Lower case *feminine* and *masculine* will, from now on, refer to gender and gender identification, while upper case *Feminine* and *Masculine* will refer to attitude or outlook, regardless of sex.

With *Orlando* Woolf not only breaks down the boundary between the sexes, she also underscores the need for the Feminine outlook as a means to achieve Selfhood. As *Orlando* shows, the Feminine has the capacity to hurdle fact and thus gain vision; it replaces intellect with intuition and creativity; it has the power to mend psychic fragmentation and thus produce wholeness; it stands beyond gender differentiation and operates within the realm of androgyny.[6]

To learn more about Woolf's theory of androgyny, consider

her use of time in *Orlando*. Woolf follows only twenty years of the protagonist's life, but over three hundred years elapse. Through the three centuries, the biographer points out superficial differences in the various ages: the Elizabethan Age, the Restoration, the Neoclassical Age, and the Victorian Age. But by doing so, as Naremore says, she "exposes the relative emptiness of empirical data."[7] Despite the passage of so many centuries, Orlando still exists, he-she continues to return to the oak tree on the family's estate, he-she continues to write the poem "The Oak Tree." Even certain other characters reappear. For instance, the writer Nicholas Greene complains in the seventeenth century of the dearth of literary genius, and takes Cicero as his model; then in the nineteenth century he voices a similar lament about his contemporaries and refers to Addison as his model. Despite the superficial changes in Nick Greene's personality, he remains the same. Similarly, despite any changes in Orlando, including the apparently major one of sex, he-she retains a single identity. As the biographer explains, "Orlando had become a woman — there is no denying it. But in every other respect, Orlando remained precisely as he had been. The change of sex, though it altered their future, did nothing whatever to alter their identity" (*O*, 138). In other words, the physical change, along with its resultant change in dress and social behavior, has no real significance. The identity stays consistent through both of Orlando's sexes; it therefore is androgynous.

Woolf's obliteration of time highlights Orlando's androgyny. But it also underscores the need for Feminine priorities. As Woolf says in her diary, she intended a portrayal of "some semi-mystic very profound life of a woman" (*AWD*, 101). Therefore, Orlando, as a man, though he acts out of his preoccupation with the ego in that he thrives on his life in Queen Elizabeth's court and in his role as Ambassador to Constantinople, nevertheless frequently yearns for solitude so as to escape the superficiality of this existence. These momentary excursions into solitude, however, do not provide enough ballast for

Orlando's psychological stability. The more dominant Masculine forces obviate any spiritual growth. Not until Orlando becomes a woman can she permit full expression to her spiritual needs. As a woman, Orlando gradually loses interest in fame and vanity, the issues of the ego, and concentrates on her own integrity and spiritual development. These priorities of the Feminine — and only these priorities, according to Woolf's fiction — supply the spiritual and emotional strength to contact the Self. Only by operating on the principles of the Feminine can Orlando seek "the true self . . . compact of all the selves we have it in us to be" (*O*, 310) and commune with it in blissful silence (*O*, 314).

Throughout the novel, Orlando, whether male or female, seeks wholeness. Woolf indicates this by her retention of certain elements that Orlando consistently regards with much respect and affection, despite all of the extraordinary episodes in the plot and apparent permutations in the identities of certain characters. These elements are three: the old poet, whom Orlando sees in the beginning of the novel and who occasionally re-enters Orlando's consciousness during the novel's progress, the oak tree where Orlando frequently returns for moments of solitude and meditation, and Orlando's poem "The Oak Tree," which he-she often returns to so as to add certain lines and emend others. These three recurring elements furnish the novel's walls with studs that strengthen and support the entire construction. The overall construction consists of Orlando's experimentation with many life styles as he-she attempts through all of them to detect and acquire psychic wholeness.

As in *To the Lighthouse*, Woolf uses the symbol of the house to represent the self. Whereas in *To the Lighthouse* she presents two houses to symbolize both the self without God and the Self with God, in *Orlando* she only uses one. Orlando's house has greater similarity to the Ramsay home than to the lighthouse in that it stands for Orlando's superficial identity, or persona, as C. G. Jung calls it.[8] At first Orlando conceives of his whole identity as wrapped up in the house, or persona. But as Orlando grows psychologically, she discovers that her Self lies beyond this superficial identity. The novel's opening scene presents Orlando at his most undeveloped or unevolved stage. He slices at the head of a Moor that swings from the rafters in his attic room. Either his father or grandfather struck the head from the shoulders of some pagan in Africa. Here, Orlando identifies with his fathers: "Since he was sixteen only, and too young to ride with them in Africa or France, he would steal away from his mother and the peacocks in the garden and go to his attic room and there lunge and plunge and slice the air with his blade" (*O*, 13). In his identification with the masculine models in his family, Orlando turns barbarian by taking pleasure from an act of gross inhumanity. Yet Woolf follows this scene with imagery repeated from her earlier novels: the house, or Orlando's selfhood, "was so vast that there seemed trapped in it the wind itself" (*O*, 14), the wind representing God or at least Orlando's spiritual potential. In short, Orlando's Selfhood, his psychic integrity, lies trapped in the house of his ego-centered fathers. *Orlando* depicts his evolution out of this world of the ego.

Orlando's poetry reflects his psychological state. Because of his psychic distance from the God within, his poetry has no secure foundation to support his thoughts. As Woolf writes, "He was fluent, evidently, but he was abstract. Vice, Crime, Misery were the personages of his drama; there were Kings and Queens of impossible territories; horrid plots confounded them; noble sentiments suffused them" (*O*, 16). Orlando's poetry eventually acquires greater concreteness and verisimilitude, but now he has no secure contact with his spiritual core.

Orlando, however, does demonstrate a need for this contact. Out of a desire for solitude, he leaves the house and climbs a hill upon which stands an oak tree. After reaching the tree,

> He sighed profoundly, and flung himself—there was a passion in his movements which deserves the word—on the

earth at the foot of the oak tree. He loved, beneath all this summer transiency, to feel the earth's spine beneath him; for such he took the hard root of the oak tree to be; or, for image followed image, it was the back of a great horse that he was riding; or the deck of a tumbling ship — it was anything indeed, so long as it was hard, for he felt the need of something which he could attach his floating heart to; the heart that tugged at his side; the heart that seemed filled with spiced and amorous gales every evening about this time when he walked out. (*0*, 19)

In his attraction to the tree, Orlando reveals his need for Selfhood, that state of being that develops out of a firm contact with one's spiritual core. Just as Woolf replays the imagery of the house and the wind from earlier novels, so she here too uses the image of a tree to symbolize the Self as she does elsewhere. For example, Rachel Vinrace, in *The Voyage Out*, leaves the dance to enjoy solitude in the midst of nature. She sees one tree stand out boldly from the others and seem to rise from the ground. This single tree, fully integrated within itself and capable of emerging boldly as a singular entity, symbolizes Rachel's Self (*TVO*, 174). Similarly, Lily Briscoe, in *To the Lighthouse*, sits at dinner and contemplates how to complete her painting so as to harmonize two opposing masses. She has a vision that will achieve such totality: "I shall put the tree further in the middle; then I shall avoid that awkward space" (*TTL*, 128). This vision relieves Lily from her discomfort over these two dissociated masses. It relieves her because it shows that the Self unites opposites.

So far, then, Woolf presents the opposites that conflict in Orlando: the Moor's head, or that victim of the Masculine ego that identifies with barbarity, and the oak tree, or that spiritual segment that yearns for wholeness. Woolf unites these two when she introduces the old poet. Orlando, returning to his home to greet the visiting Queen Elizabeth, sees this old man deeply contemplating an idea he wishes to translate into poetry. As Orlando catches a glimpse of this man, who sits in a servant's room in Orlando's house, he stops dead: "Was this a poet? Was he writing poetry? 'Tell me,' he wanted to say, 'everything in the whole world' " (*0*, 21). In this man, Orlando sees the union of those two forces he thinks must remain separate: his identification with his father and his need for solitude. Orlando cannot reconcile these two now, but eventually he will. And on his way to this wholeness, he will occasionally recall this glimpse he now has of the old poet.

Unfortunately, Orlando is not yet prepared for the psychic integration represented by the poet. He must first play out, and thus move through, his Masculine identity. This identity takes him away from the visions of the old poet, who imagines "ogres, satyrs, perhaps the depths of the sea" (*0*, 21), and into the arms of Queen Elizabeth, who hears only the "sound of cannon" and sees "always the glistening poison drop and the long stiletto" (*0*, 23). For the Masculine self permits the sights and sounds of humanity's outrages to crowd out the human capacity for creation and fantasy. And because Orlando fully enters this Masculine world, his capacity for feeling freezes. The Great Frost comes. All life stops: birds freeze in mid-air, corpses freeze and cannot be drawn from the sheets, a herd of swine freezes immovably upon the road, and people are "struck stark in the act of the moment." Woolf describes the effect of the Great Frost as a "petrifaction" (*0*, 34). Likewise, as Orlando becomes fully immersed in his life in court, as Treasurer, Steward, and member of the order of the Garter, his feelings, his humanity, and thus his creativity and his potential for wholeness, petrify. In such a state, then, Orlando can thrill with the other courtiers in "a carnival of the utmost brilliancy," as "the country people suffered the extremity of want, and the trade of the country was at a standstill" (*0*, 34). Furthermore, King James orders that the frozen river "be swept, decorated and given all the semblance of a park or pleasure ground," while an old woman who was carrying her fruit to market sits frozen on the river, her lap full of apples.

The suspension of animation caused by the Great Frost represents the suspended state of Orlando's feelings. In the midst of this he meets Sasha. In Sasha, Orlando confronts an externalized version of his own present psychological state. At a dance, just as Orlando finishes the steps of a quadrille, he notices Sasha: "He beheld, coming from the pavilion of the Muscovite Embassy, a figure, which, whether boy's or woman's, for the loose tunic and trousers of the Russian fashion served to disguise the sex, filled him with the highest curiosity" (*O*, 37). Woolf clearly draws a parallel here between Orlando and Sasha, because she introduces Orlando on the novel's first page in a similar manner: "There could be no doubt of his sex, though the fashion of the time did something to disguise it" (*O*, 13). The point of similarity between Orlando and Sasha exists in the suggestion of seeming androgyny. And this suggested androgyny hints at Orlando's potential psychic wholeness that, when fully developed, defies gender identification and operates in a realm that extends beyond sexual distinctions. But the androgyny in Sasha, and initially in Orlando, works strictly on a superficial level; it actually arises from mere dress fashion. Though Sasha's androgyny remains on that level, Orlando eventually develops his on a psychic plane, where it has the depth and strength to define him totally.

This eventual transformation depends first upon Orlando's ability to discard the ego's priorities and adopt instead those of the Self. As long as Orlando's feelings stay suspended during the Great Frost, what androgyny he possesses himself or sees in Sasha will remain superficial. Consequently, what Orlando sees in Sasha as "the extraordinary seductiveness which issued from the whole person" (*O*, 37), soon, after Orlando recognizes the full womanliness of Sasha, turns into a sexual attraction with Orlando fully a man and Sasha fully a woman. Orlando's "manhood woke" (*O*, 40); he assumes the identity of "a nobleman, full of grace and manly courtesy" (*O*, 42). Though Orlando apparently matures, he does so socially rather than psychologically. Therefore, Sasha represents Orlando's potential Selfhood in her seeming androgyny, but her presence also arouses in Orlando a gender identification nurtured by the egocentric world of the court. His identity becomes one-sided in its strictly Masculine attitude, and as a result, covers his true Self with a thin facade of courtly grace and courtesy.

Such a social facade inevitably leads to a conflict; the hidden true nature of an individual, in its struggle for recognition, creates tremors on the surface. The resultant conflict then manifests itself in apparently contradictory behavior. Orlando, understandably, suffers from such contradictions in his relationship with Sasha. For example, at the ecstatic height of his lovemaking, "suddenly Orlando would fall into one of his moods of melancholy . . . and would fling himself face downwards on the ice and look into the frozen waters and think of death" (*0*, 45). From his ecstasy, Orlando falls into melancholy; and from his act of love and regenerative life, he sinks into thoughts of death. Evidently some force steals from him the freedom of self-acceptance, for only self-hatred destroys such happiness. That force within him is the ego that he cultivates in his court life, and which takes him further from the Self. The ego interrupts his happiness with thoughts of death, so Orlando can only see "frozen waters." At court, in other words, he wanders far from the visions of the old poet who could see into "the depths of the sea."

Because Orlando cannot contact his own psychic depths, he suffers from a delusion similar to Othello's. Orlando sees a performance of Shakespeare's last scene in *Othello*, and he identifies: "The frenzy of the Moor seemed to him his own frenzy, and when the Moor suffocated the woman in her bed it was Sasha he killed with his own hands" (*0*, 57). As Iago deludes Othello, and Othello cannot see beyond the deceit, so Orlando cannot see beyond the superficial demands of the ego in his existence at court. But the frenzy Orlando identifies with indicates his awareness, if only an unconscious one, that the ego deludes. Though Orlando cannot now grasp the truth behind the ego, he will do so when he becomes a woman and has successfully pulled away all the many layers of deluded behavior imposed on the Self by the ego. Until that time, however, Orlando remains a victim of the ego that denies him any access to the Self.

During the Great Frost Orlando experiments with court life. After the thaw, King James exiles Orlando from court and he now returns to his home. At court he experiences the romantic layer of the ego and discovers its vacuity. At home, he experiences the ego's second layer, that of ambition. Orlando's biographer articulates the correlation between these two layers:

> Once before he had paused, and love with its horrid rout, its shawms, its cymbals, and its heads with gory locks torn from the shoulders had burst in. From love he had suffered the tortures of the damned. Now, again, he paused, and into the breach thus made, leapt Ambition, the harridan, and Poetry, the witch, and Desire of Fame, the strumpet; all joined hands and made of his heart their dancing ground. (*0*, 80-81)

As in his first stage, where Orlando awakes into manhood, here he wishes to purify this manhood by ridding his life of all despicable feminine elements that impede his growth: the harridan, the witch, and the strumpet. He errs in this assumption, but does not realize the error immediately because such recognition demands greater growth. At this point, Orlando must learn to reconcile his love for poetry with his need for fame. This reconciliation takes place in Orlando's second stage of growth, which opens with an occurrence as fantastic as that of the Great Frost: Orlando enters a death-like trance from which he does not awake until the seventh day. Through this trance he drops down into a new level of awareness, from which point he has "an imperfect recollection of his past life" (*0*, 66).

The two elements that now cause conflict in Orlando, nobility and poetry, alternate throughout this part of the book. Woolf begins this section with Orlando's descent into his ancestors' crypt. This scene reveals the emptiness of the noble life: he finds the ghastly sepulchre "dug deep beneath the foundations of the house as if the first Lord of the family . . . had wished to testify how all pomp is built upon corruption; how the skeleton lies beneath the flesh; how we that dance and sing above must lie below" (*O*, 71). The noble life has substance only so long as the flesh lives. With the death of the flesh goes the basis for vanity, and only vanity sustains nobility.

Orlando now sits in his room, pen in hand and inkstand within reach, about to work on his poem "The Oak Tree." In this confrontation with the poem, a connection appears between two prominent elements in the novel. Sasha and the old poet:

> Thus it was that Orlando, dipping his pen in the ink, saw the mocking face of the lost Princess and asked himself a million questions instantly which were as arrows dipped in gall . . . All of which so drove their venom into him that, as if to vent his agony somewhere, he plunged his quill so deep into the inkhorn that the ink spirted over the table, which act, explain it how one may . . . at once substituted for the face of the Princess a face of a very different sort. But whose was it, he asked himself? . . . 'This is the face of that rather fat, shabby man who sat in Twitchett's room ever so many years ago when old Queen Bess came here to dine.' (*O*, 79)

Sasha, a member of the court life, represents Orlando's potential wholeness reduced to vacuous gestures of love and shallow expressions of devotion. Such conditions devastate wholeness. The poet, on the other hand, represents Orlando's potential wholeness elevated to a level of vision and creativity. In these two figures, then, are the two forces that conflict in Orlando's mind: the noble, that seeks fame, and the creative, which seeks psychic integration. Because of Orlando's psychologically unevolved state at this point, he yearns for the former, with all of its insincerity and deceit. But his unconscious mind reveals the truth, for it sees in the ink smear, as a mind under analysis reacts to a Rorschach test, Sasha replaced by the old poet.

Orlando's mind, therefore, shows him what priorities he should adopt to acquire wholeness.

Although Orlando does reject his ancestors for all their vanity, his love for writing still retains some of his vanity. He lets pride in his identity as a scholar and a writer sidetrack him away from the actual compostion of the poetry. The image of one involved in a creative act carries more weight for Orlando, at this point, than the act itself. As a result, he wants to associate with famous writers. He invites Nicholas Greene to visit him, and in his attempt to appear as a writer himself, Orlando scorns his noble life style. He thus becomes "unaccountably ashamed of the number of his servants and of the splendour of his table" (*O*, 85-86). Greene, however, knows as little about poetry as Orlando does, though Greene can tell entertaining anecdotes about Shakespeare, Ben Jonson, and other writers whom he supposedly knows intimately. But concerning poetry itself, Greene has little to teach: "Of the nature of poetry itself, Orlando only gathered that it was harder to sell than prose, and though the lines were shorter took longer in the writing" (*O*, 87). Greene, the opportunist, with as little concern for human feeling as for poetry, later proceeds to write a pamphlet in which he satirizes Orlando's life, mannerisms, and even one of his written tragedies.

Orlando reacts to this heartless work with much disgust and a decision to be "done with men" (*O*, 96). He sees love, ambition, women, and poets as equally vain, and so turns to the only two things in life he can trust: dogs and nature. The pain Orlando suffers in his exposure to Greene, says the biographer, resembles that which he experienced with Sasha: "In our belief, Greene's ridicule of his tragedy hurt him as much as the Princess' ridicule of his love" (*O*, 102). Once again, Orlando permits some outside source to devastate his self-concept. Unable to accept himself and reliant on some superficial role in life to determine his whole identity, Orlando crumbles under the weight of ridicule and turns from humanity.

Orlando, at this point, needs solitude so that he can free his world of all distractions and delusions. As the biographer says, "Feeling quit of a vast mountain of illusion, and very naked in consequence, he called his hounds to him and strode through the Park," where he flings himself under "his favourite oak tree" (*O*, 97). Orlando consistently turns to the oak tree for consoling solitude. It provides him with an emotional stability that the world of society denies. This stability strengthens Orlando to commit himself to self-reliance; he decides to write for himself, rather than for anyone else. This truly is, as the biographer says, "one of the most remarkable oaths of his lifetime" (*O*, 103), for no longer, swears Orlando, will he try to fashion himself after some role model. He, in other words, determines to grow beyond his need to slice at a Moor's head swinging from the rafters, an act based on Orlando's wish to identify with his father and grandfather; and he determines to grow beyond his need for Sasha's affirmation of him as a man and Greene's affirmation of him as a poet. He will, from now on, write for no one else but himself. This admirable commitment takes enormous courage, because, as Orlando discovers, once one tears down the role models, the fear arises that nothing else remains: "Memory ducked her effigy of Nick Greene out of sight; and substituted for it — nothing whatever" (*O*, 103). This nothing arises from Orlando's fear that he has no identity of his own. But, as he will find out at the end of the novel, a Self does exist, and it replaces the ostensible nothingness with a most commanding force.

Having rid himself of all impediments, such as "rejected love" and "vanity rebuked, and all the other stings and pricks which the nettle-bed of life had burnt upon him when ambitious of fame" (*O*, 105), Orlando can now turn to his self, symbolized by the house. In this image of his self, Orlando, for the first time, sees coherence and integration: "It looked a town rather than a house, but a town built, not hither and thither, as this man wished or that, but circumspectly, by a single architect with one idea in his head" (*O*, 105). But he does not consciously understand the symbolic value of the house; he sees it as simply a house, rather than an image of his self. He, therefore, fills the nothingness left in the absence of Nick's effigy with another effigy: that of his ancestors. He feels shame over his attempt to make himself better than his ancestors. Consequently, he raises them to the position of role models and devotes himself to lavishly furnishing the home they built. Pleased with his work of filling rooms with elegant furniture and art work, he now feels the need to add the human element, without which the elegant furnishings would have no purpose. Accordingly, Orlando begins to entertain with great splendor.

Regardless of all his attempts to fill in the nothingness, Orlando cannot immerse himself in this new life. Some part of him, that part which needs the Self to thrive, encourages him to leave the lavish feasting and the revelling guests, and go to his room to work on his poem. And Orlando sees himself in the poem: "As he scratched out as many lines as he wrote in, the sum of them was often, at the end of the year, rather less than at the beginning, and it looked as if in the process of writing the poem would be completely unwritten" (*O*, 113). He fears, in other words, that despite his many alterations in his life styles, he ends up no better than when he started. However, as the biographer says, "He had changed his style amazingly. His floridity was chastened; his abundance curbed" (*O*, 113).

Because of these improvements, one day as he works on his poem, a "shadow" or an "apparition" crosses the paper. The Archduchess Harriet, who rides through his court to catch a glimpse of Orlando, with whom she has fallen hopelessly in love after seeing his portrait, casts the shadow. Harriet reappears later in the novel, but now, in her first appearance, she represents Orlando's hidden feminine component. Up to this point in the book, Orlando concentrates on developing his manhood. To compensate for this one-sidedness, then, Harriet enters his life as a phantom that relentlessly plagues him. Unfortunately, Orlando does not recognize Harriet's psychological significance, so he flees from her by requesting that King Charles send him to Constantinople in the capacity of Ambassador Extraordinary (*O*, 118).

In Constantinople Orlando enters another deathlike trance, also lasting seven days. And from this trance he awakes as a woman. With this event begins the third major section of the book, all three of which started with some fantastic occurrence. By way of this sex change, as James Hafley says, Orlando "adds intuitive to intellectual knowledge, and the gradual development of that intuitive faculty leads her to her final perception of reality."[9] But the interpretation cannot stop here. Though the diametric faculties of intellect and intuition do characterize Woolf's frequent distinction between the typically masculine and feminine attitudes, these opposites only marginally explain the overall import of Orlando's sex change. Orlando becomes a woman because of his long suppression of the feminine component within his own psyche. Any element pushed down in one spot will push back up with compensatory strength in another spot. Thus, Orlando does not now take on a female identity at the exclusion of the masculine one. Instead, she approaches the androgynous nature of the Feminine.

This theory accounts for the fantasy played out, during Orlando's trance, between the figure of Truth on one hand and the Ladies of Purity, Chastity, and Modesty on the other. These last three present the typical characteristics of the individual who only exercises the feminine aspect of her personality. They possess as little depth and as much superficiality as the masculine traits of courtly courtesy and chivalry. Truth, however, who significantly does not carry the title of Lady, which limits the other three figures to the female gender, chases out Purity, Chastity, and Modesty with a series of trumpet blasts. Having rid Orlando of all feminine manacles, Truth now peals out the last trumpet blast, which awakens Orlando and announces that he has become a woman (*O*, 137). As a woman now, Orlando enters the androgynous world of the Feminine. The biographer makes clear that Orlando has this androgynous quality: "His form combined in one the strength of a man and a woman's grace" (*0*, 138); and "Orlando had become a woman — there is no denying it. But in every other respect, Orlando remained precisely as he had been. The change of sex, though it altered their future, did nothing whatever to alter their identity" (*0*, 138). Androgyny comprises this constant identity.

As a consequence of Orlando's entrance into the Feminine realm, some very major changes occur in her life. Prior to Orlando's trance, all the structure, ceremony, and formal ritual of an Ambassador's life determined his behavior. He had to sneak away, often in disguise, to enjoy some solitude and, on occasion, to write his poem. But after the sex change, Orlando leaves Constantinople and all the insincerity of an Ambassador's life to join a tribe of Gypsies. The change in life thrills Orlando; as she approaches the Gypsies' campground, located in the mountains outside of Constantinople, the biographer says that Orlando often had "looked at those mountains from her balcony at the Embassy; often had longed to be there" (*0*, 140). Now Orlando can luxuriate in the "pleasure of having no documents to seal, or sign, no flourishes to make, no calls to pay" (*0*, 141). When Orlando leaves Constantinople, she leaves the Masculine world. She has not yet overcome the Masculine force — that which demands one act as gender dictates, and thereby places distance and even distrust between the sexes. Nevertheless, as a woman, Orlando can escape the clutches of these demands, and, from a point of safety, complete her task of working through all the many layers of social fabrication that cover over the Self.

With the Gypsies, then, Orlando has the freedom to commune with nature without first sneaking away from a society crowd or even donning a disguise:

> When, from the mountain-top, she beheld, far off, across the Sea of Marmara the plains of Greece, and made out (her eyes were admirable) the Acropolis with a white streak or two which must, she thought, be the Parthenon, her soul ex-

panded with her eyeballs, and she prayed that she might share the majesty of the hills, know the serenity of the plains, etc., etc., as all such believers do. Then, looking down, the red hyacinth, the purple iris wrought her to cry out in ecstasy at the goodness, the beauty of nature; raising her eyes again, she beheld the eagle soaring, and imagined its raptures and made them her own. (*0*, 143-44)

She wonders if this happiness or beauty "was in things themselves, or only in herself; so she went on to the nature of reality, which led her to truth, which in its turn, led to Love, Friendship, Poetry . . . which . . . made her long, as she had never longed before, for pen and ink" (*0*, 145). Orlando shows here her determination to penetrate to that core where all apparent disagreements and disparities coalesce into truth. The figure of Truth has awakened Orlando into the Feminine, and it is Truth that Orlando seeks. She seeks it because, as the biographer states, "It is not love of truth, but desire to prevail that sets quarter against quarter and makes parish desire the downfall of parish. Each seeks peace of mind and subserviency rather than the triumph of truth and the exaltation of virtue" (*0*, 149). Orlando knows now what she most needs: truth. So she resolves to return to England and there continue her growth at the point where the masculine part of her fled in fear.

On board a merchant ship sailing to England, Orlando accustoms herself to her female identity and in doing so finds greater happiness in womanliness. At first she wonders, "Which is the greater ecstasy? The man's or the woman's?" She discards the idea that the two ecstasies have equal appeal, but quickly decides that "this is the most delicious . . . to refuse, and see him frown" (*0*, 155). Her first instinct, then, is to revel in the feminine power over a man. Orlando soon sees, however, that woman, in other respects, is also powerless: "Lord! Lord! . . . must I then begin to respect the opinion of the other sex, however monstrous I think it? If I wear skirts, if I can swim, if I have to be rescued by a blue-jacket, by God!. . . I must!' (*0*,

156). Having lived as both a man and a woman, and now knowing the secrets and weaknesses of both sexes, Orlando decides she prefers to be a woman for three simple reasons: as a woman she can enjoy "contemplation, solitude, love." For the sake of these three luxuries, Orlando willingly leaves "the rule and discipline of the world to others" (*0*, 160).

She also finds that she can love another woman much better as a woman herself than as a man. As the biographer explains, when a woman loves another woman, "the obscurity, which divides the sexes and lets linger innumerable impurities in its gloom, was removed, and . . . this affection gained in beauty what it lost in falsity" (*0*, 161). The obscurity and falsity that separate the sexes arise from what Woolf repeatedly characterizes as the Masculine attitude. A man or a woman who has no contact with the Feminine element acts out of the Masculine attitude. Consequently, this individual, blind to the relatedness of all people, imposes different social and psychological identities on the two sexes. The ideal, then, is androgyny. Only through androgyny will the obscurity and falsity that lie between two people of opposite sexes disappear. Orlando contacts this androgyny when she becomes a woman, and thus tempers the masculine one-sidedness she lived by before her sex change. As an androgyne she can love a woman without any impediment.[10]

Because Orlando has contacted that power within herself that sees the relatedness of both sexes, she begins to experience, even more, those recurring signs of the Self. For instance, she imagines that a "dome of smooth, white marble" emerges out of her hurried thoughts. This dome soon recalls "that earliest, most persistent memory—the man with the big forehead in Twitchett's sitting-room" (*0*, 163-64). Thoughts of the old poet, who represents Orlando's Self, calm and remind Orlando of her own act of creation, the poem. This poem, which she works on throughout the novel, reflects her growth toward the Selfhood that Orlando sees in the old man. Therefore, when she reaches for the poem, which she safely hides near her breast, Orlando feels the "distraction of sex" subside: "She thought now only of the glory of poetry" (*0*, 164). Poetry, in other words, takes part in a world beyond gender and beyond human differences. As Orlando concludes, "The ear is the antechamber to the soul . . . The poet's then in the highest office of all" (*0*, 173). Poetry not only takes Orlando beyond gender distinctions but it also gives her a means into the soul. A vital confluence of thoughts occurs here: creativity, androgyny, truth, the soul, and God all ultimately merge into one concept.

When Orlando arrives back in England, she takes up the process of growth where, as a man, she left off. Consequently, she faces two desires: one for a lover, and the other for life. Orlando, however, does not realize that she cannot combine these two desires. Rather, she believes that she can find both life and a lover in London, amongst society. But, as the biographer says, Orlando discovers that in society "truth does not exist. Nothing exists. The whole thing is a miasma — a mirage" (*0*, 192). Within this miasma, Orlando satisfies only one of her wishes: "Lovers she had in plenty, but life, which is after all of some importance in its way, escaped her" (*0*, 195).

Life escapes her now because she mistakenly looks for it in society. She thinks she can find life by marrying Archduke Harry. Harry, who earlier impersonated the Archduchess Harriet so as to better his chances to win Orlando's love, now reveals himself as a man. He proposes to Orlando and returns daily for her answer. But Orlando finds Harry a bore, and Harry, unable to win Orlando's affections, finally gives up. Though Orlando does not regret the loss of his fortune or of his title, she does see in his departure a loss of both a lover and life. Clearly, she has lost a lover, but Harry could not give her the life she wants. No one can; only Orlando can give it to herself. She does not realize this now, but will later.

Orlando as a woman, therefore, finds an abundance of lovers, as she did when she was a man. But life still eludes her and she continues to look for it in the wrong places. For example, she looks for it in great men, such as Addison, Dryden, and Pope. As the biographer says, "Her experience with Nick Greene had taught her nothing" (*0*, 197). Because she worships genius, she accepts Lady R.'s invitation to a reception that great men of literature may attend. But the miasma of society permeates such receptions, and all becomes an illusion:

> The guests thought that they were happy, thought that they were witty, thought that they were profound, and, as they thought this, other people thought it still more strongly; and so it got about that nothing was more delightful than one of Lady R.'s assemblies; everyone envied those who were admitted; those who were admitted envied themselves because other people envied them; and so there seemed no end to it. (*0*, 200)

Eventually, however, after Lady R.'s reception and after entertaining men of genius herself, Orlando learns that "where the Mind is biggest, the Heart, the Senses, Magnanimity, Charity, Tolerance, Kindliness, and the rest of them scarcely have room to breathe" (*0*, 213). And with this revelation comes another major statement of Woolf's theory on androgyny. The exclusive concentration on the mind, which Woolf repeatedly identifies as a Masculine trait, cancels out those humanistic and loving qualities of the Feminine. One must temper the one so as to absorb the other and thus integrate the two.

Orlando applies this theory to herself. No longer content with the role of the Lady who entertains and worships men of genius, she completely reverses her situation. Dressed like a man, she visits a prostitute. But Orlando does not swing from one extreme to the other, for once alone with the prostitute, she reveals herself as a woman. Before this, Nell, the prostitute, feigns timidity, hesitancy, and clumsiness, all in order to appeal to Orlando's masculinity. But once Nell finds Orlando to be a woman, she laughs out of relief and immediately "dropped her plaintive, appealing ways" (*0*, 218). Nell now talks freely with Orlando, and Orlando "had never known the hours speed faster or more merrily, though Mistress Nell had not a particle of wit about her" (*O*, 218). In this scene, then, Orlando proves to herself her own theory that an overdeveloped mind suffocates the heart. All the Feminine traits—heart, senses, magnanimity, charity, tolerance, and kindliness—come out only when Orlando drops her masculine identity.

Furthermore, in this scene Orlando demonstrates the need to break down all distinctions based on sex that divide people. Between two women sex poses no barrier. It follows, then, that if Orlando tears down sexual distinctions in herself, no barrier would block her emotional relation to another person equally androgynous. Orlando, therefore, frequently changes her sexual identity: "She reaped a twofold harvest by this device; the pleasures of life were increased and its experiences multiplied. From the probity of breeches she turned to the seductiveness of petticoats and enjoyed the love of both sexes equally" (*O*, 221). Orlando has truly grown into the androgyny of the Feminine. As J. B. Batchelor writes, Orlando, as a woman, can relate indiscriminately to both sexes outside of herself and also combine both male and female qualities within herself.[11]

Having recognized her own need for androgyny, Orlando now seeks it. At first she errs by believing she can contrive a practical means to this wholeness. A couple walking hand in hand down the street move as one piece, male and female together (*O*, 242). She concludes from this that marriage will supply her needed wholeness. But the more she considers marriage the more Orlando deprives herself of total personhood by seeking someone to lean on and by feigning ineptness and weakness so as to appeal to a man (*O*, 247). But while straying out into the park alone, Orlando has a vision that shows that faith, rather than contrivance, creates wholeness. As she walks,

there were only the rooks flaunting in the sky. A steel-blue plume from one of them fell among the heather. She loved wild birds' feathers . . . As the rooks went whirling and wheeling above her head and feather after feather fell gleaming through the purplish air, she followed them, her long cloak floating behind her, over the moor, up the hill . . . Six feathers had she picked from the grass and drawn between her finger tips and pressed to her lips to feel their smooth, glinting plumage, when she saw, gleaming on the hill-side, a silver pool, mysterious as the lake into which Sir Bedivere flung the sword of Arthur. A single feather quivered in the air and fell into the middle of it. Then, some strange ecstasy came over her. Some wild notion she had of following the birds to the rim of the world and flinging herself on the spongy turf and there drinking forgetfulness, while the rooks' hoarse laughter sounded over her. She quickened her pace; she ran; she tripped . . . Her ankle was broken. She could not rise. But there she lay content. (*O*, 247-48)

Her vision of Excalibur, like that of Lily Briscoe's (*TTL*, 266-67), conveys the importance that one relinquish a materialistic hold on life and replace it with one of faith. The wedding ring that just prior to this vision Orlando had considered essential to her life now becomes insignificant. Instead, Orlando finds real ecstasy in her identification with the rook's feather. She flings herself onto the spongy turf, as a single feather falls into a mysterious lake. And just as Sir Bedivere's act of faith evokes a vision of the hand that reaches out of the lake to grasp the sword, so Orlando's emotional abandonment, as she flings herself to the ground, effects a miraculous answer to her needs — Marmaduke Bonthrop Shelmerdine. He rides by on horseback and when he sees Orlando stretched out on the ground, stops to see if she needs help. Then, "a few minutes later, they became engaged" (*O*, 250).

With Marmaduke, Orlando finds an ideal in human relationships because both share in an androgynous nature. Being androgynous within, neither of them suffers from the obscurity and falsity that, according to Orlando, typically separate the sexes. They sense each other's androgyny: she cries, "You're a woman, Shel!" and he cries, "You're a man, Orlando!" (*O*, 252). And a little later each questions the other:

"Are you positive you aren't a man?" he would ask anxiously, and she would echo,
"Can it be possible you're not a woman?" . . . For each was
so surprised at the quickness of the other's sympathy, and it
was to each such a revelation that a woman could be as
tolerant and free-spoken as a man, and a man as strange
and subtle as a woman, that they had to put the matter to
the proof at once. (*0*, 258)

Because of the psychic totality each enjoys, Orlando joyously
exclaims to herself, "I am a woman . . . a real woman, at last"
(*0*, 253). She exults at having found in Marmaduke the perfect
complement to her womanhood.

Though this marks an enormous advance in her psychic
growth, Orlando must take one last step. Here she thrills in her
womanhood as it is complemented by Marmaduke's combination of masculine strength and feminine sympathy. However,
Orlando has yet to discover that she alone possesses the two
complements. In other words, at this point, she thanks "Bonthrop from the bottom of her heart for having given her this
rare and unexpected delight" (*0*, 253). After Orlando takes her
last step in psychic growth, however, she will be able to thank
herself for the same gift.

But before Orlando does this and becomes psychically "one
and entire" (*0*, 320) within herself, she faces the conflict between her role as wife and her love of poetry. Just after Marmaduke leaves to sail around Cape Horn, Orlando sits down to
her poem. Filled with trepidation, she slowly begins to write:
"The words were a little long in coming, but come they did" (*0*,
264). But before she can permit herself any feeling of satisfaction, Orlando immediately questions whether her words make
any sense. She begins to panic and self-doubts paralyze her
creative powers. These self-doubts appear as a "power . . .
which had been reading over her shoulder" (*0*, 265). And this
power tells her to stop writing. It speaks out of her own sense
that a woman finds completion only in the presence of a man,
someone to lean on. Alone, Orlando thinks, a woman has no

self-sustaining identity. To attempt such an identity in the absence of a man, Orlando believes, amounts to a prohibited act: "She was extremely doubtful whether, if the spirit had examined the contents of her mind carefully, it would not have found something highly contraband for which she would have to pay the full fine" (*0*, 265).

This spirit, which Woolf also discusses in her essay "Professions for Women,"[12] leads Orlando to seek masculine approval. When she finishes the poem, then, she immediately sets out for London to find someone who will read her work. She accidentally meets Nick Greene on the street. While they sit at a restaurant together, the upper part of Orlando's dress suddenly bursts open, and out upon the table falls her poem. Greene immediately picks it up, reads it, and declares its brilliance. Insisting that they submit the manuscript for publication, he talks of royalties and of a possible publisher, and then folds the manuscript and slips it into his pocket. In a matter of minutes, the poem that Orlando has always held so close to her heart, both physically and emotionally, is gone. She leaves the restaurant, feels the poem's absence and wonders, "What then, was Life?" (*0*, 282). In other words, there is no satisfaction in someone reading her work. Rather, the whole experience robs her of the "life" she seeks.

Orlando walks off by herself into Hyde Park, questioning where she can find "life." Sitting by the Serpentine, she reads an article of criticism written by Greene. But Orlando finds such articles so manly and thinks to herself, "though I'm spiteful enough, I could never learn to be as spiteful as all that, so how can I be a critic and write the best English prose of my time?" (*0*, 286). Because Orlando has not yet taken the last step toward individuation, she turns to a man, Nick Greene, for approval. But Greene, in his reaction to her poem, as well as in his overall reaction to literature, violates all of Orlando's spiritual and emotional sensibilities. With this realization, Orlando exclaims, "Damn it all!" and vigorously launches a toy boat into the bronze-colored waves of the river (*O*, 286).

This act gives Orlando a vision that supplies her spiritual and emotional sensibilities with the sustenance she has always craved:

> If one looks at the Serpentine in this state of mind, the waves soon become just as big as the waves on the Atlantic; the toy boats become indistinguishable from ocean liners. So Orlando mistook the toy boat for her husband's brig; and the wave she had made with her toe for a mountain of water off Cape Horn; and as she watched the toy boat climb the ripple, she thought she saw Bonthrop's ship climb up and up a glassy wall; up and up it went, and a white crest with a thousand deaths in it arched over it; and through the thousand deaths it went and disappeared — "It's sunk!" she cried out in agony — and then, behold, there it was again sailing along safe and sound among the ducks on the other side of the Atlantic.
> "Ecstasy!" she cried. "Ecstasy!" (*0*, 286-87)

Orlando's vision draws to itself a previous vision, and, furthermore, encourages her on to the final enlightenment in which she discovers her fully integrated Self. The act that evokes this vision recalls again Sir Bedivere's act in Malory's *Morte Darthur*. Like Sir Bedivere, Orlando thrusts out into the water a material object that the water, at first, appears to engulf. Orlando initially, then, sees death. But because Sir Bedivere finally does release the material wealth of King Arthur's sword, and, similarly, because Orlando violently dismisses Nick Greene's egocentric approach to literature, a symbol of rebirth appears: a hand rises out of the lake in *Morte Darthur*, and Orlando's boat rises out of the waves' threat of death. In psychological terms, then, Woolf suggests that only by one's willingness to let fall the values of the ego can one deprive the ego of its tyrannical supremacy and permit the Self to ascend.

For the rest of the novel Orlando advances more rapidly

than ever toward that Self. Two major occurrences mark this progress. First, she gives birth to a son (*0*, 295). Not only does this act demonstrate Orlando's creative powers, but it also shows that she can bring to life that complementary masculine part of herself that, until now, she relied on others to provide.[13] Second, the time of the novel reaches the present moment. For the first time, Orlando lives in the present, and not just the biographer's temporal present, but her own psychological one as well. And only in the Now, the culmination and concentration of all the past, can one approach the Self.

These two occurrences, which not only mark but also result from her psychological growth, emotionally equip Orlando to extend her reach into the Self's domain. She drives out of London and keeps moving until she reaches a cottage on a farm: "When this happened, Orlando heaved a sigh of relief, lit a cigarette, and puffed for a minute or two in silence. Then she called hesitatingly, as if the person she wanted might not be there, 'Orlando!' " (*0*, 308). She calls out for her Self. Yet she questions if a response will come, because all of the many identities she assumes throughout the novel leave her wondering if a core identity has survived, or even existed to begin with. So she keeps calling out. She does not need the "boy who cut the nigger's head down; . . . the boy who sat on the hill; the boy who saw the poet; . . . the young man who fell in love with Sasha; or . . . the Courtier; or . . . the Ambassador; or . . . the girl in love with life; the Patroness of Letters" (*0*, 309), or any other superficial identity she has assumed. Rather, Orlando seeks "the Captain self, the Key self, which amalgamates and controls them all" (*0*, 310). But only when she stops looking for it and thus lets it appear "of its own accord" does she reach this Self (*0*, 313-14). And having reached it, Orlando can return home and roam from room to room in search of "the heart of the house" (*0*, 317), the pulsating, life-giving core of her Selfhood.[14]

Having become "one and entire" (*0*, 320), Orlando leaves the house, walks through the garden and out into the park, and ascends a hill. While climbing she identifies herself with the little boat in the river that surmounts "the white arch of a thousand deaths" (*O*, 322). Still following the ferny path, Orlando now nears the oak tree at the hill's summit. As she flings herself down onto the tree's roots, feeling as if she rides the "back of the world," out from her jacket falls the poem. She wants to bury it at the base of the tree as a symbolic celebration of her acquired Selfhood (*O*, 324).

When night falls and Orlando remains on the hilltop, she envisions two symbols of her Self. For one, she sees the Self's birth in the boat that pushes through the wave's arch of death and emerges triumphantly on the other side. And secondly, at midnight, she sees the Self's ascension symbolized by the wild goose that soars out into the sky. This wild bird recalls the wild rook that she wanted to follow to "the rim of the world" (*O*, 248). Running after the rook, she fell on the spot where Marmaduke found her. Now, on the novel's last pages, just before Orlando sees the goose, she calls out for Marmaduke and imagines that he leaps down from the sky to her side. At this precise moment, as the clock sounds the twelfth stroke of midnight, the point where night and day, dark and light, and, therefore, feminine and masculine, meet, the wild goose springs up into the sky. Opposites unite, and out of this union soars all that the goose symbolizes—"life," "truth," the Self.

*Orlando: A Biography* presents Woolf's composite being's search for the Self as the five previous novels also do. But like all the other novels, it introduces a new element. Just as *Night and Day* continues the growth process begun in *The Voyage Out*, and just as *Jacob's Room* and *Mrs. Dalloway* rid the psyche of the mother and father imagoes respectively, *To the Lighthouse* reveals the Godlike powers inherent in the Self, and *Orlando* depicts the androgynous nature of that Self. Therefore, by the end of *Orlando*, the composite being reaches the Self in all of its complexity. *The Waves*, Virginia Woolf's next novel, describes the psychological and spiritual reasons why humankind, though capable of understanding the Self, cannot completely and exclusively attain full Selfhood.

# NOTES

1. Virginia Woolf, "The New Biography," *Granite and Rainbow* (New York: Harcourt Brace Jovanovich, 1958), p. 149.

2. Virginia Woolf, *Orlando: A Biography* (New York: Harcourt Brace Jovanovich, 1928), pp. 133-34. All further quotations and references to the novel will be cited within the text as *0*.

3. Woolf, *Granite and Rainbow*, p. 155.

4. James Naremore, *The World without a Self: Virginia Woolf and the Novel* (New Haven, Conn.: Yale University Press, 1973), p. 217.

5. Virginia Woolf, *A Room of One's Own* (New York: Harcourt, Brace & World, 1929), p. 102. All further quotations and references to this work will be cited within the text as *AROO*.

6. Today, Woolf is not alone with this theory. Erich Neumann, writing almost thirty years after *Orlando* was published, says, "It is no accident that analytical psychology defines the totality of consciousness and the unconscious as the 'psyche.' This psyche as the whole of the personality must be characterized in man as well as in woman as feminine, because it experiences that which transcends the psychic as numinous, as 'outside' and 'totally different.' " Neumann, then, proceeds to explain what he means by that which transcends the psychic: "It is an emotional reality, a metapsychic situation that is constellated when the human psyche is united with its divine partner." Neumann, however, overlooks the suggestion of androgyny present in the *feminine*, even in the evidence he himself provides. That is, he says "the mandala figure, which appears in man and woman as the totality of the psyche, is feminine in its symbolism as circle and round, or uroboric as that which contains the opposites." If Neumann took one more step beyond this point, he would have been faced with the androgyny implied in totality; the mandala does contain opposites in that it integrates the circle with the square, as androgyny contains the opposites of masculine and feminine. See *Amor and Psyche:The Psychic Development of the Feminine*, trans. Ralph Manheim (Princeton, N.J.: Princeton University Press, 1956), pp. 141-42.

7. Naremore, *The World without a Self*, pp. 193-94.

8. Jung defines *persona* as a *mask* or an "*ad hoc* adopted attitude." He derives the word from "the name for the masks worn by actors in antiquity." The persona, according to Jung, "is exclusively concerned with the relation to objects." He defines an object as an "outer attitude." Such an exclusive concern with one's "outer attitude" leads to a denial of the unconscious world. As a result, "the persona is characterized by a lack of relatedness, at times even a blind inconsiderateness, that yields only to the harshest blows of fate." See *Psychological Types*, trans. R. F. C. Hull (Princeton, N.J.: Princeton University Press, 1971), pp. 465-67.

9. James Hafley, *The Glass Roof:Virginia Woolf as Novelist* (New York: Russell & Russell, 1963), p. 103.

10. Joanne Trautmann comments on Orlando's ability as a woman to love a woman. She says Woolf illustrates that a woman discovers her own androgynous nature by loving another woman. Joanne Trautmann, "*Orlando* and Vita Sackville-West," *Virginia Woolf: A Collection of Criticism*, ed. Thomas S. W. Lewis (New York: McGraw-Hill Book Co., 1975), p. 91.

11. J. B. Batchelor, "Feminism in Virginia Woolf," *Virginia Woolf: A Collection of*

*Critical Essays,* ed. Claire Sprague (Englewood Cliffs, N.J.: Prentice-Hall, Inc., 1971), p. 177.

12. In this essay, written a few years after the completion of *Orlando,* Virginia Woolf describes how when she began to write her first book review, a phantom appeared: "Directly, that is to say, I took my pen in hand to review that novel by a famous man, she slipped behind me and whispered: 'My dear, you are a young woman. You are writing about a book that has been written by a man. Be sympathetic; be tender; flatter; deceive; use all the arts and wiles of our sex. Never let anybody guess that you have a mind of your own. Above all, be pure.' " Soon thereafter, Woolf comments, "Had I not killed her she would have killed me. She would have plucked the heart out of my writing. For, as I found, directly I put pen to paper, you cannot review even a novel without having a mind of your own, without expressing what you think to be the truth about human relations, morality, sex." See *The Death of the Moth and Other Essays* (New York: Harcourt Brace Jovanovich, 1942), pp. 237-38.

13. The symbolic value of Orlando's son has its roots in primitive beliefs and mysteries. Erich Neumann explains the significance of such a birth: "With the birth of her son, the woman accomplishes the miracle of nature, which gives birth to something different from itself and antithetical to itself . . . Not only does he engender, while she conceives and bears; he is also light in contrast to her natural darkness, motion in contrast to her static character. Thus the woman experiences her power to bring forth light and spirit, to generate a luminous spirit that despite all changes and catastrophes is enduring and immortal." Much of Neumann's interpretation stays within the confines of actual gender. Woolf, on the other hand, speaks of the sexes in a far more metaphysical sense. Despite this difference, however, Neumann's distinction does illumine, if only partially, the psychological significance of Orlando's son. See *The Great Mother: An Analysis of the Archetype,* trans. Ralph Manheim (Princeton, N.J.: Princeton University Press, 1955), p. 320.

14. Woolf uses this image of the heart of the house in a similar way in her short story "A Haunted House." See *A Haunted House and Other Short Stories* (New York: Harcourt, Brace & World, 1921), pp. 3-5.

7

# *The Waves*
## They Fall and Break

By the end of *Orlando*, Virginia Woolf's composite personality
reaches its goal. This personality, embodied by major
characters in the novels, can now identify the goal's object, the
Self, or that key or captain self that Orlando calls out for (*0*,
310). The personality can identify it and so complete the
penultimate step to the acquisition of full Selfhood. In *The
Waves*, Woolf explains why her composite personality must
descend from the realm of Selfhood and drop back into the
world of psychic dissolution.

When Virginia Woolf first conceived of *The Waves*, her
seventh novel, she described it as a "very serious, mystical
poetical work" (*A WD*, 104). All three qualities she intended to
incorporate into the novel—seriousness, mysticism, and
poetry—do indeed appear in the finished work. Her prose has
poetic imagery and syntactic concentration, the characters
move in a deeply serious psychological direction, and the
theme revolves around certain complex mystical concepts.
Whereas many critics see little depth and coherence in *Orlando*'s
theme, very few lodge the same complaint against *The Waves*.
Most readers consider *The Waves* one of Woolf's greatest
novels, if not her greatest.[1] Essentially, the profundity of the

novel operates on two levels: religious and psychological. The religious import of the novel centers on the Genesis account of humankind's fall from God's grace, while the psychological theme follows the psyche's disintegration. And the first causes the second: because Adam and Eve disobey God, all of humankind suffers a severance from God; and because of this separation from God, the human psyche falls into fragments. The wholeness sought by Woolf's composite being and envisioned by Orlando, therefore, collapses and shatters. In other words, as Woolf implies in *The Waves*, psychic wholeness depends upon an individual's steady and direct relationship with God. Also, according to Woolf's novel, and as the sin of Adam and Eve illustrates, the human ego sunders this relationship. In sum, as one follows the lives of the novel's six characters, who together comprise the present embodiment of the composite personality, one watches their original psychic harmony fall into discord, both among themselves and within them individually.

The novel's style and structure provide a foundation for this theme. Woolf writes in prose, but she injects into her prose specific poetic techniques such as repetition of words or phrases, syntactic cadence, and alliteration. Illustrations of these techniques abound. So, for the time being, some brief examples taken only from the work's opening pages will suffice. Louis, for instance, uses repetition to describe a noise he hears: "A great beast's foot is chained. It stamps, and stamps, and stamps."[2] And Rhoda uses both repetition and alliteration when she speaks of birds: "Off they fly. Off they fly like a fling of seed" (*TW*, 180). And last, Jinny describes with both peotic rhythm and repetition of sounds a sensation she feels in her hands: "the palm is clammy and damp with dew" (*TW*, 181). A reader can point blindly to almost any passage in the book and land upon more illustrations of Woolf's poetically conceived prose. But the question remains, does Woolf extend her prose into the poetic realm merely to stretch her artistic talents? Or does her style reflect more than just an artistic exercise? If one sets the theme of humankind's fall from God — and therefore from the Self — by the side of the novel's poetic style, a correlation between the two comes to light. One can envision human existence after Adam and Eve's fall from grace as prose-like, with its emphasis on the intellect and practicality. Before the fall, however, life has a poetic quality, ordered by the emotions and senses. Over all, then, Woolf suggests stylistically that deep within the prose-like existence of fallen humankind lies a poetic accord with God. And until an individual can vanquish the ego that buries the poetry, that poetry will remain forever encased in prose.

The novel's structure sets up a similar contrast between prelapsarian and postlapsarian existence. Woolf structures her novel upon two concurrent stories. One deals with the lives of six characters, beginning with their nursery school years and staying with them into old age. The second story depicts the stages of the sun from dawn to dawn. These two stories contrast in that one deals with human existence and the other with nature. Also, one presents itself by way of the characters' soliloquies and interior monologues, whereas the other comes as objective fact. These two stories establish the essential contrast operating in *The Waves*. The story of the sun's course during the day has no end; the conclusion of one day begins another in an eternal continuance of God's design. But the lives of the six characters do end, or will, because Adam and Eve's fall brings on mortality: "For dust thou art, and unto dust shalt thou return" (Genesis 3:19).

Not only does original sin cause actual death, but it also brings about a figurative death — the death of Selfhood at the hands of the ego. Such death manifests itself as self-consciousness, a characteristic of postlapsarian existence, which Woolf captures by her use of interior monologues. And these interior monologues, as well as the soliloquies, reflect a self-consciousness that verges on self-preoccupation. Such a self-preoccupation characterizes Adam and Eve after they eat the fruit of the tree of knowledge — the eyes of them both were

opened, and they knew that they were naked; and they sewed
fig leaves together, and made themselves aprons" (Genesis 3:7).
Adam and Eve's self-consciousness, therefore, inevitably leads
to not only physical but also psychological separation from
each other. Such a fate also befalls Woolf's six characters while
the sun follows its eternal course.

The interludes that open each of the novel's nine chapters,
and which mark the sun's stages, represent more than just the
eternal life forfeited by Adam and Eve. Not only do these interludes, in other words, stand in contrast to the story of the six
characters; they also symbolically depict the progression of the
characters' lives. More specifically, if the sun is a symbol of
human consciousness, in the beginning it has not yet risen.
Similarly, in the beginning of human existence, self-
consciousness docs not operate. But the further the sun rises,
the more distinct, therefore the more separate, the objects in
the world appear. The sunlight reveals definite boundaries
around objects and distances between them. Jean Love sees this
process as paralleling that of the human psyche out of primordial sensory experience and into consciousness.[3] And Woolf extends this notion even further by implying that the more self-
consciousness takes over, the more people see themselves as different and distinct. Finally, such psychic separation and, at its
extreme, solipsism, ends in darkness and dissolution, while the
sun disappears and takes with it the light.

Throughout the novel, primarily in the interludes, but in the
interior monologues and soliloquies as well, one watches and
hears the waves. This central image contains the duality implied by the juxtaposition of the interludes and the characters'
words. Specifically, the sea represents the original state of the
world; when God created the world, the earth was without
form and He "moved upon the face of the waters" (Genesis
1:2). From this formless void arise individual waves that swell
with awesome assertion and then fall, spread into dissolution,
and return to the sea. Humankind follows a similar progression. Out of the depths of a primordial accord with eternity,

individuals arise and assert their differences, only to dissolve and return to eternity. Therefore, the novel's prevalent symbol of the waves captures Woolf's overall philosophical theory. Woolf's title on the holograph manuscript for the novel also reflects this philosophical duality: "The moths? or the life of anybody; life in general or Moments of being or The waves."[4] In Woolf's attempt to find an appropriate title she reveals her essential concern. When she first considered "The Moths" she apparently intended to convey the short-lived existence of someone, anyone, or humankind in general. But this title would eliminate the complementary concept of eternality that underscores human life's ephemerality. Thus, she finally chose "The Waves" perhaps because it contains both concepts.

The psychic fragmentation prevalent in a fallen world becomes manifest in Woolf's six characters, who are segments of a single individual. If the characters are seen as parts of a whole, two points in Woolf's theory emerge: not only does the human fall from grace psychically separate individuals, but it also drives a wedge into the single psyche and splits it into fragments. Though no critic attributes this fragmentation to humanity's fall from grace, most do agree that the six characters comprise a whole.[5] As will become clearer, Jinny represents sensuality, and as such she complements Neville's emphasis on the intellect. Susan has a strong maternal drive and craves the world of the senses, whereas Bernard feels numbed by his role as father and fears his own senses. And last, Rhoda finds the immediate world frightening and thus escapes into mystical and ethereal visions, whereas Louis needs to keep a firm grip on the hard, fast roots of his own existence.

Other differences among the six also exist. For example, whereas Jinny indiscriminately has sexual relations with many men, Susan waits for the love of that one, special man, and Rhoda eludes all sexuality completely. Likewise, whereas Bernard fears he has no essential identity of his own, Louis feels what identity he does have, because of its difference, separates him from the other characters, and Neville envisions his own identity as deriving its substance only from Percival's love. These differences between the six characters have several consequences: each character senses his or her own inadequacies, and, as a result, suppresses the inadequacies. Such suppression hides from each character those personality traits that would, if acknowledged, contribute to psychic wholeness; moreover, such suppression makes each character project a false impression to others. In short, the characters, through suppression, further their own psychic fragmentation, which keeps others from knowing them and, even more tragically, precludes self-knowledge. Just as Adam and Eve sew fig leaves to hide the bodies of which their fall has made them self-conscious, so Woolf's six characters hide those parts of themselves about which their self-consciousness makes them feel shame.

Percival, on the other hand, the seventh character in *The Waves*, has no self-consciousness and thus feels no shame. He represents pure Being that totally accepts itself. Unlike the other characters, he never speaks; yet through his power as Being he draws the other six together. He serves as linchpin for the others. Yet with his death the center can no longer hold. When alive, Percival represents that lack of self-consciousness — and therefore that lack of shame — that characterizes Edenic humanity. But he must die, for humanity dies in its fall from grace.

The chapters in *The Waves* take the reader through each step in the entire progression from psychic wholeness to psychic disintegration. At first all six characters appear united; then the sexes separate; then individuals separate from each other; then individuals splinter psychically within themselves; and, finally, Bernard, in the last chapter, presents himself as the isolated individual with neither identity nor Selfhood.

The original psychic wholeness shows up in the imagery of the opening interlude. This interlude describes the sun as not yet risen, for human consciousness has not yet developed. Before the sun rises, the setting bears a strong resemblance to that of the world on the first day of God's act of creation: "The earth was without form, and void; and darkness was upon the face of the deep" (Genesis 1:2). But as the sun rises in Woolf's interlude, a dark line on the horizon divides the sea from the sky. Likewise, on the second day, God created a firmament that "divided the waters which were under the firmament from the waters which were above the firmament" (Genesis 1:7). And, just as in Woolf's interlude, individual waves rise and heap themselves, so on the sixth day God created the human being (Genesis 1:27). Woolf's interlude then concludes with the symbol of the house that consistently, in *The Waves* as well as in *To the Lighthouse* and *Orlando*, represents human selfhood. As the sun casts greater light, it sharpens the walls of the house.

All of these details in the first interlude foreshadow the psychological movement of the six characters in the novel's first chapter. When the characters first speak, they describe what imaginatively they see and hear. For instance, Bernard says he sees a ring that "quivers and hangs in a loop of light," while Susan sees "a slab of pale yellow" and Rhoda hears a "cheep, chirp; cheep, chirp; going up and down" (*TW*, 180). It seems as though each character freely associates to a diffuse, undifferentiated world. Even Bernard's particular reaction characterizes the world as still undifferentiated, for his words recall those of Henry Vaughan's opening lines in his poem "The World": "I saw eternity the other night/ Like a great ring of pure and endless light."[6] Next, the characters each take a turn to express their impressions, but this time they react to some actual object rather than to an undifferentiated world. Bernard, for example, notices a spider's web, while Susan looks at the leaves and Louis watches a shadow that falls along a path (*TW*, 180). The next set of associations reveals a greater connection between the thing perceived and the person who perceives: Neville feels cold stone against his feet, Jinny has a burning sensation on the back of her hands, and Susan hears birds singing all around them (*TW*, 181). In the fourth set of associations, each of the children begins to see the house from the outside. And, last, in the fifth set of associations, they speak of what they see inside the house. Through these five sets of impressions, in each of which all the children have a turn to speak, one witnesses the gradual emergence of human awareness and of the human relation to external objects. The fact that this awareness draws the children closer and closer to the house — Woolf's symbol for the self — further indicates that with growing awareness comes self-consciousness. Similarly, Adam and Eve know no differences between themselves until they gain a comparable self-consciousness.

Because the children gain self-consciousness, they no longer react to the world outside. Instead, now they begin to see themselves, and with this self-awareness comes a certain emotional insecurity. Louis, for example, now feels alone. To compensate for this loss of union with the other five children, he imagines himself a stalk whose "roots go down to the depths of the world" (*TW*, 182). Jinny, out of a need to make human contact, impetuously kisses Louis. Susan, who shares Jinny's need, sees the kiss, and, out of a sense of exclusion, decides, "I will wrap my agony inside my pocket handkerchief. It shall be screwed tight into a ball" (*TW*, 183). All three of these children, Louis, Jinny, and Susan, feel the loneliness that results from their loss of accord with eternity.

Bernard tries to console Susan, and in so doing he brings to the novel a vision of the lost Eden. He suggests that he and Susan "sink like swimmers just touching the ground with the tips of their toes" (*TW*, 185) into the world of Elvedon. Elvedon, a "ringed wood with the wall round it" (*TW*, 185), resembles Eden, which, after God expells Adam and Eve from the garden, is sealed off with cherubims and a flaming sword (Genesis 3:24). Bernard delights in Elvedon, until suddenly he sees it as a hostile country; he fears the gardener will shoot them. Bernard recognizes in the gardener the same anger expressed by the God of Genesis. So he flees and tells Susan, "Follow without looking back" (*TW*, 186). Elvedon, once a newly discovered country of delight, reminiscent of Eden, turns into a fearsome world, like that of Sodom once God condemns it. And just as Bernard escapes with Susan out of the dangerous Elvedon and tells her not to look back, so God tells Lot to take his family out of Sodom, and never look back (Genesis 19:17). The loss of Eden, then, causes not only self-consciousness and the loneliness that results from this self-consciousness, but fear as well.

Before the novel's first chapter ends, Neville has his own vision that explains the source of all this loneliness and fear. He recalls a story he once heard of a man found beneath an apple tree with his throat cut. This mental picture plagues Neville, and he thinks of this tree as "immitigable" and "implacable." He feels unable to pass by: "There was an obstacle. 'I cannot surmount this unintelligible obstacle,' I said. And the others passed on. But we are doomed, all of us by the apple trees, by the immitigable tree which we cannot pass" (*TW*, 191). In this vision lies the source of the children's loneliness and fear; Adam and Eve disobey God when they eat of the tree of knowledge, and from their act comes death. Though the Bible does not specify the kind of fruit Adam and Eve eat, it is commonly spoken of as an apple. So, Neville sees humankind dead beneath the apple tree, that source of knowledge of good and evil that God reserves for Himself.[7] Having attempted to arrogate God's powers, humankind now faces that immitigable obstacle that divides the mortal from the immortal, the temporal from the eternal. Thus, the first chapter of *The Waves* now ends with a picture of humanity's spirit covered over with flesh: as Mrs. Constable bathes Bernard and squeezes the sponge above him, he feels the water run down his spine and thinks to himself, "Bright arrows of sensation shoot on either side. I am covered with warm flesh" (*TW*, 192).

The novel's second chapter depicts the next consequence of the loss of God's grace. The sexes separate. Whereas in the first chapter all six children lived together at the nursery, now the boys go to one boarding school and the girls to another. The interlude forebodes this stage: the strain or two of the birds' song suddenly fall silent and the waves break with the force of a concussion. The order of the interior monologues reinforces this concept of separation: first, all the men speak, then all the women, then back to the men again, and so on. At no point, that is, do the voices of the sexes mingle. And Woolf draws clear lines of demarcation by providing extra spacing on the page to indicate that a major shift occurs between the masculine and feminine voices.

Moreover, the concept of separation gains further reinforcement from the content of the monologues. They open with Bernard and his dependence on making phrases to keep himself distinct from the world: "I must make phrases and phrases and so interpose something hard between myself and the stare of housemaids, the stare of clocks, staring faces, indifferent faces, or I shall cry" (*TW*, 195). As the other characters deliver their monologues, the reader learns more about the results of this state of separation. For example, Rhoda, Louis, and Neville express their individual needs for God or a godlike figure in their lives. Rhoda feels attracted by the purple light in Miss Lambert's ring as it passes across a page in the Prayer Book (*TW*, 197). She endows Miss Lambert with a spiritual power here, as well as shortly afterwards, where Rhoda says that the teacher's presence makes everything change and become luminous. Also, as Rhoda says, "All is solemn, all is pale where she stands, like a statue in a grove" (*TW*, 205). She needs to project this spiritual power onto Miss Lambert because of her own loss of identity, due to humanity's expulsion from Eden. The loss of identity, another manifestation of the state of separation, comes from the loss of God and leads to a need for God. As Rhoda says, "We are all callous, unfriended. I will seek out a face, a composed, a monumental face, and will endow it with omniscience" (*TW*, 197). Louis also experiences a need for God. Sitting in chapel, he watches Dr. Crane mount the pulpit and rejoices in the man's presence: "Now all is laid by his authority, his crucifix, and I feel come over me the sense of the earth under me, and my roots going down and down till they wrap themselves round some hardness at the centre. I recover my continuity, as he reads" (*TW*, 198). Neville, who also craves a godlike figure in his life, finds Dr. Crane a menace to his liberty. Neville, therefore, turns toward Percival, whom he idolizes: "He sees nothing; he hears nothing. He is remote from us all in a pagan universe. But look—he flicks his hand to the back of his neck. For such gestures one falls hopelessly in love for a lifetime" (*TW*, 199). The needs of Rhoda, Louis, and Neville reflect humanity's wish to return to the paradisaical accord with God.

If a person feels unaccepted by God, then difficulty in self-acceptance is a natural consequence. The three women in the novel cannot accept themselves. On their way to play tennis, each stops at the mirror in the stairs. As Susan looks into the mirror she envies Jinny; "Jinny dances. Jinny always dances in the hall . . .; she turns cartwheels in the playground; she picks some flower forbiddenly, and sticks it behind her ear so that Miss Perry's dark eyes smoulder with admiration, for Jinny, not me" (*TW*, 202). But, when Jinny passes the looking-glass, she sees her face as ugly, particularly as it compares with Susan's "grass-green eyes which poets will love" (*TW*, 203). Rhoda, worse than disdaining her own appearance, wishes to deny its very existence. She ducks behind Susan to avoid seeing herself. And because Rhoda believes she has no face, no identity, she patterns her behavior after the other two women: "See now with what extraordinary certainty Jinny pulls on her stockings, simply to play tennis. That I admire. But I like Susan's way better, for she is more resolute, and less ambitious of distinction than Jinny. Both despise me for copying what they do" (*TW*, 204). None of these three women can accept herself. Each one's envy of the others illustrates this lack of self-acceptance and results from, psychologically speaking, the ego's ascension into power and its usurpation of God.

Without self-acceptance, fears arise and a dependence on an outside source of strength develops. Rhoda, for example, says, "Alone, I often fall down into nothingness" (*TW*, 204). She

fears solitude because she believes that deep within her exists a
void, the void left by the absence of God. Jinny, likewise, suffering from a lack of self-acceptance, needs the constant attention of men to prove to herself her own worth: "I begin to feel
the wish to be singled out; to be summoned, to be called away by
one person who comes to find me, who is attracted towards
me, who cannot keep himself from me" (*TW*, 206). If someone
singles her out, Jinny feels affirmed. She has no concern for the
man himself, but merely for his affirmation of her own power
to attract. Louis also suffers from an inability to accept
himself. Because he cannot accept himself, he desperately
craves to participate in some group that shares a single cause.
By his very espousal of that cause, Louis thinks, he assures
himself that others will accept him. So, as he watches the other
boys he thinks, "They are the volunteers; they are the
cricketers; they are the officers of the Natural History Society . . .
How majestic is their order, how beautiful is their obe-
dience! If I could follow, if I could be with them I would
sacrifice all I know" (*TW*, 206).

The state of separation, therefore, caused by the
psychological and spiritual act of original sin committed by
Adam and Eve, creates a need for some godlike force, a lack of
self-acceptance, a fear of no psychic core to affirm and reinforce one's own selfhood, and a dependence on some outside
source of strength. Eventually all of these symptoms result in a
split within the individual. In other words, separation may first
manifest itself in envy or fear of others, but its damage spreads
until an internal, psychological fragmentation also occurs.

For the remainder of the novel's second chapter, the
children reveal the form of their own particular states of
fragmentation. Neville, for one, knows his need for a god, but
has no one to whom he can admit this need. He fears Bernard
would make a story of it, and he finds Louis too "cold" and
"universal." Thus Neville's "absurd and violent passion" for Percival must remain a secret: "Nobody guessed the need I had to
offer my being to one god; and perish, and disappear" (*TW*,

210). Keeping such a secret creates a psychic breach; in Neville's case, he hides his passion beneath his intense studies of Shakespeare and Catullus. Bernard too wishes to cover up his own fragmented state. He becomes preoccupied with his phrases in order to give life some coherence. Susan suffers from her own peculiar conflict. She despises any imposed order on life that worships "restrictions that wrinkle and shrivel — hours and order and discipline" (*TW*, 211), preferring instead the world of imagination and nature. She therefore tears the days from the calendar and screws them up in her hand so they no longer exist. Then, though the days feel like a weight in her side, she has the freedom to imagine "phantom riders," see "the swallow skim the grass," and watch "the fish slip in and out among the reeds" (*TW*, 211). Jinny's conflict occurs between her day and night worlds: "I hate darkness and sleep and night . . . and lie longing for the day to come. I long that the week should be all one day without divisions" (*TW*, 212). Rhoda, in contrast to Jinny, fears contact with the immediate world. She, thus, can barely tolerate the day, as she waits longingly for the night world: "There are hours and hours . . . before I can put out the light and lie suspended on my bed above the world, before I can let the day drop down" (*TW*, 213). And, whereas Rhoda sees the present moment as an "emerging monster" (*TW*, 219), and thus pursues visionary dreams as a means of escape, Louis forces himself to concentrate on the present moment. If he shut his eyes, Louis fears, he would fail to "realise the meeting-place of past and present" (*TW*, 220). He uses this vision as an escape from the dark world of the past, where he imagines his buried envy and bitterness rage. Each character, then, feels split in two. And because each can accept only one part of himself or herself, the unacceptable part undergoes suppression. The character fears this part, and so buries it deep into the unconscious.

The more extensive this suppression, the less the individual knows himself. Therefore, in the novel's third chapter, the characters repeatedly ask "Who am I?" The interlude here marks a further stage in the sun's ascension, which parallels the growing power of the ego that imprisons an individual into self-doubts. And to combat the reign of the ego the characters attempt to find their individual identities that would give them a sense of completion and wholeness. In their search, however, each finds greater fragmentation. And, concurrent with the growing internal separation, even wider distances form between the individuals: Bernard and Neville go to college, while Louis begins his business career. And Susan leaves the other two women so she can continue her education in Switzerland.

Bernard is the first to question his identity. When he asks, "What am I?", he decides, "I am not one and simple, but complex and many" (*TW*, 227). Yet, he also senses, "Underneath, and, at the moment when I am most disparate, I am also integrated" (*TW*, 228). However, though sensing his own integration, he finds it difficult to clearly identify that singular self that combines all the others. So, at the end of his meditation, he asks himself the final question: "When I say to myself, 'Bernard,' who comes?" But Bernard now only sees "a faithful, sardonic man, disillusioned, but not embittered. A man of no particular age or calling" (*TW*, 230). In other words, though Bernard senses, or hopes for, a psychically integrated identity that unites all of his apparent selves, when he actually seeks this core he finds only a shell. Once he removes all of the "several different men who alternately act their parts as Bernard" (*TW*, 227), he finds that only the container of these men remains.

Neville likewise lacks a psychic core. He derives his apparent identity through identification with those he envies. Sitting on the bank of the river, he looks through the willow tree out onto the water where powerful young men stretch out in boats, as they eat fruit and listen to the gramophone. Because Neville envies these men, he identifies with them. And as long as his identification lasts, he can exclaim, "Oh, I am in love with life!" (*TW*, 231). But once he realizes that his life really plays no part in theirs and that without these figures to envy and identify with he has no particular selfhood of his own, Neville despairs. He feels his frenzy become artificial and insincere and concludes, "I do not know myself sometimes, or how to measure and name and count out the grains that make me what I am" (*TW*, 232). So when Bernard approaches, Neville greets him with the question, "Who am I?" (*TW*, 232).

Louis, like the others, refuses to confront what he disapproves of in himself and buries it deeper into his unconscious. His conflict stems from his sense of inferiority to the others. An Australian accent makes him different from the others and marks him as an outsider. Therefore, Louis describes himself this way: "I, who desire above all things to be taken to the arms with love, an alien, external" (*TW*, 240). To compensate for this sense of exclusion, Louis wants to reduce the world to order. With order imposed, he will be an integral part of the world. But this imposition of order can only pull him further away from the alien world. That is, Louis's refusal to submit to the "ordinary" gives him a most disagreeable countenance: "Hence my pursed lips, my sickly pallor; my distasteful and uninviting aspect as I turn my face with hatred and bitterness upon Bernard and Neville, who saunter under yew trees; who inherit arm-chairs; and draw their curtains close" (*TW*, 241). Louis thus disparages those who exclude him; he refuses to join with the others and accept them as he wishes they would accept him.

Susan also covers up her true identity. Louis, out of a wish for order, had retreated into his translation of poetry and thus away from the immediate world, but Susan immerses herself in nature. This immersion initially makes her feel content and complete: "I am the trees; mine are the flocks of birds, and this young hare who leaps" (*TW*, 242). But soon she realizes that her identity is derived from the surroundings. She therefore has no answer for the question, "But who am I?" (*TW*, 242). Susan only knows that she identifies more with the light that falls on the gate than with womanhood. Because of this, Susan waits for her lover. Some day, she feels, her lover will come, and then she will bear children and as wife and mother finally acquire an identity. She, like the other characters, looks to some outside source of selfhood because she fears that within herself no such source exists.

Jinny and Rhoda have a similar need for some outside source of fulfillment, but their individual searches take them in opposite directions. Jinny needs reinforcement of her physical attractiveness. She therefore depends on the attention others pay her for her own feeling of completion. For example, she sits at a dance and beckons men to approach. This compulsion reflects Jinny's fear that she has no soul beneath her physical self and therefore nothing to offer. She thus craves physical intimacy in order to be "admitted to the warmth and privacy of another soul" (*TW*, 247). Though this is achieved with one man, as other people brush by, the ecstasy of the moment slackens and indifference invades. The moment having vanished, Jinny returns to her post and watches the door for another person to come in. Rhoda, conversely, fears the opening door, for through it she imagines "the tiger leaps . . . terror rushes in; terror upon terror, pursuing me" (*TW*, 247). To escape the terror that some man will scorn her, she longs "for marble columns and pools on the other side of the world where the swallow dips her wings" (*TW*, 248). Jinny and Rhoda, then, run away from that which could complete them psychologically. As long as Jinny seeks the privacy of the soul in someone else, her moments of ecstasy will remain fleeting and her own spirit will atrophy. Similarly, as long as Rhoda skittishly flees from the immediate world of sensation, the more "naked" and "broken into separate pieces" (*TW*, 248) she will feel. The answer to the question "Who am I?" inevitably becomes more elusive.

In the novel's fourth chapter, the six characters hold a farewell dinner for Percival, who will leave for India shortly. Woolf's choice of the name Percival links this character with that medieval knight who quests for the Holy Grail. Such an association has two effects: one, Percival's connection to the

Grail legend characterizes him less as a personality than a symbol or life force; and second, his roots in the medieval world
distance him in time from the other six characters. These
associations help to explain Percival's role in *The Waves*. Most
critics agree that he unifies the other six because all the
characters assemble, after years of separation, for the farewell
dinner. Opinions do differ, however, on Percival's effect on the
others.[8] Percival symbolizes that state of being before the fall
because he lacks the self-consciousness of the other characters.
And, as a symbol of a prelapsarian man, Percival is
characterized by silence and a disregard for the human intellect. He is in stark contrast to the other six and embodies that
long-lost form of existence of the Garden of Eden.

Because Percival represents all that the others have lost, they
admire him and recall their fall into psychological fears and
fragmentation. Neville suggests that he and the other five
reveal "brutally and directly" their moments of terror and
ecstasy. As each character briefly refers to an early moment in
his or her life at the nursery before separation set in, they each
uncover the natures of their own peculiar state of separation.
Bernard recalls the bath that Mrs. Constable gave him and the
arrows of sensation that struck his flesh, from which he has run
ever since. Susan remembers seeing the boot boy make love
with the scullery-maid. Her reaction at the time made her feel
different from all the others, for she, unlike the others, had no
fear "of heat, nor of the frozen winter" (*TW*, 192). Susan, in
other words, prided herself as the only one unafraid of extremes in passion. Rhoda recalls fear of the terrifying tiger—
physical passion—that pursues her. Next, Neville remembers
the man dead among the apple trees. This picture has ever
since locked Neville into a desire for a god that would demand
his self-sacrifice. And Jinny remembers the leaf that danced in
the hedge, the sight of which compelled her to race after Louis
and kiss him. This desperate need for physical intimacy with a
man has since dictated Jinny's behavior. Louis in his turn
recalls his vision of petals that swam on depths of green, a vi-

sion that portrays Louis's feeling of isolation and need to have roots that drive deep into the earth. And, last, Bernard thinks of Elvedon, the lost paradise that suddenly turned hostile; with this image Bernard closes the series of recollections of terrors and ecstasies.

So far, the characters remember the first step or manifestation of their progression toward psychic separation and fragmentation. The next step to recount involves how, as Louis puts it, "We changed, we became unrecognisable" (*TW*, 262). So Louis, the first to speak in this set of monologues, distinguishes between himself and the others by saying, "I am not single and entire as you are. I have lived a thousand lives already" (*TW*, 263). Jinny then says that, unlike the others, she does not hide her body. For that matter, she says, "I can imagine nothing beyond the circle cast by my body" (*TW*, 264). Neville next says that his life has a rapidity that the others lack. By rapidity he means that he anxiously seeks physical love. However, Neville says, "I shall have riches; I shall have fame. But I shall never have what I want, for I lack bodily grace and the courage that comes with it" (*TW*, 264). Rhoda talks of her fear of everyone else because she dreads the shock of sensation. This reaction to sensation is something that makes her different from the others: "I cannot deal with it as you do" (*TW*, 265). And Susan, who thrills in her happiness with the cycles of nature, says, "No day will be without its movement. I shall be lifted higher than any of you on the backs of the seasons" (*TW*, 266). And finally, Bernard admits to his fear of solitude, and that, unlike the others, his very existence depends on "the stimulus which other people provide" (*TW*, 267). In sum, all the characters have an indomitable fear that distinguishes them from each other and keeps them all separate.

Because of their isolation, not one of the characters has the strength to reverse the process of separation in order to reunite them all as they existed on the novel's opening pages. Therefore, they now turn to Percival, the only one who has remained unharmed by psychic disintegration. And, for each character, Percival represents the quality that would mend the separation. For example, Rhoda attributes to Percival that power to draw the distant to the near. And for Louis, Percival reveals that no separation need distance people. Louis has learned that "we have tried to accentuate differences. From the desire to be separate we have laid stress upon our faults, and what is particular to us. But there is a chain whirling round, round, in a steel-blue circle beneath" (*TW*, 270). But the knowledge that these two characters gain, and all that the others learn as well, can last only as long as Percival does. For he, as a symbol of humankind's existence before the expulsion from Eden, remains only a symbol, something outside of the characters and something lost long ago.

In the novel's next chapter, the six characters lose this only model of integration that remained in their lives: Percival dies. Out of his death comes even greater separation, which Woolf captures structurally; she distances the characters by having only three of them speak in one chapter, while leaving the other three for another chapter. In these two chapters, the first three characters reflect on what psychological deprivation Percival's death has inflicted on them, and the second three show how they cope with this deprivation. To Neville, Percival's death means a loss of the past. Because of this loss, Neville resolves to remain forever solitary and never to attempt any spiritual ascension. He resigns himself to doom (*TW*, 281). Bernard sees in Percival's death the world's loss of a leader. The loss of such a leader makes Bernard incapable of distinguishing between joy and sorrow (*TW*, 281). Furthermore, Bernard now finds his own existence empty and barely tolerable. And Rhoda feels deserted and left to her own inadequate devices with which to adapt to the immediate world. But she does recognize that Percival, by his death, has given her some consolation for the torment and terror she encounters in the world; she imagines a square placed upon an oblong, which she interprets as the dwelling place humankind has made for itself. Rhoda thus learns through Percival to derive some satisfaction from this structure of opposites, though she cannot know "the thing that lies beneath the semblance of the thing" (*TW*, 288). For all three of these characters, then, Percival's death forces them to relive humankind's original separation from God and a series of natural reactions to this loss—the sense of doom, then the pain of isolation, and finally the search for some new dwelling place to replace the lost one of God's garden.

When the next three characters present their soliloquies, the reader learns of various fabricated dwelling places people construct to protect themselves against their worst enemy—themselves. Louis, for example, finds his dwelling place in order. He thrives on punctuality and a time schedule, for, in his words, "I roll the dark before me, spreading commerce where there was chaos in the far parts of the world." Then he explains why he adopts this purpose: "If I press on, from chaos making order . . . I expunge certain stains, and erase old defilements" (*TW*, 292). The shame he feels over his accent and the fact that his father is a banker disappears because he replaces it with order. But Louis also admits that although he imposes order on his life, his true desires defy order. He really would like, for instance, that the typist cuddle by his knees, and that he go to public-houses where he could have his favorite dish. Since Louis sees these desires as weaknesses, he dismisses them whenever possible by reminding himself of engagements with business associates and the letters he must sign. He cannot permit himself to dwell outside of order.

Susan finds her dwelling place in her role as mother. As such she protects her infant from "all who rattle milk-cans, fire at rooks, shoot rabbits, or in any way bring the shock of destruction near this wicker cradle, laden with soft limbs, curled under a pink coverlet" (*TW*, 294). But as she sings the baby to sleep, Susan feels a dark, wild violence rush up inside her. She, of course, holds this violence back so as not to disturb her child, but in so doing suppresses it. As a result, when she wishes that "life shall sheathe its claws and gird its lightning and pass by, making of my own body a hollow, a warm shelter for my child to sleep in" (*TW*, 295), she speaks not only of protecting her infant but also of protecting herself from her own violence. Therefore, just as Louis covers his shame with a business man's order, Susan covers her violence with a mother's protection.

Jinny dwells in the body. Through sexual promiscuity she avoids all steadfast social roles that, to her mind, would stifle her. She much prefers, instead, to thus "see with the body's imagination things in outline" (*TW*, 297). Such an existence assures Jinny that she will never have to look deeply into anything, anyone, or even herself, and thereby understand. In short, she protects herself from herself, as Louis and Susan do as well. Neville concludes the novel's sixth chapter by revealing his own protective dwelling place. He insists on neatness: "One must slip paper-knives, even, exactly through the pages of novels, and tie up packets of letters neatly with green silk, and brush up the cinders with a hearth broom" (*TW*, 300). Neville uses this neatness to oppose "the waste and deformity of the world" (*TW*, 300). But again, just as in Susan's case, Neville projects his own dreaded shortcomings onto the world. Therefore, because he sees himself as "ugly" and "weak," he imagines the world threatens him with its "waste" and "deformity." And while he feels protected from the world, Neville actually covers up what he senses in himself.

With Percival's death, then, the characters see their lives robbed of something essential and therefore compensate by trying to make their own psychic solidity. As a result, the characters lock themselves into their own artificial dwelling places. Thus confined, they experience the discomfort and unhappiness of their own existence and recognize all of life that they have denied to themselves and that now lies beyond their reach. The interlude that opens the seventh chapter describes the characters' current state with its picture of the dense clouds that draw themselves across the setting sun while casting a net of deep shade upon the earth. Then each character speaks of his or her own unhappiness and needs.

Bernard and Susan have similar present states. Bernard

recalls his complacent happiness in his family life. He felt secure with children, wife, house, and dog. But now, he says, "that lovely veil has fallen. I do not want possessions now" (*TW*, 305). He recognizes that his need for possession rather than love motivated him toward family life. And this need served the same purpose as his phrase-making and story-telling; both imposed an arbitrary design on life. Bernard, therefore, yearns for a vision of spontaneity, something that arises for no apparent rational reason. He does have this vision as he leans over a parapet, looks out at the waste of water, and sees a fin turn. Bernard, in other words, imagines his life a waste and so seeks some unexpected, unplanned occurrence, something that would cut through the waste. Susan, likewise, at first feels content in her role as mother. She sought in this role "security, possession, familiarity" (*TW*, 308), but also now needs and waits for some shock that can loosen her "laboriously gathered, relentlessly pressed-down life" (*TW*, 308). She feels imprisoned by "the unscrupulous ways of the mother who protects, who collects under her jealous eyes at one long table her own children, always her own" (*TW*, 308-9). She feels enclosed by life, and, in a prison of glass, sometimes thinks of Percival and Rhoda, who escaped the world of the body that encloses her. So both Bernard and Susan regret the manacles they placed on themselves out of their need for emotional security and possession. Now both wait for something or someone to release them.

Jinny and Neville also have similar attitudes towards life. Jinny realizes that she has grown old and that perhaps because of her age cannot attract men as easily as in the past. Nevertheless, since she has locked herself in the body's prison, she knows of no other alternative. So she prepares her home for a visitor. The identity of the visitor has no importance to Jinny. She merely wants in that visitor some eagerness that she can say she has aroused. Similarly, Neville sits in his room and waits for a visitor. He also has no interest in who visits, but does need someone, anyone, to whom he can say, "Come closer, closer" (*TW*, 314). Both Jinny and Neville place enormous emphasis on the body. Though Jinny needs to arouse someone sexually and Neville needs only the intimate closeness of another body, they both thrill in the uncharted, unreasoned procession of life.

Louis and Rhoda occupy comparable emotional dwelling places in that both crave solitude. And both fear physical intimacy. Louis can allow himself no spontaneity, but rather must torturously labor beneath the level of natural happiness, which he has never known. And there, below the surface of life, that level to which Jinny and Neville bind themselves, Louis "must weave together, must plait into one cable the many threads . . . There is always more to be understood; a discord to be listened for; a falsity to be reprimanded" (*TW*, 316). Unlike Jinny and Neville, then, Louis seeks a "continuity and permanence" (*TW*, 317) in life but fears he may never attain it. Rhoda also dreads the hectic, rushing life on the streets, which she says demands a "dissolution of the soul" (*TW*, 317). In the past she yielded to this dissolution while she concealed her rage. Now, she must give up this pretense. Both Louis and Rhoda have locked themselves into a solitude in which they fearfully avert their eyes away from the darkness of the immediate world and look out into a realm beyond the immediate, where hopefully the sun shines. Meanwhile, they sit caught between the two.

In the novel's eighth chapter, all six characters come together for the last time. At their meeting at Hampton Court they admit to each other their differences and the various emotional prisons into which they have locked themselves. They also admit to the emotional crutches they have leaned on. By each admission of the truth to the others, that character admits it to himself or herself, for all six represent the fragments of a single identity that the ego and self-consciousness have split. So Bernard speaks of his reluctance to order life arbitrarily through his story-telling. He sees that this crutch can never stay the perpetual flux in life's patterns. He also realizes its futility in that despite all the stories he constructs around all the scenes of life—the wave of a hand, a hesitation on a street corner, or a cigarette dropped in the gutter—he still does not know the one true story (*TW*, 327). Neville imagines that a door will open, but now no lover will enter his room. He sees all his credentials to prove his superiority as useless; they arouse no more applause than a "faint sound like that of a man clapping in an empty field to scare away rooks" (*TW*, 323). Susan, however, cannot fully admit to her own unhappiness. But the violence within, which she has strained to suppress, admits the truth for Susan. This violence comes out in her attack against Neville, whom Susan sees as her opposite. She discredits Neville: "You see one inch of flesh only . . . but nothing entire . . . But I have seen life in blocks, substantial, huge" (*TW*, 325). Susan wishes to abrade the softness in Neville with her hardness to assure herself that her life has substance. Though her words do not show any of Susan's suspicion that her life has failed, the violence behind her speech does. The crooning, protective mother is now proud of her hardness. Unlike Susan, Louis freely admits to his own limitations. He begs the others to notice his cane and waistcoat, symbols of his business success, and then acknowledges, "This is the arch and ironical manner in which I hope to distract you from my shivering, my tender, and infinitely young and unprotected soul" (*TW*, 328). Then Jinny admits to her way of protecting her own vulnerable identity; she tells the others that the torments and divisions of human existence are solved by her sexual relationships. And though, as Jinny says, her body cannot conjure up fine and pure visions, she nevertheless does not suffer from fear (*TW*, 330). Finally, Rhoda admits to her unhappiness brought on by the company of others. She sees the other characters as having individual identities, whereas "I have no face" (*TW*, 330). Therefore, she refuses to fake comfort at this dinner at Hampton Court: "I must go through the antics of the individual" (*TW*, 331).

When the six characters leave Hampton Court, they leave each other forever. But the unity experienced during this last dinner together, where differences dissolved with their in-

dividual admissions, lives on in a single character, who concludes the novel by summing up all that has passed. Bernard is
the perfect vehicle for this because he, unlike all the other
characters, derives his identity from the people and actions he
observes. So the novel's last chapter shows Bernard sitting in a
restaurant with a stranger, telling the story of his life, and, as a
consequence, telling the life stories of all six characters. For, as
Bernard says, "I am not one person; I am many people; I do
not altogether know who I am—Jinny, Susan, Neville, Rhoda,
or Louis: or how to distinguish my life from theirs" (*TW*, 368).

Bernard's monologue begins with an account of how the six
once-united characters split away from each other. So he first
comments that "in the beginning, there was the nursery" (*TW*,
342) echoing the Bible's first words—"In the beginning God
created the heaven and the earth." In the nursery no self-
consciousness separates the children. But then Bernard recalls
that when Mrs. Constable squeezed the sponge over his head,
the arrows of sensation awakened him to self-consciousness and
his difference from the others. Not only did Bernard awake to
self-consciousness but they all did. Bernard, then, marks the
dissolution of human harmony and solidity—that tragic effect
of the ego's ascension—with the time of Percival's death. When
Percival died, according to Bernard, symmetry turned to
nonsense and the world lost the justice and protection Percival
could have provided (*TW*, 345). Thus, to Bernard's mind, Percival's death represents humankind's severence from God.
Because of Adam and Eve's sin, the solidity and integrity of
Selfhood become buried under illusion. Bernard symbolizes
these heavy layers of illusion as the "leaden waste of waters."
And though he keeps watching for something to break through
these waters, "nothing, nothing, nothing broke with its fin that
leaden waste of waters" (*TW*, 346).

Bernard recalls the vision of the fin for the second time at
the conclusion of his summing up. He associates the initial appearance of this image with one day in his life when, as he says,
"a space was cleared in my mind. I saw through the thick leaves

of habit" (*TW*, 373). At that moment Bernard addressed himself as "one would speak to a companion" (*TW*, 373). The self he addressed was his apparent self, the identity he presents to others. And this self did not answer. Because Bernard has mistaken his apparent identity for his true identity, he feels deserted and destroyed by its absence. He thus asks himself, "How can I proceed now . . . without a self, weightless and visionless, through a world weightless, without illusion?" (*TW*, 375). But having experienced the loss of illusion, Bernard now realizes that it provided a specious support in his life. For, as he says, "my being seems . . . deep, tideless, immune, now that he is dead, the man I called 'Bernard,' the man who kept a book in his pocket in which he made notes" (*TW*, 379). Being freed of the heavy layers of illusion, Bernard gets a sense of his Selfhood and of that divine power that infuses his Self. He therefore imagines himself as a pursuer of eternal rather than temporal truth: "So now, taking upon me the mystery of things, I could go like a spy without leaving this place" (*TW*, 379). Bernard here uses the words of Lear who, after learning of all the illusion that has permeated his life, tells Cordelia, "And take upon's the mystery of things,/ As if were God's spies" (William Shakespeare, *King Lear*, act 5, sc. 3, lines 16-17).

Now that Bernard has discovered the Self, he inevitably must fight to protect that Self from the dissolution inflicted by the ego. The ego asserts itself by reminding Bernard of the stranger in his presence. Bernard says, "I catch your eye. I, who had been thinking myself so vast, a temple, a church, a whole universe, unconfined and capable of being everywhere on the verge of things and here too, am now nothing but what you see — an elderly man, rather heavy, grey above the ears" (*TW*, 379). Bernard's contact with the "mystery of things" makes him aware of his Self and the God within that Self. He therefore rightly conceives of himself as a place of worship and as vast as the universe. But the ego destroys this conception, as the ego destroyed the holiness of Adam and Eve's existence in Eden. So Bernard sees this ego as his enemy.

Though the ego does replace the power of the Self in Bernard, he does feel strengthened by his momentary glimpse into the Self, which has fortified him enough that he no longer fears solitude. For that matter, he repeatedly states, "Heaven be praised for solitude!" (*TW*, 381), because now he feels prepared to face it and the waiting enemy—the ego. With this feeling of being awakened, which Bernard calls "a sense of the break of day" (*TW*, 382), he prepares to fight the enemy:

> And in me too the wave rises. It swells; it arches its back. I am aware once more of a new desire, something rising beneath me like the proud horse whose rider first spurs and then pulls him back. What enemy do we now perceive advancing against us, you whom I ride now, as we stand pawing this stretch of pavement? It is death. Death is the enemy. It is death against whom I ride with my spear couched and my hair flying back like a young man's, like Percival's, when he galloped in India. I strike spurs into my horse. Against you I will fling myself, unvanquished and unyielding, O Death! (*TW*, 383)

In his fight against the psychic death that the ego threatens, Bernard identifies with Percival, who consistently represents that pure Being, undistorted by illusion, that grows from the Self. But just as his horse stumbles and Percival dies, so Bernard loses his fight. The ego triumphs because humankind willingly forfeited Selfhood.

This is the meaning of the novel's last sentence: "*The waves broke on the shore.*"[9] Out of the waters, the original state of the world, rise the waves, or individual identities, that arch their backs in a surge of power, only to fall in upon themselves and dissolve. But Woolf, with the novel's last sentence, not only implies that these individual identities dissolve but also that they return to eternity. The last line, therefore, carries not only despair, but also hope, for the sea will always sweep up the broken waves and receive them again into its awesome vastness.

*The Waves*, then, portrays the cause of the Self's elusive quality. God bestowed Selfhood on humanity when He created the world. This Selfhood, or psychic totality, lacks all self-consciousness and thus has freedom from shame or pride, both of which the ego instills. This psychic totality also appears in the androgynous form that humankind originally takes: "God created man in his own image, in the image of God created he him; male and female created he them" (Genesis 1:27).[10] But when humankind permits the ego to make demands, this original totality splits. Adam and Eve become aware of themselves as different sexes. And, as Virginia Woolf shows in *The Waves*, after the split between the sexes, comes the split between individuals and finally the psychic fragmentation of the single individual. So, in *The Years*, Woolf's next novel, the individual struggles to retrieve, if only momentarily, the original psychic wholeness out of an ego-dominated existence.

# NOTES

1. For instance, E. M. Forster says *The Waves* is Woolf's greatest book (*Virginia Woolf: A Collection of Critical Essays*, ed. Claire Sprague (Englewood Cliffs, N.J.: Prentice-Hall, Inc., 1971), p. 18). And Leonard Woolf agrees (preface to *A Writer's Diary: Being Extracts from the Diary of Virginia Woolf* (New York: Harcourt Brace Jovanovich, 1953), p. ix. Alice van Buren Kelley speaks more specifically when she says that the very serious theme of *The Waves* is of the human "journey from unconscious vision to fact to conscious vision" (*The Novels of Virginia Woolf: Fact and Vision* (Chicago: University of Chicago Press, 1971), p. 178.

Certain readers, however, withhold such praise. Dorothy M. Hoare, for one, says the novel's theme lacks emotional validity. See *Some Studies in the Modern Novel* (London: Chatto & Windus, 1953), p. 66. Likewise, W. H. Mellers claims that Woolf's statement about people lacks depth. See "Virginia Woolf: The Last Phase," *Kenyon Review* 4 (Autumn 1942): 383.

2. Virginia Woolf, *The Waves* in *Jacob's Room & The Waves* (New York: Harcourt, Brace & World, 1931), p. 180. All further quotations and references to the novel will be cited within the text as *TW*.

3. Jean Love, *Worlds in Consciousness: Mythopoetic Thought in the Novels of Virginia Woolf* (Berkeley, Calif.: University of California Press, 1970), p. 46.

4. This first manuscript for *The Waves* is presently owned by The New York Public Library and can be found in the Berg Collection.

5. See Nancy Topping Bazin, *Virginia Woolf and the Androgynous Vision* (New Brunswick, N.J.: Rutgers University Press, 1973), p. 144. Also, Robert Collins, *Virginia Woolf's Black Arrows of Sensation: The Waves* (Ilfracombe, Devon, England: Arthur H. Stockwell, 1962), p. 9. And Irma Rantavaara, "Virginia Woolf's *The Waves*," *Societas Scientiarum Fennica: Commentationes Humanarum Litterarum* (Helsinki, 1960), p. 9.

6. *The Norton Anthology of English Literature*, ed. M. H. Abrams, rev. ed. (New York: W. W. Norton & Co., 1962), 1:976.

7. Robert Collins reaches the same conclusion in his interpretation of this scene. See *Virginia Woolf's Black Arrows of Sensation*, p. 20.

8. Nancy Topping Bazin says that Percival's "attitude creates an atmosphere which draws each of the other six from a conscious to an unconscious state of mind. They then can experience unity and harmony" (*Virginia Woolf and the Androgynous Vision*, p. 150).

Ethel F. Cornwell holds a slightly different view in that she sees Percival as the complete being to which all the others aspire. See *The "Still Point" : Theme and Variations in the Writings of T. S. Eliot, Coleridge, Yeats, Henry James, Virginia Woolf, and D. H. Lawrence* (New Brunswick, N.J.: Rutgers University Press, 1962), p. 168.

James Hafley also distinguishes between Percival and the rest when he says that although the six characters reflect, Percival acts (*The Glass Roof: Virginia Woolf as Novelist* (New York: Russell & Russell, 1963), p. 107).

9. Critics explain the novel's last line in different ways. William Troy says this sentence signifies that all the characters have died. See "Virginia Woolf: The Novel of Sensibility," *Virginia Woolf: A Collection of Critical Essays*, ed. Claire Sprague (Englewood Cliffs, N.J.: Prentice Hall, Inc., 1971), p. 33.

Manly Johnson writes that Woolf implies that humankind, though broken, gathers forces to resist defeat (*Virginia Woolf*, p. 91).

And Michael Payne claims that the words suggest that "flux is an ultimate reality." See "The Eclipse of Order: The Ironic Structure of *The Waves*," *Modern Fiction Studies* 15 (Summer 1969): 210.

10. Besides the first account of creation, which implies the androgyny of the first human being, both Judaism and Christian gnosticism assert explicitly that androgyny characterizes humankind's primal state. Mircea Eliade discusses this point in *The Two and the One*, trans. J. M. Cohen (New York: Harper & Row, 1962), pp. 104-5.

# 8

## *The Years*
### Fear or Love

Virginia Woolf envisioned *The Years*, originally called *The Pargiters*, as a natural sequel to *The Waves*. In her diary she wrote, "This is the true line, I am sure, after *The Waves—The Pargiters*" (*AWD*, 184). Therefore, since Woolf depicts in *The Waves* the dissolution of humankind's original wholeness, one can expect in the present novel some continuation of this theme. What one finds in *The Years* involves the psychological fragmentation caused by the ego's supremacy: people cannot converse with each other about anything emotionally or spiritually significant, for something always interrupts such conversations; people have difficulty penetrating through their own egocentric armor, so they cannot know another's pain and thus cannot begin to help heal that pain; and because individuals are split within themselves, they cannot even heal their own pain.

Originally, Woolf intended this work to take the form of an "Essay-Novel" (*AWD*, 183), in which she would fictionally present a situation and then comment on it in her essay. The two, in other words, were to alternate. She never completed this idea but instead wrote the novel and the essay separately;

thus, one has *The Years* and *Three Guineas*.[1] Though the two works do not dovetail perfectly, an understanding of the thesis in *Three Guineas* does help explain the fictional theme in *The Years*. *Three Guineas* follows in the line of *A Room of One's Own* in that it contains Woolf's feminist concerns. The occasion for *Three Guineas* centers on three letters Woolf has received. Each asks for a donation for a particular cause: one for the prevention of war, another for the building fund of a women's college, and another for the employment of women in the professions. Woolf decides in *Three Guineas* that before she can make any donation to help prevent war, she must first give a guinea to each of the other two causes. She reasons that men create war (*TG*, 6) and only women can prevent it; therefore, unless women are helped to enter college and then the professions, "those daughters cannot possess an independent and disinterested influence with which to help . . . prevent war" (*TG*, 84). Just as in *Three Guineas* Woolf states the necessity to cultivate women's growth both educationally and professionally in order to protect the world from masculine belligerence, so in *The Years* she portrays the world's need for the Feminine power.

She does not, of course, imply that the Feminine should totally supplant the Masculine, but believes that the two need to combine. And in *The Years* she does show the union of the two, for the novel works up to a concluding vision of androgyny. So in *The Years* Woolf portrays that ideal, which she expresses in *Three Guineas*:

> If it were possible not only for each sex to ascertain what laws hold good in its own case, and to respect each other's laws; but also to share the results of those discoveries, it might be possible for each sex to develop fully and improve in quality without surrendering its special characteristics. (*TG*, 185)

Androgyny has concerned Woolf since *To the Lighthouse*, and in her eighth of nine novels, she not only sets up androgyny as an ideal, but describes the forces that threaten this ideal. The Feminine must temper the Masculine, Woolf suggests, if humankind at all hopes for social peace and psychic wholeness.

Woolf considered many possible titles: *The Pargiters, Here and Now, Music, Dawn, Sons and Daughters, Daughters and Sons, Ordinary People, The Caravan,* and finally *The Years* (*AWD*, 183-224). Before deciding on the last title, Woolf seemed most fond of the first, *The Pargiters*. Mitchell A. Leaska writes that the word *Parget* appears in the *English Dialect Dictionary* compiled by Joseph Wright, whom Woolf knew personally and respected highly. According to Wright's dictionary, *Parget* means "to plaster with cement or mortar." It also means "to whitewash."[2] Besides the word's literal definition, which reads, "glosses or smooths over," the *OED* gives a figurative definition of *pargeter*: "One who 'bedaubs' with flattery; a sycophant." With all these meanings in mind, one can safely guess at Woolf's intention in selecting her first title. Apparently she wished to capture the superficial quality of life that characterizes humankind's fallen nature. After the spiritual and psychological fall from God's grace, as depicted in *The Waves*, society and the individuals that comprise that society are left with only pieces. As seen in *The Waves*, the fall, caused by the ascension of the ego that usurps God's position in the Self, creates a self-consciousness that necessarily separates people and splits individuals. Such fragmentation divorces the individual from his unconscious realm, within which lies the potential for wholeness, and leaves him to operate strictly on the conscious level. Consequently, the individual becomes desensitized and superficial. He appears covered with impenetrable cement or mortar and tends to whitewash his own feelings and the needs of others.

Colonel Pargiter and his daughter Delia, for example, demonstrate such an act of emotional pargeting in their similar reactions to the severe illness suffered by Rose Pargiter, the colonel's wife. Both the colonel and his daughter feel only inconvenience because of the illness. Rose Pargiter's ill health burdens them, so they can only wait, as if their own lives must remain suspended until the burden of someone else's illness falls away. Another illustration of pargeting appears in the characters' repeated inability to converse with each other. Either no desire exists to share one's innermost feelings, or attempts to do so meet with some interruption. This emotional whitewashing results from humankind's worship of the ego, which introduces the fragmenting force of fear. Therefore, as North Pargiter so succinctly sums up the human predicament, "That's what separates us; fear" (*TY*, 414).

To leave the novel entitled *The Pargiters* would have, however, omitted an essential element in Woolf's theme. That title clearly conveys the postlapsarian human nature, but Woolf wanted to combine fact with vision (*AWD*, 191). Fact, the product as well as the focus of the conscious mind, may have gained supremacy from humanity's fall, but Woolf does not merely wish to depict the ravages of this fall. She also introduces the possible healing element — vision. Both, therefore, are suggested through the title *The Years*. As Woolf recorded in her diary, she intended with her title to present "*The Waves* going on simultaneously with *Night and Day*" (*AWD*, 191). In other words, she intended that the fact-oriented, socialized world of *Night and Day* unite with the vision-oriented, personal world of *The Waves*. Therefore, Woolf chose a title that takes its form from *The Waves* and its suggestion of the passage of time from *Night and Day*.

The novel's overall theme of fact and vision, or Masculine and Feminine, appears also in the dichotomy between public and private existence. Woolf speaks of this dichotomy in *Three Guineas*, where she parallels it to the distinction between masculinity and femininity. In *Three Guineas* she addresses the man who requested a donation for the prevention of war and says that ruin is inevitable "if you in the immensity of your public abstractions forget the private figure, or if we in the intensity of our private emotions forget the public world. Both houses will be ruined, the public and the private, the material and the spiritual, for they are inseparably connected" (*TG*, 142-43). This necessary connection between the two, then, shows up in the title. Since *The Years* combines *Night and Day* and *The Waves*, it unites the public and private worlds. Katharine Hilbery, in *Night and Day*, lives in the social world of tea parties and class distinctions and therefore wages her fight for Selfhood against this public world. *The Waves*, on the other hand, depicts the individual's struggle within himself, where he fights on the private plane against psychic disintegration. Thus, in *The Years* the struggle operates on both levels. The characters quest for wholeness within themselves, as in the case of Eleanor, who seeks the balance between her Masculine and Feminine components, and for peace in the social world, as seen in Nicholas Pomjalovsky whose hope for the "New World" lies in the soul's ability "to expand; to adventure; to form — new combinations" (*TY*, 296).

The needed harmony between the public and private worlds not only appears in Woolf's choice of title but also in the structural and stylistic changes she makes from *The Waves* to *The Years*. Because Woolf saw *The Years* as a natural sequel to *The Waves*, so the suggestions of the private realm made in *The Waves* find their public complements in *The Years*. For instance, the interludes in *The Waves* describe the individual's gradual emergence into self-consciousness. The movement of the sun and the shadows cast in the house symbolize private psychological dynamics. *The Years* also opens its chapters with interludes, but these passages describe London and the motion of civilization. So, in contrast to *The Waves*, the interludes in *The Years* conjure up the public world. Furthermore, the private world of the interior monologues in *The Waves* finds its complement in the public atmosphere created by the omniscient narrator of *The Years*.

In short, then, *The Years* underscores the present state of Woolf's composite personality's search for Selfhood. Through all the novels up to this point, the composite personality struggles through the impediments to Selfhood and finally reaches the knowledge that humankind's fallen nature prevents an individual from sustaining any firm hold on such psychic wholeness. Now, in *The Years*, Woolf depicts the fallen world and the individual's struggle to regain some glimpse of that lost wholeness. And as the novel progresses, Eleanor Pargiter emerges as the embodiment of Woolf's composite personality who seeks to unite the Feminine and the Masculine, the private and the public.

The novel's opening interlude contrasts markedly with the first interlude of *The Waves*. In the earlier novel the sun has not yet risen, while in *The Years* the sun sets and the moon begins to rise. Whereas the just-rising sun in *The Waves* suggests the awakening of consciousness, the setting sun in *The Years* signifies that human consciousness has gone through its full swing, attained the full height of its power, and now sinks into darkness. Not only does this first interlude contrast with the opening of *The Waves*; it also differs from the end of that novel. Whereas *The Waves* ends with "a sense of the break of day" (*TW*, 382), *The Years* opens with the onset of darkness. This darkness, which follows the full swing of consciousness, constitutes that spiritual blindness caused by humankind's fall from God's grace. And in this state, *The Years* opens.

In the first interlude, Woolf depicts this state of blindness with her picture of civilization: "Interminable processions of shoppers in the West end, of business men in the East, paraded the pavements, like caravans perpetually marching" (*TY*, 3). This rush of people, driven on by their sense of "I," or the ego, drowns out the crooning pigeons whose "lullaby," Woolf says, "was always interrupted" (*TY*, 3). This lullaby, which sounds intermittently throughout the novel as the words "Take two coos," constantly reminds the reader that the soft sounds of maternal love fall faint under the cacophony of civilization.

After the interlude and with the start of the actual narrative, Woolf continues this contrast between the privacy of maternal love and the public motion and noise of civilization. Colonel Abel Pargiter sits with his companions in the men's club speaking of some possible political appointment while his wife, Rose Pargiter, lies at home unable to regain full health, yet unable to die. Just as the pigeons' sounds always meet with interruptions, so Rose Pargiter's health at times improves, but then inevitably worsens. Woolf, in other words, begins her account of three generations in the Pargiter family by establishing a contrast between the first set of parents: she associates the father with the public life, or the Masculine domain, and the mother with the private life, or the Feminine domain. The Feminine, however, is dying. And to emphasize the absence of the Feminine from life, Woolf never shows Rose Pargiter. Instead, there is only her portrait, which gradually becomes more soiled and less a picture of the mother than a distant work of art.

Colonel Pargiter and his children evidence the effect of this increasing distance between life and the Feminine in three significant ways. They, first of all, appear to wait for something, as if full satisfaction lies just outside their grasp; they also seem to exist in a state of emotional suspension; and, third, as a consequence of the waiting and suspension, they fantasize unrealistic situations. For instance, Colonel Pargiter has no purpose in life. Whereas "everybody in the crowded street, it seemed, had some end in view . . . for him there was nothing to do" (TY, 5). So the colonel waits. He imagines that some purpose will enter his life once his wife dies. So he waits for "one of these days" (TY, 6). But while he waits he turns to his mistress, Mira, for he craves the presence of someone who "would be glad to see him" (TY, 6). In other words, the colonel, ironically, needs feminine acceptance while he awaits the death of the Feminine. Delia, one of the colonel's daughters, also awaits Rose's death, for she sees her mother as "an obstacle, a prevention, an impediment to all life" (TY, 22). Although the colonel demonstrates an ambivalence toward the Feminine, Delia despises it because the Feminine blocks her need to identify with and be accepted by the Masculine. So, while Delia waits for her mother's death, she fantasizes giving a speech before a large crowd with Charles Parnell, the Irish nationalist, by her side (*TY*, 23). When she does not fantasize about Parnell, she imagines a secret bond between herself and her father. For instance, at one point when her mother's health wanes, Delia sees herself and the colonel as feigning concern: "We're both acting, Delia thought to herself, stealing a glance at him, but he's doing it better than I am" (*TY*, 38).

Conversely, Rose — another daughter — refuses to wait. She wants to walk into town, and though Eleanor tells her to wait until their brother Martin can come along, Rose goes alone. She needs to go alone to compensate for her feeling, constantly reinforced by Eleanor's maternal protectiveness, that she is too young and therefore incapable of taking care of herself. And she fantasizes on the way into town, also to compensate for this feeling. Upon leaving the house, Rose imagines herself " 'Pargiter of Pargiter's Horse' . . . riding by night on a desperate mission to a besieged garrison . . . She had a secret message . . . to deliver to the General in person. All their lives depended upon it" (*TY*, 27). Rose's fantasy of self-importance and of being a savior comes not only from a need to compensate for her youthful innocence, but also to make up for the absence of her mother. Without the protective Feminine principle present, Rose must see herself in the Masculine role of hero. But this fantasy is rudely interrupted when Rose comes upon a man in the street who exposes his genitals to her. This incidence of masculine force in real life totally destroys her fantasy of self-importance. And the fear aroused by the incident stays with Rose, for even when she returns to the safety of her home and bed, she imagines that this man still pursues her.

While the mother lies in bed, wavering between life and death, periodically returning to consciousness long enough to ask, "Where am I?" (*TY*, 23), her family suffers from the same uncertain suspension. The colonel waits for her death so he can make his long-awaited move from London to the country (*TY*, 6); Delia waits for her death so that she can actually live; and Rose waits in fear for some relief from her pursuer. All of this suspension stems from the gradual and certain diminution of the Feminine force. As Woolf proposes in *Three Guineas*, however, an individual inevitably suffers in the absence of either the Feminine or Masculine. So Woolf now turns to Kitty Malone, the Pargiter children's cousin, to show the consequences of the absent Masculine force.

Kitty's Masculinity receives no encouragement from either her mother or her father. For that matter, she cannot even verbalize what she senses as her own problem. Woolf makes this point clear in the exchange between Kitty and her tutor, Lucy Craddock. Miss Craddock, pointing out the peculiar inconsistency between the poor written work Kitty does and what the tutor senses as her "original mind," asks why Kitty does not use her mind. When Kitty begins to respond eagerly with the words, "my mother," however, the tutor stops her immediately: "Confidences were not what Dr. Malone paid her for" (*TY*, 65). Though Miss Craddock interrupts her, Kitty reveals by inference that Mrs. Malone discourages her intellect.

Not only does Miss Craddock refuse to hear Kitty out, but so does Mrs. Malone. Or at least Kitty senses that her mother lacks the understanding to appreciate her true wishes. When Mrs. Malone does ask her daughter, "Why don't you take more interest in things here, Kitty?", all she can say is "Mama, dear—." And when the mother pressures her with the question, "But what is it you want to do?", Kitty can only repeat, "Mama, dear—" (*TY*, 80-81). She cannot explain what she wants to do for two reasons: one, her mother shows little tolerance and, two, Kitty herself does not really know what she wants. All she does know is that she cannot confide in either her tutor or her mother; and even if she turns to her father, offering to help him write his history of the college, she knows he will rebuff her interest with "Nature did not intend you to be a scholar, my dear" (*TY*, 81). With so little encouragement, naturally Kitty feels unfulfilled and psychologically stymied.

The encouragement denied Kitty in her home and with her tutor, however, comes to her when she visits her friend Nelly Robson and her family. Though terribly awkward in their home because the Robsons do not occupy as high a social rank as do the Malones, Kitty feels a freedom in their presence that she cannot enjoy elsewhere. For instance, when Mr. Robson asks Kitty about her studies with Lucy Craddock, she finds that his "bright blue eyes, gazing straight at her rather fiercely, seemed to make her say quite shortly what she meant" (*TY*, 69). Though her responses to Mr. Robson are brief, she completes her thoughts, rather than aborts them as she does with her mother and her tutor. Kitty leaves the Robsons's home, but the naturalness of their lives stays with her, forcing her to see repeatedly the emptiness of her own life.

The Robsons may lack the social graces of the Malones, but this is precisely what attracts Kitty to them. The Malones's insistence, conversely, on Kitty's proper marriage to Lord Lasswade and on the proper pastimes for a young woman of the wealthy and mannered class deprives Kitty of her own Masculinity, the part of her personality that values the intellect and would provide the psychic balance that could free Kitty from the confines of social stereotypes. Thus, the comfort Kitty experiences at the Robsons's home remains with her as a fond memory.

The formality of the Malones supplants the naturalness of the Robsons, so the regimen of the dinner bell drowns out the gentle crooning of the pigeons: "The pigeons were cooing Take two coos, Taffy. Take two coos . . But there was the dinner bell." And the bell also interrupts Kitty: "She plucked up courage and said to her father: 'Father ...' He looked up very kindly over his spectacles . . . 'I want ...' she began . . . But here a bell struck" (*TY*, 75).[3] Kitty will continue to suffer from her unexpressed wishes, for she does marry Lord Lasswade and thus forfeits psychic wholeness. Only once, and not until twenty-three years after her marriage, does she permit herself much-needed freedom from her stifling and restrictive role as Lady Lasswade. After hostessing a party, Kitty changes clothes and dashes to catch a train out of London. Alone on the train, away from guests and social responsibilities, Kitty feels the

same freedom she experienced with the Robsons: in both instances, she imagines herself a little girl who has escaped from
her nurse for an adventure on her own (*TY*, 71, 270). In both
instances, she escapes the egocentric world that assigns
stereotypic social roles to the two sexes.

The enforcement of these socialized roles results from an imbalance between the Feminine and Masculine forces. In particular, too much emphasis on social roles in public life indicates an imbalance in favor of the Masculine force. The
novel's second chapter, "1891," reflects this stress on public life
with its immediate introduction of social facts: Kitty marries
Lord Lasswade, Milly Pargiter marries Hugh Gibbs, and Morris Pargiter becomes a lawyer. Rose Pargiter, the mother and
representative of the Feminine force, dies near the end of the
first chapter, "1880," so now the Masculine asserts its
supremacy. Besides Kitty's, Milly's, and Morris's entrances into
public roles, Eleanor Pargiter's present life also suggests the
rise of Masculine priorities. Eleanor, who supplied her family
with the maternal care it needed during Rose's illness, now,
after the mother's death, feels as if she "did not exist; she was
not anybody at all" (*TY*, 95). This feeling comes while she sits
at a committee meeting. So she stays removed from the discussion until Major Porter asks for her opinion. Then she discovers
that her feeling that "she was not anybody at all" has no basis.
She thus makes a reversal; she drops her overdeveloped
feminine identity, which tries to convince her that she had
nothing to contribute in the Masculine public world of
business, and asserts her own Masculinity: "She pulled herself
together and gave him her opinion. She had an opinion — a
very definite opinion. She cleared her throat and began" (*TY*,
96). And Eleanor continues to operate out of her own
Masculine strengths when she confronts Duffus, the
superintendent at the apartment house she owns.

However, Eleanor's swing from Feminine protectiveness to
Masculine assertiveness throws her off balance; she passes the
middle ground where the two forces unite to form full per-

sonhood and enters the domain dominated by the Masculine. She therefore loses sight of the Feminine priorities on interpersonal relations: she forgets her promise to her father that she buy him a birthday gift to give to Maggie. So she races to Mrs. Lamley's shop and blurts out, "Something pretty, something to wear" (*TY*, 102), repeating her father's words when he asked Eleanor to do this errand. By using his words with Mrs. Lamley, Eleanor reveals that she has identified with her father. This identification grows so strong that she refers to Maggie as her niece rather than her cousin (*TY*, 103). In short, Eleanor swings from complete identification with her Feminine component to a similarly unhealthy absorption in her own Masculinity.

As the novel progresses, Eleanor attempts to bring back Feminine concerns into her life and thus reach some equilibrium. Colonel Pargiter, on the other hand, has no awareness of such a psychic equilibrium; his Masculine ego demands too much attention from others for him to ever consider the needs of anybody else. For example, when Delia's hero, Parnell, dies, Eleanor instantly becomes concerned for Delia's sorrow: "She must go to Delia. Delia had cared. Delia had cared passionately . . . She must go to her. This would be the end of all her dreams" (*TY*, 114). Conversely, the colonel has no concern for his daughter's sorrow. He only says sternly, "Perhaps it will bring her to her senses" (*TY*, 123). Such a reaction, compounded by the colonel's discomfort in the presence of his niece Sara, who has a physical deformity, highlights the inadequacy of the one-sided Masculine temperament. And this one-sidedness will increase, unless some healing element is introduced.

In the third chapter, "1907," Woolf suggests the nature of this healing element by presenting Sara Pargiter and the story of Antigone. While Sara's sister Maggie and her parents, Sir Digby and Eugénie, attend a dance, she stays home and reads her cousin Edward's translation of *Antigone*. What she reads parallels her present situation. The contrast between

Antigone's private determination to bury her brother and
Creon's "estimable court" (*TY*, 136) parallels the distinction
between Sara, alone in her room, and the festive dance in a
nearby house. As Sara reads, the sounds of laughter and music
intrude on her privacy. Likewise, as Antigone flings sand over
the corpse of her brother, horsemen from Creon's court approach her, seize her, bind her wrists, and bear her off to
Creon. And just as Sara lays herself out straight in her bed and
pulls the pillow over her ears, so Antigone is buried alive by
Creon, laid "straight out in a brick tomb" (*TY*, 136). These
parallels imply the contrast between public and private existence and the overpowering of the private by the public life.

To understand these two points one must turn to *Three
Guineas*, where Woolf becomes more explicit. As mentioned
earlier, Woolf proposes in *Three Guineas* that the Feminine
force operates in the private domain and the Masculine in the
public. She reinforces this idea not only in *The Years*, where
she symbolizes the private life with the character Antigone and
the public life with Creon, but also in *Three Guineas*, where
she again discusses the drama of *Antigone*. First she describes
the egocentric tyranny of Creon:

> Consider the character of Creon. There you have a most
> profound analysis by a poet, who is a psychologist in action,
> of the effect of power and wealth upon the soul. Consider
> Creon's claim to absolute rule over his subjects. That is a far
> more instructive analysis of tyranny than any our politicians
> can offer us. (*TG*, 81)

Here Woolf describes the Masculine force that threatens
destruction to the psyche and the spirit. And the power and
wealth that comprise the public life make this force destructive. Woolf then introduces the figure of Antigone as the antidote to this destruction:

> You want to know which are the unreal loyalties which we
> must despise, which the real loyalties which we must

honour? Consider Antigone's distinction between the laws and the Law. That is a far more profound statement of the duties of the individual to society than any our sociologists can offer us. (*TG*, 81-82)

Then, in a note, Woolf gives the English translation of what Antigone describes as her Law: "'Tis not my nature to join in hating, but in loving" (*TG*, 170). Thus, Woolf not only connects the Masculine attitude to the public life and the Feminine to the private, but she also attributes tyranny to the first and love to the second. And then she completes the distinction by associating Antigone with Christ: Woolf says Antigone did not want "to break the laws, but to find the law" (*TG*, 138), just as Christ says, "Think not that I am come to destroy the law, or the prophets: I am not come to destroy, but to fulfil" (Matthew 5:17). And, as Antigone espouses love over hatred, so Christ says, "A new commandment I give unto you, That ye love one another; as I have loved you, that ye also love one another" (John 13:34).

In her next chapter, "1908," Woolf describes the diminution of the Feminine force under the tyranny of the Masculine and the need to recapture that Feminine power. One sees the fading of the Feminine temperament in Woolf's description of Rose Pargiter's portrait: as Martin Pargiter stands before the portrait, he sees that "in the course of the past few years it had ceased to be his mother; it had become a work of art. But it was dirty" (*TY*, 149). The personal aspect of the Feminine principle grows more remote from the actual world and even becomes soiled as the Masculine principle takes over. Eleanor, who adopts Masculine powers in her professional life, yet retains some contact with Feminine concerns in her private life, reveals her curiosity about Christianity: "She had always wanted to know about Christianity—how it began; what it meant, originally. God is love, The kingdom of Heaven is within us, sayings like that, she thought . . . what did they mean?" (*TY*, 154). The biblical passages that intrigue her reflect all the meaning that Woolf attaches to the Feminine principle: love and the power of redemption that resides within the privacy of the individual. As the novel proceeds, Eleanor cultivates, more and more, these inchoate interests. And as her need for the Feminine principle develops greater strength, she draws closer to a vision of psychic wholeness.

The novel's next chapter, "1910," surrounds Eleanor's need for wholeness with instances of the world's loss of the Feminine component. For example, one sees an individual's refusal to listen to the pain of another. Specifically, as Sara and Maggie hear Rose approach their apartment, one reads, "'This is the worst torture . . .' Sara began, screwing her hands together and clinging to her sister, 'that life . . .' 'Don't be such an ass,' said Maggie, pushing her away, as the door opened" (*TY*, 164-65; Woolf's ellipses). Sara, the struggling Antigone figure in search of the Feminine law that lies beyond the Masculine laws, finds neither compassion nor tolerance in her sister. Frustrated in her attempts to find Feminine love in others and cultivate it in herself, Sara, at the end of the chapter, concludes, "In time to come . . . people, looking into this room — this cave, this little antre, scooped out of mud and dung, will hold their fingers to their noses . . . and say, 'Pah! They stink!' " (*TY*, 189). The words Sara chooses to describe her disgust for her surroundings echo Hamlet's remark in the grave-digging scene: "And smelt so? Pah!" (*Hamlet*, act 5, sc. 1, line 187).[4] Just as Hamlet lifts a skull, the remains of a human head, out of the dirt and finds it repulsive, so Sara envisions the room she lives in as a grave and her life as repulsive in its decay.

Yet Eleanor yearns to discover the psychic wholeness made possible only by the introduction of Femininity. At a meeting, presumably about the woman's suffrage movement, formal speeches create a counterpoint with Eleanor's private musings. As the others publicly voice their opinions, Eleanor sits quietly doodling on her blotting-paper. She first digs a hole, then draws spokes that extend out from the hole. And as more people enter the meeting room and more speakers give their opinions, Eleanor continues to draw more spokes and blacken

them. The significance of this doodle becomes more apparent
when one reads: "They were all at loggerheads. Eleanor listened.
She became more and more irritated. All it comes to is: "I'm
right and you're wrong, she thought. This bickering merely
wasted time. If we could only get at something, something
deeper, deeper, she thought, prodding her pencil on the
blotting-paper" (*TY*, 177-78). That something deeper that
Eleanor seeks appears in her doodle: the core from which all
else extends. Eleanor wishes to find what lies below all the
words of public debate and the verbal battle of egoes. She seeks
the quiet, deep, private center of life, the integrative Feminine
principle.

Despite many instances of Masculinity, the chapter "1911"
ends with another example of Eleanor's need for wholeness and
relatedness. Lying in bed, she opens a book and by chance
comes upon a passage from Dante:

> For by so many more there are who say 'ours'
> So much the more of good doth each possess. (*TY*, 212)

When her eyes fall upon these two lines, their meaning "seemed to scratch the surface of her mind." Within this short
passage lies the essential remedy to all the separation and
superficiality that plague life. Virgil speaks here of precisely
the same predicament that Woolf develops in *The Years*. As
long as one relies exclusively on the ego, which permits the
supremacy of "I" or "mine," the more impoverished becomes
the soul and the more darkness reigns. Yet, the individual who
can say "we" or "ours" enriches his soul. Eleanor, through her
search for "something deeper" and through her attraction to
Dante's words, exhibits a need to experience the expansion of
her soul. And she will eventually have this experience. But for
now the book slips onto the floor: "Darkness reigned" (*TY*,
213).

Woolf now proceeds in the chapter "1914" to show the incompatibility between the private concerns with the spirit and

the public concerns with the ego. And she does so through the figures of Martin and Sara. Martin represents the Masculine preoccupation with earthly concerns. His spirits are high solely because he plans to visit his stockbroker in the city. When in London, he catches a glimpse of Sara, who has become involved in the particular activity that keeps her own spirits high—she stands by a pillar at St. Paul's talking to herself while listening to the religious service. Because Martin's life has only an earthly orientation, he fears Sara's religious interests. As they sit in a restaurant together, Sara opens her prayer book and reads, "The father incomprehensible; the son incomprehensible." Since Martin cannot tolerate these private words and Sara's unabashed display of her religious beliefs, he immediately tells her to "hush," for he fears that "somebody's listening." Sara, finding her private world blocked, falls into the traditional role expected of her as a public individual: "In deference to him she assumed the manner of a lady lunching with a gentleman in a city restaurant" (*TY*, 229). The demand Martin places on Sara, out of his fear of spirituality, forces Sara to comply with the Masculine attitude.

A further illustration of Martin's inability to accept public exposure of privacy occurs after they leave the restaurant and pass a woman selling violets. The woman wears a hat drawn over her eyes, but Martin catches sight of her face: "She had no nose; her face was seamed with white patches; there were red rims for nostrils" (*TY*, 235). Martin finds the sight repulsive, particularly because he has seen it in Sara's presence. Being in someone else's company when faced with what the public world deems grotesque frightens Martin. He cannot bear to look at it, for "he had buried his feeling" (*TY*, 236).

Because the public world cannot tolerate an exposure of someone's private life, people end up talking to themselves. Others refuse to listen, but this does not erase the need to speak. Martin and Sara witness this loneliness as they walk through Hyde Park; three people pass them, all talking to themselves. Even the orators in the park, who wish to draw an audience to hear their speeches, end up talking to themselves, for the public world, embodied in Martin, refuses to hear them out. As they walk, Martin directs Sara to listen first to one speaker, then to another. But he never stays long enough to know the purpose of any one speech. As they walk, one voice fades away as another becomes audible, only to be replaced by a third voice. The principle that makes Martin embarrassed by Sara's religiosity, fearful of deformity, and incapable of listening, also makes him ask, "What would the world be . . . without 'I' in it?" (*TY*, 242).

Although up to this point Woolf has used two figures — Martin and Sara — to show the incompatibility between the public and private orientations, she now concludes the chapter with a picture of the same conflict concentrated in one individual. Kitty Lasswade holds a dinner party at which she tries to assume the role of a perfect hostess. For instance, when she sees a young girl, Ann, standing alone, she immediately beckons her and says, "Come and talk to us, Ann" (*TY*, 259). And when she sees Tony Ashton she decides that "he would like to talk to some smart woman — Miss Aislabie, or Margaret Marrable." But when Kitty sees both women already engaged in conversation, she concludes that she has failed: "She was not a good hostess, she reflected; this sort of hitch always happened at her parties" (*TY*, 261). She feels she has not succeeded in her public responsibilities as hostess because she could not assure the comfort, at every moment, of all her guests.

Because of Kitty's discontent with her role, she craves an escape from her public image. After the party, she quickly changes clothes, boards a train, and heads off for her country home. Out in the country, away from guests and fawning servants, she finally can achieve some peace in the privacy of her soul. Even on the train, just barely outside of London, Kitty begins to experience the freedom she needs: "All the tension went out of her body. She was alone; and the train was moving. The last lamp on the platform slid away. The last figure on the platform vanished" (*TY*, 269). Only in solitude can Kitty luxuriate in the freedom she has longed for since she met the Robsons. A most conclusive sign that Kitty needs solitude and needs to rid herself of her public life in order to become psychically at peace occurs as the train continues to rush on and Kitty sinks into the present moment:

> *Now* where are we, she said to herself. Where is the train at this moment? *Now*, she murmured, shutting her eyes, we are passing the white house on the hill; *now* we are going through the tunnel; *now* we are crossing the bridge over the river . . . A blank intervened; her thoughts became spaced; they became muddled. Past and present became jumbled together. (*TY*, 271; Woolf's ellipsis)

Kitty, in other words, can now permit herself to drop into the privacy of her own Selfhood, for she has shed the public role that demands she attend only to the social comforts of others.

Her freedom continues to grow as she approaches the country and the seclusion it offers. And having arrived at the house and breakfasted, Kitty walks out through the terrace and climbs a hill. At its top, she experiences a spiritual calm that her public life denies her. The sensation Kitty has that her "body seemed to shrink; her eyes to widen" (*TY*, 277) suggests a spiritual awakening. It implies that Kitty no longer conceives of herself as a body, an object functioning in the world, and an object scrutinized by others. Rather, she now can become the perceiver: she can look out from herself, instead of being on public display, and she can visually and spiritually absorb the natural surroundings. In nature she sees a world "uncultivated, uninhabited, existing by itself, for itself" (*TY*, 278) that supplies the perfect antidote to a public life in London among her sophisticated guests. So, high on the hill, she joyously opens all her senses to the quiet and solitude that encompass her. Kitty cannot combine her public and private existences. She must keep both distinct, because in public her private needs make her resent the pretense of the socially cultivated individuals who inhabit London. Only in private can Kitty's psyche and spirit expand into full freedom and happiness.

Woolf elaborates on this concept, that psychic freedom has a spiritual basis, in her next chapter, "1917." Sara, Nicholas, and Eleanor have dinner at Maggie and Renny's home. But a German bomb raid interrupts their evening. The sounds of war introduce death, and death destroys the calm of privacy. And the more rare the calms become, the less effect they have. For that matter, as seen in Eleanor's experience, the threat of war immunizes her against the calm: "Robbed by the presence of death of something personal, she felt—she hesitated for a word—'immune?' " (*TY*, 294). Nicholas suggests a cure for this immunity. He tells Eleanor that now they all live "screwed up into one hard little, tight little—knot," and Eleanor agrees. However, Nicholas recommends that to unknot oneself, one must permit the soul "to expand, to adventure; to form new combinations" (*TY*, 296). So here Nicholas articulates the spiritual basis of psychic wholeness.

This link between the psyche and the spirit comprises the crux of Woolf's theme, throughout her novels, of an individual's need to discover Selfhood. The link shows the necessary connection between the person's private and public worlds. If an individual, in other words, permits his soul to expand and reach out to the world and the people outside himself, then the private spirit achieves peace. It does not suffice to develop one's soul only in solitude and thus have internal accord. The soul must also extend into the social world. As a result, then, no one will need to hide his private beliefs and wishes, for he will have attained the sense that the outside world accepts his private being. Loneliness will no longer threaten the individual, and his private being will no longer frighten others. Woolf brings out this point in the scene that concludes "1917." Eleanor, after leaving the dinner party, stands outside on the street and sees an old man eating something out of a paper bag. He says to her, "Like to see what I've got for supper, lady?", and holds "out for her inspection a hunk of break on which was laid a slice of cold meat or sausage" (*TY*, 301). This scene recalls two earlier ones, the one in which a man exposes his genitals to Rose and the one in which Martin sees the deformed face of a lady selling violets. All three scenes show a person exposing something private. Yet this last scene differs from the other two in that although Martin is repulsed at the sight of the woman's face and Rose feels pursued by the strange man, Eleanor has no negative reaction to the old man. The man, rather, provides Eleanor's soul with an opportunity to expand, adventure, and form new combinations. Because she realizes her psychic peace rests in her soul's expansion, she does not run away from the old man. And significantly, because of Eleanor's growth, the privacy she sees in the stranger proves not as grotesque or as frightening as what Martin and Rose see.

Before the "Present Day" chapter, in which a vision of the harmonious coexistence of the private and public worlds forms, Woolf interjects the short chapter, "1918." in order to make two points. She devotes this chapter entirely to Crosby, who has become physically weakened in her old age and extremely lonely. This idea of loneliness, as seen in Crosby's newly acquired habit of talking to herself (*TY*, 302), comprises the first of Woolf's intentions in this chapter; she presents Crosby as a symbol of the loneliness that tortures human beings. Woolf also introduces Crosby because the novel has brought the reader to a significant height of awareness; Eleanor realizes that the cure for fear and loneliness comes from the soul's extension into the public world. Crosby is a temporary respite from the emotional intensity of this truth and is included in accordance with a suggestion Woolf makes in *Three Guineas*. In *Three Guineas* she imagines a conversation in which the question arises concerning the admission of woman to the Church or the Stock Exchange. Woolf presumes that such a suggestion would alarm the men involved in the conversation to such a degree that there would be "a strong desire either to be silent; or to change the conversation; to drag in, for example, some old family servant, called Crosby, perhaps, whose dog Rover has died . . . and so evade the issue and lower the temperature" (*TG*, 129; Woolf's ellipsis).

The novel's last chapter, "Present Day," restates the entire theme of the public life in conflict with the private life, and the individual's need to integrate the two. It exposes the inevitable psychic fragmentation that occurs when the public or Masculine attitude predominates and thus overpowers the private, or Feminine, attitude. Yet the last chapter also places a special emphasis on the need to exercise the Feminine principle, which provides an individual with the insight and strength to cultivate an androgynous being.

First, Woolf establishes the consequences of a predominantly Masculine principle. She shows, for example, the isolation of individuals unable to communicate with each other. When North, the son of Morris and Celia, visits Sara, for instance, something always interrupts their conversation. When North and Sara begin to talk of the last time they met, the voice of a singer in a nearby apartment intrudes on their conversation. Then, when North questions Sara as to why she chooses to live in a slum, the maid suddenly comes into the room (*TY*, 314). And when North finally seems to reach some depth in his conversation by referring to Nicholas's philosophy of life, the maid again bursts into the room (*TY*, 316). With all the interruptions, North can find nothing to say to Sara other than, "D'you know . . . that you've a smudge on your face?" And Sara, equally trapped in her own isolation, first touches the wrong cheek, then leaves the room without looking in the mirror (*TY*, 317).

At the same time that North visits Sara, Peggy, North's sister, dines with Eleanor. Just as North tries to prompt Sara to talk of the vision she once had that led her to see war as psychically harmful (*TY*, 322), so Peggy tries to get Eleanor to speak of her past. But both Sara and Eleanor refuse to recall the past in which they felt a greater optimism about life, for they both have lost their visions. But where Sara shows no vestige of her old beliefs in the way she behaves now—she merely shakes her head at proddings for her to continue talking—Eleanor reveals that she still retains some of her old vision by violently throwing a newspaper to the floor that carries a front-page picture of Hitler. Peggy rightly interprets this action: "It was as if she still  believed with passion — she, old Eleanor — in the things that man had destroyed" (*TY*, 331). In short, the younger generation, North and Peggy, look to the older generation, Sara and Eleanor, for some guidance out of the world devastated by war and a society fragmented by the ego.

The ego dominates at Delia's party, which all of the novel's principal characters attend and with which the novel ends. When Peggy arrives, she forces herself into a state of "comparative insensibility" (*TY*, 351) so she can leave the comfort of her solitude and enter the social world of the party. And even when she does enter some conversation, no communication of any sort, deep or superficial, takes place. She asks Uncle Patrick about the gardener who cut his toes off with a hatchet, and her near-deaf uncle responds, "Oh, the Hackets! . . . Dear old Peter Hacket — yes" (*TY*, 352). Uncle Patrick's physical deafness symbolizes the emotional deafness that prevails in the social world. The deafness not only results from the social world, but becomes a prerequisite for anyone who wishes to function in it. For this reason Peggy desensitizes herself. She finds that "to smile, to bend, to make believe you're amused when you're bored, how painful it is"; so she wishes that "the merciful powers of darkness would obliterate the external exposure of the sensitive nerve" (*TY*, 354).

The need to desensitize highlights the need for self-protection when one participates in a world ruled by the public or Masculine attitude. Yet the more one obliterates the nerves, the more one withdraws from others and enters the realm tyrannized by the ego. This is noticeable when Peggy begins a conversation with a young man she thinks she knows. Once the young man begins to talk, Peggy loses all interest in him because he cannot see beyond his own ego:

Her attention wandered. She had heard it all before. I, I, I — he went on. It was like a vulture's beak pecking, or a

vacuum cleaner sucking, or a telephone bell ringing. I, I, I.
But he couldn't help it, not with that nerve-drawn egotist's
face. . . . He could not free himself, could not detach
himself. . . . He had to expose, had to exhibit. . . .
"I'm tired," she apologised. "I've been up all night," she explained. "I'm a doctor—"
The fire went out of his face when she said, "I." That's done
it—now he'll go, she thought. He can't be "you"—he must
be "I." She smiled. For up he got and off he went. (*TY*, 361)

The ego thrives on, and therefore perpetuates, isolation.

The isolation of one individual from another assures not only
an emotional separation between people, but also a psychic
fragmentation within a single person. Eleanor now suffers from
this fragmentation. She tried to capture the pattern behind the
pieces earlier in the novel when she doodled on her blotting-
paper. Now, at Delia's party, she seeks that same integration.
Because she sees her life as comprised only of other people's
lives, her family's and her friends', she seeks the "knot" or the
"centre" that occupies the core of her own life (*TY*, 367). At
the moment she considers these things, Nicholas appears. So
she turns to him in the hope that he can carry her private year-
nings for some "gigantic pattern, momentarily perceptible" into "the open unbroken" and transform her thought into
something "whole, beautiful, entire" (*TY*, 369). Only by the
cooperation of Eleanor and Nicholas can that pattern become
lastingly perceptible. Eleanor represents the Feminine force
because of her private visions, and Nicholas represents the
Masculine force in his ability to extend the privacy of the vision
into the public world of society. And Eleanor knows that such
cooperation is necessary, for she turns to Nicholas to "finish"
her thought and "carry it out into the open unbroken."

When Sara says to Nicholas, "I will dance with you" (*TY*,
371), the novel reaches a thematic apex. The sentiment Sara
conveys here duplicates the one that Woolf, in her essay "On
Not Knowing Greek," identifies in *Emma Bovary* as signaling
the moment "which rises higher than the rest,which, though
not eloquent in itself, or violent, or made striking by beauty of

language, has the whole weight of the book behind it."[5] Similarly, the entire weight of *The Years* rests on Sara's willingness to dance with Nicholas, which demonstrates the Feminine embrace of Masculinity. Thus, as the two circle away in their dance, they embody the harmony between opposites necessary for psychic wholeness.

Such wholeness, however, cannot be sustained without love. And love cannot survive when the intellect dominates. Some of Peggy's thoughts at the party clarify this point. She says to herself, "Thinking was torment; why not give up thinking, and drift and dream? But the misery of the world, she thought, forces me to think." Because Peggy believes she cannot dispense with thought, she begins to wonder if she actually assumes a certain social pose by hanging on to her intellect; perhaps, she thinks, "I do not love my kind" (*TY*, 388). Here Peggy sets up the mutually exclusive concepts of love and intellect, concepts which characterize, respectively, the Feminine and Masculine principles. To increase an understanding of Peggy's predicament, one can turn to Woolf's short story "The Man Who Loved His Kind."[6] In this story, Prickett Ellis attends a party where he meets Miss O'Keefe. Both of these characters feel they react to other people out of love. But because they meet in the public world of the Dalloways' party, where people are "overdressed, cynical, prosperous," Miss O'Keefe assumes a haughty attitude toward Ellis and he becomes caustic. Both, in other words, use their love of their kind as a protest by which they cruelly assert their own egoes and thus deny the power of love. They become separated from each other and split within themselves.

And when the ego supplants love, a monster results, like the monster created in the game several guests play at Delia's party: "Each of them had drawn a different part of a picture. On top there was a woman's head like Queen Alexandra, with a fuzz of little curls; then a bird's neck; the body of a tiger; and stout elephant's legs dressed in child's drawers completed the picture" (*TY*, 389). The monster represents the fractured world made up of incongruous parts, each part contributed by a separate ego.

Woolf continues to reinforce her theory that love constitutes the needed element to replace separation with unity and fragmentation with wholeness. She makes this statement through North, who stands alone by the bookcase, still hurt by a comment Peggy just made to him. She said, "What's the use? . . . You'll marry. You'll have children. What'll you do then? Make money. Write little books to make money" (*TY*, 390). This remark haunts North as he stands alone, looking at the books. He picks one book out of the case and inadvertently comes upon the sentence "*nox est perpetua una dormienda*" (*TY*, 394). This line comes from Poem 5 by Catullus and with the four preceding lines, translates as

> My Lesbia, let us live and love,
> And forget the gossip of censorious old men,
> Suns may set and rise again,
> But when our own brief light descends
> We must sleep one endless night.[7]

This Latin text reminds North that only love can provide the antidote to social illness.

Shortly afterwards, North discovers why people prefer the isolation inflicted by the tyrannical ego rather than the unity and intimacy provided by love. He decides, "That's what separates us; fear" (*TY*, 414), and he confirms this conclusion after hearing Edward recite a line in Greek from *Antigone*. Though Woolf uses only the Greek in the novel, in *Three Guineas* she gives the translation: "'Tis not my nature to join in hating, but in loving." When North asks Edward to translate the line, Edward refuses, for his concern rests only with the language, not the meaning. Therefore,

> It's no go, North thought. He can't say what he wants to say; he's afraid. They're all afraid; afraid of being laughed at; afraid of giving themselves away. He's afraid too, he

> thought, looking at the young man with a fine forehead and
> a weak chin who was gesticulating, too emphatically. We're
> all afraid of each other, he thought; afraid of what? Of
> criticism; of laughter; of people who think differently . . .
> He's afraid of me because I'm a farmer (and he saw again his
> round face; high cheek bones and small brown eyes). And
> I'm afraid of him because he's clever. He looked at the big
> forehead, from which the hair was already receding. That's
> what separates us; fear, he thought. (*TY*, 414; Woolf's ellip-
> sis)

The ego, which thrives in the public world, drives people deep
into isolation because it exaggerates self-consciousness and instills a fear of disapproval. Fear, therefore, opposes love and
evokes hatred. Both the speaker in Catullus's poem and Antigone suggest that love can overcome this fear. As Fleishman
says, "For Woolf, Antigone's choice of love over aggression is
an affirmation of the power that could overcome alienation."[8]

Intimacy and wholeness, therefore, depend upon the infu-
sion of love into the cold ceremony of public life. Nicholas attempts to accomplish this with his speech, but the other guests
continually interrupt his words. He sees his speech as a
"miracle" and a "masterpiece," but no sooner does he begin
than someone interjects a comment out of fear. One never does
hear the whole speech but when Kitty Lasswade prompts him
to continue, Nicholas does explain what he wanted to say: "I
was going to drink to the human race. The human race . . .
which is now in its infancy, may it grow to maturity!" (*TY*,
426). However, he never reaches this point in his speech
because people deafen themselves to any words of hope. So
Nicholas's attempt to cut through the fear fails. And Woolf
further implies, when she introduces the unintelligible song
sung by the caretaker's children, that what words are spoken
will fall into discord and senselessness until love vanquishes
fear.

The novel ends with the only hope left to cultivate love. One
cannot impose love on others with a speech in honor of the
human race. Instead, it must come out of the privacy of one's

soul, and, from that source, emanate out into the public world. And only by freeing the privacy of one's soul can one hear what sounds of love remain in the world: " 'Listen ...' said Eleanor . . . it was the pigeons she meant; they were crooning . . . Take two coos, Taffy, take two coos . . . take . . . they were crooning" (*TY*, 433).[9] Finally, someone has heard the faint and broken sounds of the crooning pigeons, which, throughout the novel, have represented the present—though ignored— sounds of love. The sounds of love then lead Eleanor to seek the sight of wholeness achieved through love, and she finds it once she turns away from the ceremony of the party and turns toward the window from which she hears the crooning. Outside the window she sees the wholeness: a taxi stops in front of a house two doors down and she watches a young man and woman step out of it. As the man fits his key to the door, Eleanor murmurs, "There," and as the couple stand for a moment on the threshold, again Eleanor says, "There" (*TY*, 434). In this scene, she witnesses the union of the sexes and an embodiment of androgyny, which represents psychic wholeness.[10] Eleanor, in other words, first permits herself to hear the sounds of love and then to see the wholeness achieved through love.

She, therefore, can turn to her brother Morris, her hands outstretched to him, and say, "And now?" (*TY*, 435). As she watched the couple outside, Eleanor could only repeat "there," because her vision lay outside her life. But once this vision is experienced, Eleanor wishes to make it a part of her life and to enact it at the present moment. As James Hafley explains, "The private Eleanor can say that she has had her vision; the public Eleanor, recognizing that vision as a means, . . . must *behave* in the light of her response."[11] And she must act now, within the present moment that Zen Buddhists, for instance, consider the focal point of reality, in which the divine spirit moves.

# NOTES

1. Virginia Woolf, *The Years* (New York: Harcourt, Brace & World, 1937) and *Three Guineas* (New York: Harcourt, Brace & World, 1938). References to these works will be cites in the text as *TY* and *TG*, respectively.

2. Mitchell A. Leaska, "Virginia Woolf, the Pargeter: A Reading of *The Years*," *Bulletin of the New York Public Library* 80 (Winter 1977): 173.

3. The unspaced dots indicate Woolf's ellipses, and the spaced ones indicate those of this author.

4. Nancy Topping Bazin draws this connection between Sara's comment and Hamlet's remark in *Virginia Woolf and the Androgynous Vision* (New Brunswick, N.J.: Rutgers University Press, 1973), p. 176.

5. Virginia Woolf, *The Common Reader: First Series* (New York: Harcourt, Brace & World, 1925), p. 27. Joanna Lipking points out that Emma's actual words are "With you, if you will ask me." See "Looking at the Monuments: Woolf's Satiric Eye," *Bulletin of the New York Public Library* 80 (Winter 1977): 142.

6. Virginia Woolf, *A Haunted House: And Other Short Stories* (New York: Harcourt, Brace & World, 1921), pp. 112-19.

7. Knowledge of the lines' source and their translation come from Leaska's article, "Virginia Woolf, the Pargeter," p. 196.

8. Avrom Fleishman, *Virginia Woolf: A Critical Reading* (Baltimore, Md.: Johns Hopkins Press, 1975), p. 198.

9. The unspaced dots indicate Woolf's ellipses, and the spaced ones indicate those of this author.

10. In *A Room of One's Own* (New York: Harcourt, Brace & World, 1929), Woolf describes the unity of male and female by using details similar to those that appear in the final scene of *The Years*: "The sight of two people coming down the street and meeting at the corner seems to ease the mind of some strain . . . Perhaps to think, as I had been thinking these two days, of one sex as distinct from the other is an effort. It interferes with the unity of the mind. Now that effort had ceased and that unity had been restored by seeing two people come together and get into a taxi-cab" (pp. 100-101).

11. James Hafley, *The Glass Roof: Virginia Woolf as Novelist* (New York: Russell & Russell, 1963), p. 144.

# 9

## *Between the Acts*
### Love Unites


Though *The Years* ends with Eleanor Pargiter's vision of psychic wholeness, this vision remains part of only her private life. Such a vision does not suffice, for, as Virginia Woolf makes clear in *Three Guineas*, peace comes only from the harmony between the private and the public worlds (*TG*, 142-43). Nicholas Pomjalovsky's attempt to extend his private vision of wholeness into the public world fails, because the guests at Delia's party, and even Delia herself, interrupt his speech so often that he finally quits. Therefore, Woolf continues the same theme in *Between the Acts*, where she presents a further attempt to draw the two worlds together. Miss La Trobe's pageant contains her vision of wholeness, as Nicholas's speech contains his. However, although Miss La Trobe does complete her pageant, designed specifically for public view, the audience can sustain the vision, at the most, just as long as the pageant continues. Once it ends, the temporarily united audience disperses into separate identities and psychic fragments. As a consequence, the novel concludes not with wholeness permanently achieved, but with a far more advanced understanding of what steps one must take in order to attain integration.

Miss La Trobe conveys this message through her pageant, and she does so as the final representative of Virginia Woolf's composite personality in search of totality.

The novel's title carries multiple meanings. Because Woolf began writing the book in 1939, and because the book contains some references to Germany's initial steps toward the start of World War II, most critics understand the title as a reference to the time between the two world wars. The critics also agree that the title refers to the intervals between the acts in Miss La Trobe's pageant. But far more meanings, and ones that provide even greater insight into the novel's message, emerge out of the title's wording. First of all, several of the characters see themselves as emotionally trapped. For instance, Isa Oliver feels stifled by life's monotony; every year the pageant is performed and every year she hears her father-in-law, Bart Oliver, discuss with his sister, Lucy Swithin, whether it will rain or not. If it rains, they say, the servants will have to prepare the barn for the pageant; otherwise, it can be held outdoors. Such monotony fixes Isa's life so severly that she seeks an outlet. One such outlet is Rupert Haines, the gentleman farmer, whom she adores from afar. But the rigidity of Isa's life also arouses a certain violence. For example, she finds an extraordinarily strong appeal in a story from the newspaper that tells of a young girl who screams and hits a trooper about the face when he tries to rape her. Isa thinks of the girl's resistance to the assault when Bart and Lucy talk of the weather, as if their discussion violates her and as if she wishes to ferociously resist this violation.[1] But Isa does not resist and thus remains trapped in the stasis between one act and another.

Another form of emotional entrapment suffered by several of the characters appears in an inability to exercise one's true identity. Isa, for instance, hates her role as mother and loathes the domestic life (*BTA*, 19), yet she keeps up the pretense. Consequently, she hides her poetry in an account book so her husband will not suspect her true temperament (*BTA*, 50). Likewise, her husband, Giles, remains a stockbroker, the traditionally proper profession for him, though he actually yearns to farm (*BTA*, 47). Lucy Swithin, as well, constantly debates whether she should live at Kensington or at Kew but every winter does neither (*BTA*, 24-25). These and other people are trapped between two acts and emotionally die between them. Their predicament parallels a story that Bart and Isa recall, that of "the donkey who couldn't choose between hay and turnips and so starved" (*BTA*, 59).

A third meaning that arises from the title relates to the novel's structure. The book opens at nightfall and closes with the nightfall of the next day. If the day is a time for action, then the night comprises that point between acts. By opening and closing her novel with night, therefore, Woolf emphasizes the stasis of her characters. But, as becomes clear by the end of the novel, an individual has a choice between the acts: he can choose to permit this stasis to paralyze him emotionally, or he can seize the opportunity, at the time when pretenses and artificial shelters drop away, to discover and nurture his true identity.

Emotional paralysis feeds on fear, an element that Woolf introduces on the novel's first page: Mrs. Haines fears horses because, as a child in a perambulator, she was frightened by a cart-horse that brushed within an inch of her face (*BTA*, 3). This fear, which she permits to survive throughout the years, symbolizes the sort of power that robs one of any self-assurance. Fear, in general, makes one see his own identity as diminished and the identities of others enlarged in comparison. Therefore, Mrs. Haines glares at Isa, who she knows loves her husband, Rupert Haines, and thinks, "Please, Mrs. Giles Oliver, do me the kindness to recognize my existence" (*BTA*, 6).

Whereas emotional paralysis feeds on fear, emotional growth comes from love. Woolf makes this statement on the novel's last page: Giles and Isa, alone for the first time all day, have the choice to either widen the emotional gap that separates them or to overcome that separation. Enmity will on-

ly broaden the gap but love—which resides beyond enmity—will close it, for, "From that embrace another life might
be born" (*BTA*, 219). In other words, Woolf suggests as she
does in *The Years*, that an individual must choose between
fear, which leads only to hatred, and love, which promises
emotional growth and wholeness.

Another meaning carried by the title has some relation to
the preceding ones. Throughout the novel, Woolf sets up pairs
of opposites. The inability to see any pattern between the opposites results from and even aggravates fear. Conversely, a
sense of the unity that lies behind the opposites results from as
well as cultivates love. One thus can see the opposites as acts.
Each of the major characters except Miss La Trobe either
stands between these opposites, or, in conjunction with
another character, comprises the opposites. An illustration of
the latter shows up in the contrast between Bart and Lucy.
Repeatedly identified with the cross that hangs from her neck,
Lucy represents religious faith, while Bart constantly approaches life through reason. Bart frequently attacks her faith
with his barbed reason. For instance, when Lucy sees the
weather as unsettled, she says, "We can only pray." But her
brother immediately retorts, "And provide umbrellas." This
insensitive comment "struck her faith" (*BTA*, 23). And Bart
strikes another blow at her faith soon thereafter when Lucy
asks him the origin of the phrase "touch wood": he unfeelingly
responds, "Superstition" (*BTA*, 25). In all, as the narrator
says, "What she saw he didn't; what he saw she didn't" (*BTA*,
26), for "she belonged to the unifiers; he to the separatists"
(*BTA*, 118).

The opposites set up by the personalities of Bart and Lucy
comprise those poles between which other characters are
caught. Primarily, three sets of opposites operate in the novel:
that between humankind's civilized disguise and the savagery it
covers, that between the human world and nature, and that
between love and hate. And when one delves into these sets of
opposites, a most vital pattern emerges. In each category, not

only does Woolf show certain characters unable to reconcile the opposites, but she also presents some hope for the harmony between these opposites in the figures of Lucy Swithin and Miss La Trobe. Lucy privately senses the unity in all three sets of opposites, while Miss La Trobe, through her pageant, publicly portrays her vision of this unity.

Bart and his son Giles display most prominently the unreconciled conflict between humankind's civilized disguise and its deeply rooted savage nature. Bart, despite his egregious emphasis on the use of reason, exhibits a most savage quality. His need to escape the pretense of reason appears in frequent drowsiness. Halfway through the novel, he falls asleep just as the audience assembles for the pageant's opening (*BTA*, 65-66) in order to escape from the vision Miss La Trobe prepares to present. But even earlier, Bart falls asleep and dreams of his youth in India. He sees himself as a young helmeted man standing in the midst of hills, while "in the sand a hoop of ribs; a bullock maggot-eaten in the sun; and in the shadow of the rock, savages; and in his hand a gun" (*BTA*, 17). Because Bart cannot reconcile his rational and savage natures, his repressed one comes out in a dream life. Sometimes, however, it also reveals itself in some peculiar behavior in waking life. For example, hiding behind a tree, Bart is watching his grandson George, who digs in the grass. Suddenly Bart springs on George, roaring like an animal and wearing a newspaper on his head cocked into a snout. When George sees this "terrible peaked eyeless monster moving on legs, brandishing arms" (*BTA*, 12), he leaps and topples in fright. The similarity between Bart's dream and this heartless act reveals Bart's need to identify with the fearful savages hidden in the shadow of the rock. Because Bart represses his savagery under the weight of civilized rationality, both extremes become exaggerated. He is caught between the two. Reconciled, however, neither one would take on such an extreme and offensive quality.

Giles also appears caught between his civilized role and hidden savagery. When he arrives at Pointz Hall, the Oliver home, he sees a silver-plated car belonging to Mrs. Manresa, a guest of the Olivers. The sight of the car "touched his training" and the "ghost of convention rose to the surface." Thus, he changes his clothing in order to appear, as civilization demands for this occasion, as "a cricketer, in flannels, wearing a blue coat with brass buttons" (*BTA*, 46). Nevertheless, Giles is angry, for his civilized dress stands in stark contrast to the world's reality: "He was enraged. Had he not read, in the morning paper, in the train, that sixteen men had been shot, others prisoned, just over there, across the gulf, in the flat land which divided them from the continent?" (*BTA*, 46). Giles objects to but participates in humankind's pretense of civilization, for it denies the innate bestiality of human life. Civilized people's attempt to insulate themselves from bestiality enrages Giles yet he cannot reconcile the two. Rather, he is caught between them and therefore remains a stockbroker, though he wishes far more to farm.

Giles's entrapment between the two forces prevents him from acting assertively in either direction until the first interval between the acts in the pageant. At this point, more deeply submerged than ever into the abyss between acts, Giles's rage erupts when he sees a symbol for his own stasis: "there, couched in the grass, curled in an olive green ring, was a snake. Dead? No, choked with a toad in its mouth. The snake was unable to swallow; the toad was unable to die" (*BTA*, 99). Giles sees here his own predicament, and this confrontation with the truth finally forces him to act: "Raising his foot, he stamped on them. The mass crushed and slithered. The white canvas of his tennis shoes was bloodstained and sticky. But it was action. Action relieved him" (*BTA*, 99). Just as his father's repression of his own savagery leads him to act in a bestial way when he springs on George, so Giles's repression leads him to a similar act. But act he does since it is the only relief from emotional stagnation.

The second set of opposites that imprisons the novel's characters involves the human world and nature. Civilization's avoidance of nature implies its self-aggrandizement over its own origin. Because humankind has the power of reason, or so the civilized world figures, it can ignore and even dominate the elements in nature. The Oliver family, for example, bought Pointz Hall in defiance of nature: "It was a pity that the man who had built Pointz Hall had pitched the house in a hollow, when beyond the flower garden and the vegetables there was this stretch of high ground. Nature had provided a site for a house; man had built his house in a hollow" (*BTA*, 10). And when Lucy asks Bart why they built the house in the hollow, he says, "Obviously to escape from nature" (*BTA*, 8). The attempt to escape from nature amounts to a denial of human origins and a disregard for the flawless pattern of all life. In such a situation, death becomes the only certainty, and humanity must conclude, as Isa Oliver and William Dodge do, that "the future shadowed their present, like the sun coming through the many-veined transparent vine leaf; a criss-cross of lines making no pattern" (*BTA*, 114).

Another illustration of the grave results that come from humankind's disrespect for nature occurs when Bart springs on his grandson. Just before Bart comes out from behind the tree, George digs with his hands into the ground. The more he tears through the membranes of the earth, the more light replaces darkness and the more integration he sees among those things that appear distinct above the earth: "All that inner darkness became a hall . . . of yellow light. And the tree was beyond the flower; the grass, the flower and the tree were entire" (*BTA*, 11). But just then Bart jumps out and frightens George, who leaps in fear away from his discovery of nature's roots. Bart, of course, has no concern for George's activity; George merely provides Bart with an opportunity to act out his repressed fascination with savagery. So when George's fear destroys the game, Bart further demonstrates his disregard for nature by turning to Sohrab, the Afghan hound, and bawling, "Heel, you brute!" (*BTA*, 12). In short, Bart not only remains insensitive to George's wish to become involved with nature, but also asserts his dominion over an object of nature that falls victim to the cruel assertion of the human will.

The third set of opposites involves love and hate. Woolf establishes this conflict at the novel's very outset when she shows Mrs. Haines driven to hatred because she feels excluded from love. Mrs. Haines senses the love that encircles her husband and Isa, so she vehemently decides to destroy it, "as a thrush pecks the wings off a butterfly" (*BTA*, 6).

But the most extended treatment of love and hate appears in Isa's personality, for she sees no other emotion in life than these two: "Isabella felt prisoned. Through the bars of the prison, through the sleep haze that deflected them, blunt arrows bruised her; of love, then of hate" (*BTA*, 66). And as she views the pageant Isa concludes, "The plot was only there to beget emotion. There were only two emotions: love; and hate" (*BTA*, 90). Because Isa sees no alternative to these two emotions, she cannot fully exercise either one of them. Feeling imprisoned, she cannot overtly hate the monotony of life she experiences with the Olivers, nor can she strike out at her husband, to whom she feels no other allegiance than that of wife to husband. So she assuages her discomfort by secretly loving Rupert Haines, though she knows that she can never expose this love. Giles, likewise, cannot love his wife; rather, he feels a strong attraction to Mrs. Manresa. Both Giles and Isa pursue people who openly display personality traits that the other suppresses. In other words, Giles holds back his desire to farm, while Isa loves a gentleman farmer. And Isa hides her sensitivity to life expressed through her poetry, while Giles pursues Mrs. Manresa, the most sensuous member of the audience. One can assume, therefore, that if both Giles and Isa freed their true spirits, they could love each other. But until that time, both will remain imprisoned between the act of love and the act of hate, never to know the peace that arises from the reconciliation of these two acts.

Because many of the characters find themselves caught between actions, they fall into a deadly stasis. This stasis does not kill the emotions, however; it merely entraps and distorts them. Because the emotions still assert themselves, often the characters project onto others the disapproval they hold against themselves. For example, the audience laughs at the village idiot who performs a part in the pageant (*BTA*, 86). Because the audience fears that a certain idiotic quality characterizes their own civilized behavior, they turn on Albert, the village idiot, who provides a safe object for their projections. This is most evident when the audience reveals its discomfort in Albert's presence, as, for instance, when Mrs. Elmhurst fears Albert will do something dreadful and thus feels relieved once he leaves the stage. Another illustration of projection occurs in Giles's reaction to William Dodge: "He looked, once, at William. He knew not his name; but what his left hand was doing. It was a bit of luck—that he could despise him, not himself" (*BTA*, 111). Apparently, Giles sees part of himself in William. All one knows of William is that he fears expressing his true beliefs, as when he hears Mrs. Manresa incorrectly attribute a certain painting to Sir Joshua but says nothing (*BTA*, 50). One also knows that Giles sees William as "a toady; a lickspittle; not a downright plain man of his senses; but a teaser and twitcher; a fingerer of sensation; picking and choosing; dillying and dallying; not a man to have straightforward love for a woman" (*BTA*, 60). So it seems that Giles sees himself in these terms and thus hates William through projection.

The only cure for the entrapment between acts, as experienced by such characters as Bart, Giles, and Isa, involves the discovery that opposites do not necessarily have to conflict; they may also complement each other and thus become a part of some greater pattern. Lucy Swithin privately senses this fact, while Miss La Trobe publicly portrays it in her pageant.

Lucy exhibits a certain awareness that civilization does not necessarily have to conflict with savagery, nor humankind with nature. Mrs. Swithin, as Woolf most often calls her, recognizes the reconciliation between opposites mostly through her reading of the Outline of History. In this book, her favorite reading, she learns of the time that nature reigned, instead of humankind. For hours she thinks of

> rhododendron forests in Piccadilly; when the entire conti-
> nent, not then, she understood, divided by a channel, was
> all one; populated, she understood, by elephant-bodied,
> seal-necked, heaving, surging, slowly writhing, and, she
> supposed, barking monsters; the iguanodon, the mammoth,
> and the mastodon; from whom presumably, she thought,
> jerking the window open, we descend. (*BTA*, 8-9)

Mrs. Swithin's thoughts about the original primitive nature of the land humankind now inhabits help her understand the connection between civilization and its roots. She does not see them as opposites; rather, civilization is a descent from the primeval world.

Furthermore, by the end of the novel, Mrs. Swithin also learns that no distinction exists between love and hate. She has always seen herself as an opposite to her brother, Bart: "He would carry the torch of reason till it went out in the darkness of the cave. For herself, every morning, kneeling, she protected her vision" (*BTA*, 205-6). Nevertheless, Mrs. Swithin does recognize that the disruptive force represented by her brother also operates within her: "It was always 'my brother . . . my brother' who rose from the depths of her lily pool" (*BTA*, 206; Woolf's ellipsis). The lily pool symbolizes, among other things, the human psyche. So, Mrs. Swithin's reference to her brother rising from the depths of her lily pool suggests that divisiveness and insensitivity have the same roots as love and faith. Because opposites do not entrap Mrs. Swithin, she therefore can relate to William Dodge with love, rather than with Giles's hatred, and thus make William feel healed:

> He saw her eyes only. And he wished to kneel before her, to
> kiss her hand, and to say: 'At school they held me under a
> bucket of dirty water, Mrs. Swithin; when I looked up, the
> world was dirty, Mrs. Swithin; so I married; but my child's

not my child, Mrs. Swithin. I'm a half-man, Mrs. Swithin; a flickering, mind-divided little snake in the grass, Mrs. Swithin; as Giles saw; but you've healed me.' (*BTA*, 73).

Lucy Swithin's healing power comes out of her awareness that life has unity and a pattern. But this awareness remains a part of her private world. Not until Miss La Trobe's pageant does Mrs. Swithin witness her vision portrayed through a public medium.

The fact that Mrs. Swithin and Miss La Trobe share the same vision of wholeness becomes evident through Woolf's use of the symbol of the lily pond. Woolf describes the pond: "Water, for hundreds of years, had silted down into the hollow, and lay there four or five feet deep over a black cushion of mud. Under the thick plate of green water, glazed in their self-centered world, fish swam" (*BTA*, 43). The significance of the pond operates on two primary levels: the individual and the societal.[2] The history of the pond suggests the first level of significance: "It was in that deep centre, in that black heart, that the lady had drowned herself . . . drowned herself for love" (*BTA*, 44). This tragic act symbolizes the emotionally static state of several of the characters, particularly Isa who in moments of desperation over unfulfilled love, wishes that waters should cover her over (*BTA*, 103-4). The pond's societal level of significance comes out when Mrs. Swithin gazes at the lily pool and sees "ourselves" in the fish that slide on, "in and out between the stalks, silver; pink; gold; splashes; streaked; pied." In these fish she has a vision of the "beauty, power, and glory in ourselves" (*BTA*, 205). This insight comes to Mrs. Swithin after she witnesses her private vision acted out on the stage through Miss La Trobe's pageant. In the various scenes of the pageant, Miss La Trobe exposes to the audience her vision of the roots that lie beneath the deceptive vanity of civilized people. And she carries out this exposé as a representative of the unity that once held all humankind together. For she comes from the Channel Islands, the remains of the land that once joined England to the continent back in the time that

Mrs. Swithin reads about in her Outline of History.

The pageant depicts two very vital messages about human existence: first, it shows the evolution of humankind from a life based on religious devotion to one based on reason and authority; second, it shows that, despite the many apparent changes in human existence, one element remains constant — love. Miss La Trobe, paradoxically, uses illusion to reveal the illusion that characterizes the existence of the audience, an existence fragmented by the divisive force of the ego. And, in so doing, Miss La Trobe expresses precisely what Woolf wished to accomplish in her novel: "Repeating the same story: singling out this and then that, until the central idea is stated" (AWD, 276). This central idea says that love operates at the core of any and all actions, regardless of how disparate they may appear. Only by discovering this core of love can humankind recognize the pattern behind all existence and reconcile the torturous opposites in life. In short, Woolf sees love as the essential and indispensable core of life, so she places it at the center of the pageant.

To assist the audience in discovering this core, Miss La Trobe counters the seemingly severe changes in scenes by retaining certain unifying elements. She, for instance, wants her pageant performed outdoors, in nature: " 'That's the place for a pageant, Mr. Oliver!' she had exclaimed. 'Winding in and out between the trees . . . There the stage; here the audience; and down there among the bushes a perfect dressing-room for the actors' " (BTA, 57). She finds nature a perfect setting for her pageant because it constantly reminds her audience that nature and civilization do not oppose but rather complement each other. She also provides a few intervals between the acts to satisfy the audience's desire for some rest but she plays music throughout the intervals in order to sustain what unity among people the pageant has achieved: "Music makes us see the hidden, join the broken" (BTA, 120). In sum, Miss La Trobe discerns life's internal unity and wishes to convey it to her audience.

Miss La Trobe depicts the evolution of humankind by having the performers enact scenes typical of successive centuries. She begins with the Middle Ages, then goes into the Elizabethan Age, the Age of Reason, the Victorian Period, then the present day. With each new age, a certain pattern develops: religious devotion disappears with the forceful advent of rationality, which leads into a period of austere authority, all of which culminates in the isolation of individuals and psychic fragmentation within themselves.[3]

In the pageant's scene of Chaucer's time, the figure of England has "been maying, nutting. She has flowers in her hair" (*BTA*, 80). In other words, humankind, at this point in its evolution, enjoys a childlike joy in nature. The second important element in thise scene appears in the "Canterbury pilgrims," believers on their way to the shrine of the Saint (*BTA*, 80). So the pageant attributes to medieval existence a strong harmony with nature and a devotion to God. But with the Elizabethan Age humankind drops nature and religion and adopts instead material wealth. The figure of Queen Elizabeth identifies these priorities when she refers to the seafaring men who have arrived home to the Isles:

*Hawkins, Frobisher, Drake,*
*Tumbling their oranges, ingots of silver,*
*Cargoes of diamonds, ducats of gold,*
*Down on the jetty.* (*BTA*, 84)

Once humankind values material gain over spiritual gain, it ascribes more importance to itself than to God; reason replaces faith. Therefore, Miss La Trobe depicts the next age as dominated by Reason, who says, "*At my behest, the armed warrior lays his shield aside; the heathen leaves the Altar steaming with unholy sacrifice . . . No longer fears the unwary wanderer the poisoned snake*" (*BTA*, 123). In other words, because humankind has placed reason ahead of God, it has trusted to be as God; the tempting serpent and the fall from

God's grace that it instigated, therefore, no longer need be feared. With such enormous power, civilization assumes absolute authority. So the figure of a constable, outfitted with helmet and truncheon, introduces the nineteenth century (*BTA*, 160). And he pronounces that for the sake of some people's prosperity others must toil and die: "*Let'em sweat at the mines; cough at the looms; rightly endure their lot. That's the price of Empire*" (*BTA*, 163). So the unity with nature and God, known in the Middle Ages, disintegrates, as the human will and reason split humanity into the comfortable rich and the suffering poor.

This split then multiplies, leaving the inhabitants of the present world as merely "*orts, scraps and fragments*" (*BTA*, 188). Miss La Trobe portrays this state of modern existence not by having performers act the parts of "ourselves," as she does with the figures of England, Elizabeth, Reason, and the constable. Rather, she shows her audience to themselves:

> Out they come, from the bushes—the riff-raff. Children? Imps—elves—demons. Holding what? Tin cans? Bedroom candlesticks? Old jars? My dear, that's the cheval glass from the Rectory! And the mirror—that I lent her. My mother's. Cracked. What's the notion? Anything that's bright enough to reflect, presumably, ourselves? (*BTA*, 183)

The audience finds this act cruel, for the audience sees itself before it has time to assume some contrived pose (*BTA*, 184). And up to this point, the audience could remain distinct from the action on the stage; but now it becomes part of that action.

Although Miss La Trobe's portrayal of humankind's descent from unity to fragmentation has enormous significance, she includes far more in her pageant. She presents individual plays within separate scenes of the pageant, all of which contain at their center a core of love, despite their varying plots. During the scene of the Elizabethan Age, Miss La Trobe introduces a play based on a confusion between reality and appearance. The play involves a "false Duke; and a Princess disguised as a boy," who loves Ferdinando, the lost heir, "who had been put into a basket as a baby by an aged crone" (*BTA*, 88). All this confusion in identities suggests the disharmony that results from humankind's relinquishment of its unity with nature and God. This play, however, contains love at its center. The aged crone, after many years, recognizes Ferdinando by a mole on his cheek, and at the point of this recognition, Carinthia, the Duke's daughter, approaches. With the appearance of "Love embodied," Ferdinando sweeps his hat off and greets the woman with, "Hail, sweet Carinthia!" and she responds, "*My love! My lord!*" (*BTA*, 91). Thus, despite all the confusion at the play's opening, recognition of true identities follows, and brings with it fulfilled love.

In the next scene, that of the Age of Reason, Miss La Trobe interjects another play, which reveals the hypocrisy inevitable in a world geared toward material gain and the dominance of reason. Miss La Trobe calls this play *Where there's a Will there's a Way*. The plot involves Lady Harpy Harraden, who loves Sir Spaniel Lilyliver. But Sir Spaniel loves Flavinda, Lady Harpy's niece. And Flavinda and Valentine love each other. Lady Harpy, believing Sir Spaniel loves her, suggests that he marry Flavinda, but share the inheritance with her. Clearly, the play so far depicts the selfish use of rational machinations. But the plot has even deeper levels of hypocrisy. Sir Spaniel agrees to the plan because it will give him Flavinda. Meanwhile, however, he feigns affection for Lady Harpy. But, just as in the previous play, a recognition scene occurs and love ensues. Flavida and Valentine unite and the selfish machinations of Sir Spaniel and Lady Harpy are revealed: "Sir Spaniel Lilyliver has contracted an engagement with Flavinda . . . when Valentine . . . steps forward; claims Flavinda as his bride; reveals the plot to rob her of her inheritance; and, during the confusion that ensues, the lovers fly together, leaving Lady Harpy and Sir Spaniel alone together" (*BTA*, 141). With Flavinda gone, Sir Spaniel no longer has reason to pretend he loves Lady Harpy. So he rejects her proposal of marriage, and she sees his true hypocrisy: *"Off comes the sheep's skin, out creeps the serpent"* (*BTA*, 147). She compares his deceit to that of Jacob in the Bible, who appears before his blind father in a goat's skin to impersonate his hairy brother Esau and, thus, gain the father's blessing (Genesis 27: 1-19). Lady Harpy, of course, never admits to her own hypocrisy, for humankind, in the Age of Reason, continues to worship the mind over God. Nevertheless, this play, like the preceding one, contains the embrace of lovers at its very center.

The pageant concludes with a disembodied voice that emanates from the bushes. This voice sums up the pageant's message and underscores the point that, despite apparent differences in the ages, one thing remains constant — humankind's potential for love:

> *there's something to be said: for our kindness to the cat; note too in today's paper "Dearly loved by his wife"; and the impulse which leads us — mark you, when no one's looking — to the window at midnight to smell the bean. Or the resolute refusal of some pimpled dirty little scrub in sandals to sell his soul. There is such a thing — you can't deny it. What? You can't descry it? All you can see of yourselves is scraps, orts and fragments? Well then listen to the gramophone affirming.* (*BTA*, 188)

The voice says that though the audience sees itself as *"scraps, orts and fragments,"* when confronted with the mirrors and pieces of glass in the pageant's last scene, this is only a superficial quality. Beneath it all exists that unifying force of love or faith, which Miss La Trobe tries to sustain by her use of music.

Although Miss La Trobe portrays her vision of the unity that underlies the pieces, no one in the audience, except for Mrs. Swithin, can retain any hold on this vision. Whenever Miss La Trobe permits an interval between the acts, the members of the audience disperse. During the first interval, Isa says, "The wave has broken. Left us stranded, high and dry. Single, separate on the shingle." And while William Dodge cannot decide whether he should go to tea with the others or stay where he sits, Giles "remained like a stake" as the "flowing company" sweeps past him (*BTA*, 96). And during the interval just prior to the scene of "Present Day. Ourselves," the guests "were neither one thing nor the other; neither Victorians nor themselves. They were suspended, without being, in limbo" (*BTA*, 178), for the music had stopped. And when the pageant finally ends, the audience disperses into separate entities again; only this time, no music can reunite them. They go off in different groups, discussing the mechanics of the pageant and doubting the validity of its message (*BTA*, 198-200).

Even Mrs. Manresa, the one whom the others see as untouched by the separation and fragmentation that comes from unresolved conflicts, does not absorb Miss La Trobe's vision of unity. The narrator calls her "a wild child of nature" (*BTA*, 41), for she participates in the sensuousness of life and seems not to elevate human reason over anything else the world offers. Civilization, of course, finds her vulgar in her gestures, oversexed and overdressed; yet with the breach of decorum that she causes, "the fresh air . . . blew in" and the others follow her "like leaping dolphins in the wake of an ice-breaking vessel" (*BTA*, 41). Yet, Mrs. Manresa's sensuousness and sensuality are her facade. One sees this initially in her reaction to other women: "always when she spoke to women, she veiled her eyes, for they, being conspirators, saw through it." Woolf immediately explains that "it" means "her claim to be a wild child of nature" (*BTA*, 41). Because she claims this epithet, Mrs. Manresa attempts convincingly to extend this sort of personality to others. And carefully she tries to remain undetected by other women while she threads the air around her with sensation (*BTA*, 56).

Mrs. Manresa sustains this deception when she repeatedly pulls out her mirror and looks at her reflection. For instance, during the interval between the first two scenes of *Where there's a Will there's a Way*, "Mrs. Manresa had out her mirror and lipstick and attended to her lips and nose" (*BTA*, 133).

Then, during the interval between the Victorian Age and "Present Day. Ourselves," "Mrs. Manresa had out her mirror and attended to her face" (*BTA*, 178). And finally, in the pageant's last scene, while the rest of the audience shades itself from the reflections in the many forms of mirrors held up by the children, "Mrs. Manresa . . . had out her mirror; powdered her nose; and moved one curl, disturbed by the breeze, to its place" (*BTA*, 186). Bart finds this action admirable: "Alone she preserved unashamed her identity, and faced without blinking herself." Yet he cannot distinguish between Mrs. Manresa facing her own identity or her mere vanity.

Woolf makes clear that Mrs. Manresa, repeatedly raising her mirror to put on makeup, operates out of vanity. Woolf does so by not only having Bart, another victim of pride, admire her, but also through the words of the disembodied voice:

> *Don't hide among rags. Or let our cloth protect us. Or for the matter of that book learning; or skilful practice on pianos; or laying on of paint. Or presume there's innocency in childhood. Consider the sheep. Or faith in love. Consider the dogs. Or virtue in those that have grown white hairs. Consider the gun slayers, bomb droppers here and there. They do openly what we do slyly.* (*BTA*, 187)

This voice expresses what Mrs. Manresa cannot understand: despite the superficial differences caused by wealth, education, beauty, or talent, ultimately *"we're all the same."* Miss La Trobe's pageant portrays this message and Reverend Streatfield explicitly states it: "We act different parts; but are the same" (*BTA*, 192).

Of all the people in the audience, Mrs. Swithin gains the most from the pageant. She profits because she comes to the pageant with the same vision that the performance displays. Mrs. Swithin feels that Miss La Trobe "twitched the invisible strings" (*BTA*, 153) by showing that the same vibrations run throughout the centuries and varying cultures. Mrs. Swithin, therefore, can later comment to Isa, "The Victorians, . . . I don't believe . . . that there ever were such people. Only you and me and William dressed differently" (*BTA*, 174-75).

Having gained confirmation of her own private beliefs, Mrs. Swithin wishes to thank Miss La Trobe at the conclusion of the pageant. Typically, Bart disapproves of such expressed gratitude: "She don't want our thanks, Lucy" (*BTA*, 203). He disapproves of his sister's inspired wish to tell Miss La Trobe that the pageant has helped her see, but he admires Mrs. Manresa who uses her mirror and makeup to blind herself from the pageant's philosophy. Because Mrs. Swithin does not thank Miss La Trobe at the end, and because the audience disperses into fragments totally untouched by the pageant's vision of wholeness, Miss La Trobe's feeling of triumphant gift-giving does not last. She, therefore, immediately plans her next pageant in the hope that she finally can sustain the glory of the gift she offers to her audiences.

With the pageant concluded, Miss La Trobe gone, and the guests dispersed to their various homes, the novel returns its focus to the family at Pointz Hall. The pageant has not markedly altered their behavior: Giles changes his clothes again in accordance with society's conventions, Isa still cannot reconcile her emotional conflict — "Love and hate — how they tore her asunder!" (*BTA*, 215) — and Mrs. Swithin returns to her Outline of History (*BTA*, 217). But something new does happen — for the first time that day, Giles and Isa are alone. If any change will occur, says the narrator, only solitude can elicit it: "Alone, enmity was bared; also love. Before they slept, they must fight; after they had fought, they would embrace. From that embrace another life might be born. But first they must fight" (*BTA*, 219). Giles and Isa each suffer from multiple conflicts: Giles finds Mrs. Manresa far more attractive than Isa, and he would prefer to farm than sell stocks; similarly, Isa loves Rupert Haines but not her husband, and she camouflages her poetry with an account book. To find peace from these conflicts they must first bare the enmity they harbor for each other and for their own unfulfilled natures. Only then can they love each other and with their embrace destroy separation and experience their creative powers.

The novel ends with Isa and Giles about to battle through their enmity so as to reach their love. Woolf imagistically portrays the psychological state required to reach the much-needed peace: "The house had lost its shelter. It was night before roads were made, or houses. It was the night that dwellers in caves had watched from some high place among rocks" (*BTA*, 219). The night with which the novel ends represents that darkness that characterizes humankind's natural and primitive condition, still unviolated by civilization. Into this state Isa and Giles, or anyone else who lives in the fragmented and conflicted present day, must enter to recapture that unity and peace that human reason and will have devastated. But lest the readers of *Between the Acts* proudly distinguish themselves from the predicament presented in the novel, as Miss La Trobe's audience tries to separate itself from the action in the pageant, Woolf concludes her novel with the words, "Then the curtain rose. They spoke." The novel has been a pageant about us and for our viewing.

In general, one can see *Between the Acts* as Woolf's summary of all her other novels. Whereas the pageant in this work traces the ego's usurpation of love, all of Woolf's other novels show a composite personality struggling against the ego's priorities — the imposition of socialized roles on both men and women, the insistence on conformity, the dependence upon the intellect, and the ascension and supremacy of the "I." Furthermore, *Between the Acts* shows that in the absence of love comes fear, and out of fear people pull away from each other and psychically disintegrate. Virginia Woolf suggests throughout her novels that in order to draw together and make whole all the *"orts, scraps and fragments"* of present day humanity, love must depose the ego and eliminate the fear that the ego instills in people. Therefore, Isa and Giles must permit their egoes to battle each other in pure enmity until the egoes destroy themselves and let rise in their place the power of love.

And Morris Pargiter must receive the love offered to him by his sister Eleanor. In order for this love to be offered and returned, Bernard must discover the fin that breaks through the waste of waters that symbolize life's illusions. And illusion cannot be broken unless Orlando can find that central commanding Self that occupies the core of her psychic existence. This Self contains the perfect harmony between opposites, as seen in Lily Briscoe's finished painting. Clarissa Dalloway imagines this wholeness in Septimus Warren Smith's plunge to that center, which has always mystically evaded her. And Jacob Flanders finds it on top of the Acropolis, where he is free from his mother's and society's demands. This center, or Selfhood, as Katharine Hilbery discovers, becomes round, whole, and entire only when she can pursue it in solitude. For this same reason, Rachel Vinrace leaves her company so she can triumph in the wind. In short, only love can vanquish the fear that separates individuals. And only the Self, the psychic core in which opposites coalesce and the divine spirit moves, can generate the healing power of love.

## NOTES

1. Virginia Woolf, *Between the Acts* (New York: Harcourt Brace Jovanovich, 1941), pp. 20-22. All further quotations and references to the novel will be cited within the text as *BTA*.

2. Stephen D. Fox presents a thorough treatment of the lily pond symbol in "The Fish Pond as Symbolic Center in *Between the Acts*," *Modern Fiction Studies* 18 (Autumn 1972): 469-72. He sees the pond as an image of the individual mind; of couples or groups of people; of nature and its relationship to humankind; of the past and its influence on the present; and of the blending of life and death, love and fear.

3. Alan Watts, in his book *Behold the Spirit*, traces the evolution of human temperament from the Middle Ages to the present, and, in so doing, he draws precisely the same conclusions that appear in Miss La Trobe's pageant. According to Watts, "With the wisdom peculiar to children mediaeval man saw . . . what modern man does not see — that man and nature are indeed symbols of God." Then, with the advent of Humanism and Protestantism, "man was awakening to the power of his own reason." As a result, "by degrees the agrarian culture of feudalism gives place to the bourgeois, mercantile culture of cities, where man is surrounded by his own works and absorbed

in his own concerns." With reason, says Watts, comes analysis, and with analysis comes disintegration. This disintegration, characteristic of the modern day, deprives humankind "of all but habitual faith in life," which humankind compensates for with "make-believe meanings — commercial enterprise, material 'success,' absorption in political and social reform movements." See *Behold the Spirit: A Study in the Necessity of Mystical Religion* (New York: Random House, 1947), pp. 36-48.

# Selected Bibliography

*Works by Virginia Woolf:*

*Between the Acts.* New York: Harcourt Brace Jovanovich, 1941.

*The Captain's Death Bed and Other Essays.* New York: Harcourt Brace Jovanovich, 1950.

*The Common Reader: First Series.* New York: Harcourt, Brace & World, 1925.

*Contemporary Writers.* Edited by Jean Guiguet. New York: Harcourt Brace Jovanovich, 1965.

*The Death of the Moth and Other Essays.* New York: Harcourt Brace Jovanovich, 1942.

*The Diary of Virginia Woolf.* Edited by Anne Oliver Bell. New York: Harcourt Brace Jovanovich. Vol. 1, *1915-1919*, 1977; Vol. 2, *1920-1924*, 1978.

*Flush: A Biography.* New York: Harcourt, Brace & World, 1933.

*Granite and Rainbow.* New York: Harcourt Brace Jovanovich, 1958.

*A Haunted House and Other Short Stories.* New York: Harcourt, Brace & World, 1921.

*Jacob's Room.* New York: Harcourt, Brace & World, 1923.

*The Letters of Virginia Woolf.* Edited by Nigel Nicolson and Joanne Trautmann. New York: Harcourt Brace Jovanovich. Vol. 1, *1888-1912*, 1975; Vol. 2, *1912-1922*, 1976; Vol. 3, *1923-1928*, 1977; Vol. 4, *1929-1931*, 1979; and Vol. 5, *1932-1935*, 1979.

*The Moment and Other Essays.* New York: Harcourt Brace Jovanovich, 1948.

*Moments of Being: Unpublished Autobiographical Writings.*

Edited by Jeanne Schulkind. New York: Harcourt Brace Jovanovich, 1976.

*Mrs. Dalloway*. New York: Harcourt, Brace & World, 1925.

*Mrs. Dalloway's Party*. Edited by Stella McNichol. New York: Harcourt Brace Jovanovich, 1973.

*Night and Day*. New York: Harcourt Brace Jovanovich, 1920.

*Orlando: A Biography*. New York: Harcourt Brace Jovanovich, 1928.

*The Pargiters*. Edited by Mitchell A. Leaska. New York: Harcourt Brace Jovanovich, 1978.

*A Room of One's Own*. New York: Harcourt, Brace & World, 1929.

*The Second Common Reader*. New York: Harcourt, Brace & World, 1932.

*Three Guineas*. New York: Harcourt, Brace & World, 1938.

*To the Lighthouse*. New York: Harcourt, Brace & World, 1938.

*Virginia Woolf & Lytton Strachey: Letters*. Edited by Leonard Woolf and James Strachey. New York: Harcourt, Brace and Co. 1956.

*The Voyage Out*. New York: Harcourt, Brace & World, 1920.

*The Waves*. New York: Harcourt, Brace & World, 1931.

*A Writer's Diary: Being Extracts from the Diary of Virginia Woolf*. Edited by Leonard Woolf. New York: Harcourt Brace Jovanovich, 1953.

*The Years*. New York: Harcourt, Brace & World, 1937.

Books on Virginia Woolf:

Alexander, Jean. *The Venture of Form in the Novels of Virginia Woolf*. Port Washington, N.Y.: Kennikat Press, 1974.

Bazin, Nancy Topping. *Virginia Woolf and the Androgynous Vision*. New Brunswick, N.J.: Rutgers University Press, 1973.

Bell, Quentin. *Virginia Woolf: A Biography*. New York: Harcourt Brace Jovanovich, 1972.

Bennett, Joan. *Virginia Woolf: Her Art as a Novelist*. New York: Harcourt, Brace and Co., 1945.

Blackstone, Bernard. *Virginia Woolf*. London: Longmans, Green, 1952.

– – –. *Virginia Woolf: A Commentary.* New York: Harcourt Brace Jovanovich, 1949.

Brewster, Dorothy. *Virginia Woolf.* New York: New York University Press, 1962.

Chambers, R. L. *The Novels of Virginia Woolf.* New York: Russell & Russell, 1947.

Chastaing, Maxime. *La philosophie de Virginia Woolf.* Paris: Presses universitaires de France, 1951.

Collins, Robert. *Virginia Woolf's Black Arrows of Sensation: "The Waves."* Ilfracombe: Arthur H. Stockwell, 1962.

Daiches, David. *Virginia Woolf.* 2d ed. New York: New Directions, 1942.

Delattre, Floris. *Le roman psychologique de Virginia Woolf.* Paris: J. Vrin, 1932.

Fleishman, Avrom. *Virginia Woolf: A Critical Reading.* Baltimore, Md.: Johns Hopkins Press, 1975.

Gruber, Ruth. *Virginia Woolf: A Study.* Leipzig: Verlag von Bernhard Tauchnitz, 1935.

Guiguet, Jean. *Virginia Woolf and Her Works.* Translated by Jean Stewart. New York: Harcourt, Brace & World, 1962.

Hafley, James. *The Glass Roof: Virginia Woolf as Novelist.* New York: Russell & Russell, 1963.

Holtby, Winifred. *Virginia Woolf.* London: Wishart, 1932.

Johnson, Manly. *Virginia Woolf.* New York: Frederick Ungar, 1973.

Kelley, Alice van Buren. *The Novels of Virginia Woolf: Fact and Vision.* Chicago: University of Chicago Press, 1971.

Kirkpatrick, B. J. *A Bibliography of Virginia Woolf.* London: Rupert Hart-Davis, 1957.

Latham, Jacqueline E. M., ed. *Critics on Virginia Woolf.* Coral Gables, Fla.: University of Miami Press, 1970.

Leaska, Mitchell A. *Virginia Woolf's Lighthouse: A Study in Critical Method.* New York: Columbia University Press, 1970.

Lehman, John. *Virginia Woolf: And Her World.* New York: Harcourt Brace Jovanovich, 1975.

Lewis, Thomas S. W., ed. *Virginia Woolf: A Collection of Criticism.* New York: McGraw-Hill Book Co., 1975.

Love, Jean O. *Virginia Woolf: Sources of Madness and Art.* Berkeley, Calif.: University of California Press, 1977.

— —. *Worlds in Consciousness: Mythopoetic Thought in the Novels of Virginia Woolf.* Berkeley: University of California Press, 1970.

Majumdar, Robin and Allen McLaurin, eds. *Virginia Woolf: The Critical Heritage.* London: Routledge and Kegan Paul, 1975.

Marder, Herbert. *Feminism and Art: A Study of Virginia Woolf.* Chicago: University of Chicago Press, 1968.

McLaurin, Allen. *Virginia Woolf: The Echoes Enslaved.* London: Cambridge University Press, 1973.

Moody, A. D. *Virginia Woolf.* New York: Grove Press, 1963.

Naremore, James. *The World without a Self: Virginia Woolf and the Novel.* New Haven, Conn.: Yale University Press, 1973.

Nathan, Monique. *Virginia Woolf.* Translated by Herma Briffault. New York: Evergreen Books, 1961.

Noble, Joan Russell, ed. *Recollections of Virginia Woolf.* New York: William Morrow, 1972.

Novak, Jane. *The Razor Edge of Balance: A Study of Virginia Woolf.* Coral Gables, Fla.: University of Miami Press, 1975.

Pippett, Aileen. *The Moth and the Star: A Biography of Virginia Woolf.* Boston, Mass.: Little, Brown, & Co., 1969.

Richter, Harvena. *Virginia Woolf: The Inward Voyage.* Princeton, N.J.: Princeton University Press, 1970.

Schaefer, Josephine O'Brien. *The Three-Fold Nature of Reality in the Novels of Virginia Woolf.* The Hague: Mouton, 1965.

Sprague, Claire, ed. *Virginia Woolf: A Collection of Critical Essays.* Englewood Cliffs, N.J.: Prentice-Hall, Inc., 1971.

Thakur, N. C. *The Symbolism of Virginia Woolf.* London: Oxford University Press, 1965.

Vogler, Thomas A., ed. *Twentieth Century Interpretations of "To the Lighthouse."* Englewood Cliffs, N.J.: Prentice-Hall, 1970.

*Articles on Virginia Woolf:*

Baldanza, Frank. "Clarissa Dalloway's 'Party Consciousness.' " *Modern Fiction Studies* 2 (February 1956): 24-30.

Beach, Joseph Warren. "Virginia Woolf." *English Journal* 26 (October 1937): 603-12.

Beebe, Maurice. "Criticism of Virginia Woolf: A Selected Checklist with an Index to Studies of Separate Works." *Modern Fiction Studies* 2 (February 1956): 36-45.

Beja, Morris. "Matches Struck in the Dark: Virginia Woolf's Moments of Vision." *Critical Quarterly* 6 (Summer 1964): 137-52.

Benjamin, Anna S. "Towards an Understanding of the Meaning of Virginia Woolf's *Mrs. Dalloway.*" *Wisconsin Studies in Contemporary Literature* 6 (Summer 1965): 214-27.

Bevis, Dorothy. "*The Waves*: Fusion of Symbol, Style and Thought in Virginia Woolf." *Twentieth Century Literature* 2 (April 1956): 5-19.

Bowen, Elizabeth. "Between the Acts." *New Statesman and Nation* 22 (July 1941): 63-64.

Church, Margaret. "Concepts of Time in Novels of Virginia Woolf and Aldous Huxley." *Modern Fiction Studies* 1 (May 1955): 19-24.

Cummings, Melinda Feldt. "*Night and Day*: Virginia Woolf's Visionary Synthesis of Reality." *Modern Fiction Studies* 18 (Autumn 1972): 339-49.

Fortin, René E. "Sacramental Imagery in *Mrs. Dalloway.*" *Renascence* 18 (Fall 1965): 23-31.

Fox, Stephen D. "The Fish Pond as Symbolic Center in *Between the Acts.*" *Modern Fiction Studies* 18 (Autumn 1972): 467-73.

Francis Jr.. Herbert E. "Virginia Woolf and 'The Moment.' " *Emory University Quarterly* 16 (Fall 1960): 139-51.

Friedman, Norman. "The Waters of Annihilation: Double Vision in *To the Lighthouse.*" *English Literary History* 22 (March 1955): 61-79.

Gamble, Isabel. "The Secret Sharer in *Mrs. Dalloway.*" *Accent* 16 (Autumn 1956): 235-51.

Gelfant, Blanche H. "Love and Conversion in *Mrs. Dalloway.*" *Criticism* 8 (Winter 1966): 229-45.

Hartley, Lodwick. "Of Time and Mrs. Woolf." *Sewanee Review* 47 (1939): 235-41.

Hartman, Geoffrey H. "Virginia's Web." *Chicago Review* 14 (Spring 1961): 20-32.

Havard-Williams, Peter and Margaret. *"Bateau-Ivre*: The Symbol of the Sea in Virginia Woolf's *The Waves."* *English Studies* 34 (February 1953): 9-17.

— — —. "Mystical Experience in Virginia Woolf's *The Waves."* *Essays in Criticism* 4 (January 1954): 71-84.

— — —. "Perceptive Contemplation in the Works of Virginia Woolf." *English Studies* 35 (June 1954): 97-116.

Henke, Suzette. "Virginia Woolf's *To the Lighthouse*: In Defense of the Woman Artist." *Virginia Woolf Quarterly* 2 (Winter-Spring 1975): 39-47.

Hoffman, Charles G. "Fact and Fantasy in *Orlando*: Virginia Woolf's Manuscript Revisions." *Texas Studies in Literature and Language* 10 (Fall 1968): 435-44.

— — —. "From Lunch to Dinner: Virginia Woolf's Apprenticeship." *Texas Studies in Literature and Language* 10 (Winter 1969): 609-627.

— — —. "From Short Story to Novel: The Manuscript Revisions of Virginia Woolf's *Mrs. Dalloway."* *Modern Fiction Studies* 14 (Summer 1968): 171-86.

— — —. "Virginia Woolf's Manuscript Revisions of *The Years."* *PMLA* 84 (January 1969): 79-89.

Hungerford, Edward A. "Mrs. Woolf, Freud, and J. D. Beresford." *Literature and Psychology* 5 (August 1955): 49-51.

— — —. " 'My Tunnelling Process': The Method of *Mrs. Dalloway."* *Modern Fiction Studies* 3 (Summer 1957): 164-67.

Hunting, Constance. "The Technique of Persuasion in *Orlando."* *Modern Fiction Studies* 2 (February 1956): 17-23.

Kaehele, Sharon and Howard German. *"To the Lighthouse*: Symbol and Vision." *Bucknell Review* 10 (1962): 328-46.

Kelsey, Mary Electa. "Virginia Woolf and the She-Condition." *Sewanee Review* 39 (October-December 1931): 425-44.

King, Merton P. "The Androgynous Mind and *The Waves."* *University Review* 30 (Spring 1964): 221-24.

— — —. *"The Waves* and the Androgynous Mind." *University Review* 30 (Winter 1963): 128-34.

Lakshmi, Vijay. "The Solid and the Intangible: Virginia Woolf's Theory of the Androgynous Mind." *Literary Criterion* 10 (Winter 1971): 28-34.

Leaska, Mitchell A. "Virginia Woolf's *The Voyage Out*: Character Deduction and the Function of Ambiguity." *Virginia Woolf Quarterly* I (Winter 1973): 18-41.

— — —. "Virginia Woolf, the Pargeter: A Reading of *The Years*." *Bulletin of the New York Public Library* 80 (Winter 1977): 172-210.

Leavis, F. R. "After *To the Lighthouse*." *Scrutiny* 10 (January 1942): 295-98.

Lipking, Joanna. "Looking at the Monuments: Woolf's Satiric Eye." *Bulletin of the New York Public Library* 80 (Winter 1977): 141-45.

Lund, Mary Graham. "The Androgynous Moment: Woolf and Eliot." *Renascence* 12 (Winter 1960): 74-78.

Marder, Herbert. "Beyond the Lighthouse: *The Years*." *Bucknell Review* 15 (March 1967): 61-70.

— — —. "Virginia Woolf's 'Systems that Did Not Shut Out.' " *Papers on Language and Literature* 4 (Winter 1968): 106-11.

Mellers, W. H. "Virginia Woolf: The Last Phase." *Kenyon Review* 4 (Autumn 1942): 381-87.

Morgenstern, Barry. "The Self-Conscious Narrator in *Jacob's Room*." *Modern Fiction Studies* 18 (Autumn 1972): 351-61.

Overcarsh, F. L. "The Lighthouse, Face to Face." *Accent* 10 (Winter 1950): 107-23.

Page, Alex. "A Dangerous Day: Mrs. Dalloway Discovers Her Double." *Modern Fiction Studies* 7 (Summer 1961): 115-24.

Payne, Michael. "The Eclipse of Order: The Ironic Structure of *The Waves*." *Modern Fiction Studies* 15 (Summer 1969): 209-18.

Pedersen, Glenn. "Vision in *To the Lighthouse*." *PMLA* 73 (December 1958): 585-600.

Pratt, Annis. "Sexual Imagery in *To the Lighthouse*: A New Feminist Approach." *Modern Fiction Studies* 18 (Autumn 1972): 417-31.

Proudfit, Sharon Wood. "Lily Briscoe's Painting: A Key to Personal Relationships in *To the Lighthouse*." *Criticism* 8 (Winter 1971): 26-38.

Rachman, Shalom. "Clarissa's Attic: Virginia Woolf's *Mrs. Dalloway* Reconsidered." *Twentieth Century Literature* 18 (January 1972): 3-18.

Rantavaara, Irma. "Virginia Woolf's *The Waves.*" *Societas Scientiarum Fennica*: *Commentationes Humanarum Litterarum.* (Helsinki, 1960): 1-99.

Redman, Ben Ray. "Incomplete Mystic." *Saturday Review of Literature*, 23 July 1949, p. 18.

Roberts, John Hawley. "Toward Virginia Woolf." *Virginia Quarterly Review* 10 (October 1934): 587-602.

— — —. " 'Vision and Design' in Virginia Woolf." *PMLA* 61 (September 1946): 835-47.

Rosenberg, Stuart. "The Match in the Crocus: Obtrusive Art in Virginia Woolf's *Mrs. Dalloway.*" *Modern Fiction Studies* 13 (Summer 1967): 211-20.

Samuels, Marilyn Schauer. "The Symbolic Functions of the Sun in *Mrs. Dalloway.*" *Modern Fiction Studies* 18 (Autumn 1972): 387-99.

Samuelson, Ralph. "Virginia Woolf, *Orlando*, and the Feminist Spirit." *Western Humanities Review* 15 (Winter 1961): 51-58.

Savage, D. S. "The Mind of Virginia Woolf." *South Atlantic Quarterly* 46 (October 1947): 556-73.

Sears, Sallie. "Notes on Sexuality: *The Years* and *Three Guineas.*" *Bulletin of the New York Public Library* 80 (Winter 1977): 211-20.

Simon, Irene. "Some Aspects of Virginia Woolf's Imagery." *English Studies* 41 (June 1960): 180-96.

Steele, Philip L. "Virginia Woolf's Spiritual Autobiography." *Topic* 9 (Fall 1969): 64-74.

Steinberg, Erwin R. "Freudian Symbolism and Communication." *Literature and Psychology* 3 (April 1953): 2-5.

Tindall, William York. "Many-Levelled Fiction: Virginia Woolf to Ross Lockridge." *College English* 10 (November 1948): 65-71.

Toynbee, Philip. "Virginia Woolf: A Study of Three Experimental Novels." *Horizon* 14 (November 1946): 290-304.

Warner, John M. "Symbolic Patterns of Retreat and Reconciliation in *To the Lighthouse.*" *Discourse* 12 (Summer 1969): 376-92.

Watkins, Renée. "Survival in Discontinuity: Virginia Woolf's *Between the Acts.*" *Massachusetts Review* 10 (Spring 1969): 356-76.

Webb, Igor. " 'Things in Themselves': Virginia Woolf's *The Waves*." *Modern Fiction Studies* 17 (Winter 1971-1972): 570-73.

Weiser, Barbara. "Criticism of Virginia Woolf from 1956 to the Present: A Selected Checklist with an Index to Studies of Separate Works." *Modern Fiction Studies* 18 (Autumn 1972): 477-86.

Whitehead, Lee M. "The Shawl and the Skull: Virginia Woolf's 'Magic Mountain.' " *Modern Fiction Studies* 18 (Autumn 1972): 401-13.

Zorn, Marilyn. "The Pageant in *Between the Acts*." *Modern Fiction Studies* 2 (February 1956): 31-35.

*Works with Critical and Biographical References to Virginia Woolf:*

Beja, Morris. *Epiphany in the Modern Novel*. Seattle, Wash.: University of Washington Press, 1971.

Bodkin, Maud. *Archetypal Patterns in Poetry: Psychological Studies of Imagination*. London: Oxford University Press, 1934.

Burgum, Edwin Berry. *The Novel and the World's Dilemma*. New York: Russell & Russell, 1963.

Church, Margaret. *Time and Reality: Studies in Contemporary Fiction*. Chapel Hill, N.C.: University of North Carolina Press, 1949.

Cornwell, Ethel F. *The "Still Point": Theme and Variations in the Writings of T. S. Eliot, Coleridge, Yeats, Henry James, Virginia Woolf, and D. H. Lawrence*. New Brunswick, N.J.: Rutgers University Press, 1962.

Cox, C. B. *The Free Spirit: A Study of Liberal Humanism in the Novels of George Eliot, Henry James, E. M. Forster, Virginia Woolf, Angus Wilson*. London: Oxford University Press, 1963.

Daiches, David. *The Novel and the Modern World*. Rev. ed. Chicago: University of Chicago Press, 1960.

Edel, Leon. *The Modern Psychological Novel*. New York: Grosset & Dunlap, 1955.

Ford, Boris, ed. *The Modern Age: Volume 7 of the Pelican Guide to English Literature*. 3d ed. Middlesex: Penguin Books, 1964.

Freedman, Ralph. *The Lyrical Novel: Studies in Hermann Hesse,*

*André Gide, and Virginia Woolf.* Princeton, N.J.: Princeton University Press, 1963.

Friedman, Melvin J. and John B. Vickery, eds. *The Shaken Realist: Essays in Modern Literature in Honor of Frederick J. Hoffman.* Baton Rouge, La.: Louisiana State University Press, 1970.

Frye, Northrop. *Anatomy of Criticism: Four Essays.* Princeton, N.J.: Princeton University Press, 1957.

Heilbrun, Carolyn G. *Toward a Recognition of Androgyny.* New York: Alfred A. Knopf, 1973.

Hoare, Dorothy M. *Some Studies in the Modern Novel.* London: Chatto & Windus, 1953.

Johnstone, John Keith. *The Bloomsbury Group: A Study of E. M. Forster, Lytton Strachey, Virginia Woolf, and their Circle.* New York: Noonday Press, 1954.

Kaplan, Sydney Janet. *Feminine Consciousness in the Modern British Novel.* Urbana, Ill.: University of Illinois Press, 1975.

O'Connor, William Van, ed. *Forms of Modern Fiction: Essays Collected in Honor of Joseph Warren Beach.* Minneapolis, Minn.: University of Minnesota Press, 1948.

Pendry, E. D. *The New Feminism of English Fiction: A Study in Contemporary Women-Novelists.* Tokyo: Kenkyusha, 1956.

Rosenbaum, S. P., ed. *English Literature and British Philosophy: A Collection of Essays.* Chicago: University of Chicago Press, 1971.

Savage, D. S. *The Withered Branch: Six Studies in the Modern Novel.* London: Eyre & Spottiswoode, 1950.

Spacks, Patricia Meyer. *The Female Imagination.* New York: Avon, 1972.

Vickery, John B., ed. *Myth and Literature: Contemporary Theory and Practice.* Lincoln, Neb.: University of Nebraska Press, 1966.

Woolf, Leonard. *The Journey Not the Arrival Matters: An Autobiography of the Years 1939 to 1969.* New York: Harcourt Brace Jovanovich, 1969.

*Works on Related Topics:*

Alighieri, Dante. *The Purgatorio.* Translated by John Ciardi. New York: New American Library, 1957.

Bachofen, Johann Jakob. *Myth, Religion, and Mother Right: Selected Writings of J. J. Bachofen.* Translated by Ralph Manheim. Princeton, N.J.: Princeton University Press, 1967.

Cowper, William. "The Castaway." *The Norton Anthology of English Literature.* Rev. ed. Vol. 1, edited by M. H. Abrams, pp. 1783-84. New York: W. W. Norton, 1962.

Eliade, Mircea. *Myths, Dreams and Mysteries: The Encounter between Contemporary Faiths and Archaic Realities.* Translated by Philip Mairet. New York: Harper & Row, 1967.

— — —. *The Two and the One.* Translated by J. M. Cohen. New York: Harper & Row, 1962.

Harding, M. Esther. *The Way of All Women: A Psychological Interpretation.* New York: Harper & Row, 1975.

— — —. *Woman's Mysteries, Ancient and Modern: A Psychological Interpretation of the Feminine Principle as Portrayed in Myth, Story, and Dreams.* New York: G. P. Putnam's Sons, 1971.

Jewet, Paul K. *Man as Male and Female: A Study of Sexual Relationships from a Theological Point of View.* Grand Rapids, Mich.: William B. Eerdmans, 1975.

Jung, C. G. *Aion: Researches into the Phenomenology of the Self.* Translated by R. F. C. Hull. London: Routledge & Kegan Paul, 1959.

— — —. ed. *Man and His Symbols.* Garden City, N.Y.: Doubleday, 1964.

— — —. *Memories, Dreams, Reflections.* Edited by Aniela Jaffé. Translated by Richard and Clara Winston. New York: Pantheon Books, Div. of Random House, 1961.

— — —. *Psychological Types.* Translated by R. F. C. Hull. Princeton, N.J.: Princeton University Press, 1971.

— — —. *Psychology and Alchemy,* 2d ed. Translated by R. F. C. Hull. Princeton, N.J.: Princeton University Press, 1968.

— — —. *The Structure and Dynamics of the Psyche.* Translated by R. F. C. Hull. London: Routledge & Kegan Paul, 1960.

— — —. *Symbols of Transformation: An Analysis of the Prelude to a Case of Schizophrenia.* 2d ed. Translated by R. F. C. Hull. Princeton, N.J.: Princeton University Press, 1956.

— — —. *Two Essays on Analytical Psychology.* 2d ed. Translated by R. F. C. Hull. Princeton, N.J.: Princeton University Press, 1966.

Jung, Emma. "On the Nature of the Animus" (1931). In *Women & Analysis: Dialogues on Psychoanalytic Views of Femininity*, ed. by Jean Strouse, pp. 195-226. New York: Grossman, 1974.

Kluger, Rivkah Scharf. "Old Testament Roots of Woman's Spiritual Problem." A paper read in New York, 8 October 1976 as part of the "Jung Lecture Series."

Malory, Sir Thomas. *Morte Darthur. The Norton Anthology of English Literature*. Rev. ed. Vol. 1, edited by M. H. Abrams, New York: W. W. Norton, 1962.

Milton, John. *A Mask. The Complete English Poetry of John Milton*. Edited by John T. Shawcross, New York: New York University Press, 1963.

– – –. "On the Morning of Christ's Nativity." *The Complete English Poetry of John Milton*. Edited by John T. Shawcross, pp. 40-49. New York: New York University Press, 1963.

Neumann, Erich. *Amor and Psyche: The Psychic Development of the Feminine*. Translated by Ralph Manheim. Princeton, N.J.: Princeton University Press, 1956.

– – –. *The Great Mother: An Analysis of the Archetype*. Translated by Ralph Manheim. Princeton, N.J.: Princeton University Press, 1955.

– – –. "On the Moon and Matriarchal Consciousness." In *Fathers and Mothers: Five Papers on the Archetypal Background of Family Psychology*. Translated by Hildegard Nage, p. 40-63. New York: Analytical Psychology Club of N.Y., 1973.

– – –. *The Origins and History of Consciousness*. Translated by R. F. C. Hull. Princeton, N.J.: Princeton University Press, 1954.

Singer, June. *Androgyny: Toward a New Theory of Sexuality*. Garden City, N.Y.: Doubleday, & Co., 1976.

Troward, Thomas. *Bible Mystery and Bible Meaning*. New York: Dodd, Mead, 1913.

Ulanov, Ann Belford. *The Feminine: In Jungian Psychology and in Christian Theology*. Evanston, Ill.: Northwestern University Press, 1971.

Watts, Alan. *Behold the Spirit: A Study in the Necessity of Mystical Religion*. New York: Random House, 1947.

# Index

277

HS102BC

PORESKy